Pronunciation in Instruction

SECOND LANGUAGE ACQUISITION

Series Editor: Professor David Singleton, *University of Pannonia, Hungary* and Fellow Emeritus, *Trinity College, Dublin, Ireland*

This series brings together titles dealing with a variety of aspects of language acquisition and processing in situations where a language or languages other than the native language is involved. Second language is thus interpreted in its broadest possible sense. The volumes included in the series all offer in their different ways, on the one hand, exposition and discussion of empirical findings and, on the other, some degree of theoretical reflection. In this latter connection, no particular theoretical stance is privileged in the series; nor is any relevant perspective – sociolinguistic, psycholinguistic, neurolinguistic, etc. – deemed out of place. The intended readership of the series includes final-year undergraduates working on second language acquisition projects, postgraduate students involved in second language acquisition research, and researchers and teachers in general whose interests include a second language acquisition component.

Full details of all the books in this series and of all our other publications can be found on http://www.multilingual-matters.com, or by writing to Multilingual Matters, St Nicholas House, 31–34 High Street, Bristol BS1 2AW, UK.

SECOND LANGUAGE ACQUISITION: 82

Pronunciation in EFL Instruction

A Research-Based Approach

Jolanta Szpyra-Kozłowska

MULTILINGUAL MATTERS
Bristol • Buffalo • Toronto

Library of Congress Cataloging in Publication Data
Szpyra, Jolanta.
Pronunciation in EFL Instruction: A Research-Based Approach/Jolanta Szpyra-Kozlowska.
Second Language Acquisition: 82
Includes bibliographical references and index.
1. English language—Pronunciation of foreign speakers. 2. English language—
Phonology—Study and teaching. 3. English language—Study and teaching—Foreign
speakers. I. Title.
PE1137.S96 2014
428.3'4071–dc23 2014021877

British Library Cataloguing in Publication Data
A catalogue entry for this book is available from the British Library.

ISBN-13: 978-1-78309-261-1 (hbk)
ISBN-13: 978-1-78309-260-4 (pbk)

Multilingual Matters
UK: St Nicholas House, 31–34 High Street, Bristol BS1 2AW, UK.
USA: UTP, 2250 Military Road, Tonawanda, NY 14150, USA.
Canada: UTP, 5201 Dufferin Street, North York, Ontario M3H 5T8, Canada.

Website: www.multilingual-matters.com
Twitter: Multi_Ling_Mat
Facebook: https://www.facebook.com/multilingualmatters
Blog: www.channelviewpublications.wordpress.com

The policy of Multilingual Matters/Channel View Publications is to use papers that are
natural, renewable and recyclable products, made from wood grown in sustainable for-
ests. In the manufacturing process of our books, and to further support our policy, preference is given to printers that have FSC and PEFC Chain of Custody certification. The FSC
and/or PEFC logos will appear on those books where full certification has been granted
to the printer concerned.

Typeset by Techset Composition India(P) Ltd., Bangalore and Chennai, India.
Printed and bound in Great Britain by the Lavenham Press Ltd.

Contents

Preface   vii

1   English Pronunciation Teaching: Global Versus Local Contexts   1

Part A   2

A.1.1   Why Should Pronunciation Be Taught?   2
A.1.2   Why is Pronunciation Teaching Often Neglected?   4
A.1.3   Goals of Pronunciation Teaching/Learning   6
A.1.4   EFL Versus ELF: English Pronunciation Models Debate   8
A.1.5   EFL, ELF or NELF?   23
A.1.6   Which Native Pronunciation Model?   29
A.1.7   EFL Versus ESL   33
A.1.8   Diagnosing the Local Teaching Context. Learner-related and Teacher-related Determinants of Pronunciation Instruction   39

Part B   45

B.1.1   Attitudes to Accented Speech and its Users   45
B.1.2   Native Accent Models or ELF? A Questionnaire Study   49
B.1.3   Diagnosing the Pronunciation Teaching Context in Poland   55

2   Global and Local Pronunciation Priorities   67

Part A   68

A.2.1   How to Establish Pronunciation Priorities   68
A.2.2   Selected Proposals for English Pronunciation Priorities   76
A.2.3   Focus on the Pronunciation of Phonetically Difficult Words   90
A.2.4   Pronunciation and Spelling   104
A.2.5   Segmentals Versus Suprasegmentals   110

Part B   117

B.2.1 Intelligibility and Global Versus Local Errors   118
B.2.2 Other Phonetically Difficult Words   123
B.2.3 Pronunciation Priorities for Polish Learners   130

3   Pronunciation Inside and Outside the Classroom: A Holistic
      Multimodal Approach   140

Part A   141

A.3.1 Developing Concern for Good Pronunciation   141
A.3.2 A Holistic Multimodal Approach to Phonetic Training   144
A.3.3 Selected Pronunciation Teaching Techniques   170
A.3.4 Pronunciation Learning Outside the Classroom   191
A.3.5 Providing Feedback   194
A.3.6 Problems with Pronunciation Teaching Materials   198

Part B   209

B.3.1 Motor Training Versus Cognitive Training   210
B.3.2 Effectiveness Versus Attractiveness of Pronunciation
        Teaching Activities   212
B.3.3 Employing Elements of Drama   218
B.3.4 Phonetic Error Correction   220

4   Concluding Remarks   225

References   234
Author Index   243
Subject Index   246

Preface

Due to the considerable impact of the concept of English as an International Language (EIL) or English as a Lingua Franca (ELF) and its pronunciation teaching agenda, known as the Lingua Franca Core (Jenkins, 2000), the last decade has witnessed a major change of paradigms in pronunciation teaching. As a result, as argued by Levis (2005), pronunciation theory, research and practice are in transition and many widely accepted assumptions such as the supremacy of inner-circle models, the primacy of suprasegmentals and the need for native instructors have been challenged.

While most specialists agree that, in view of these facts, some modifications in English pronunciation instruction are unavoidable, it is by no means clear what they should be like in specific cases. Thus, although much attention has been given to pronunciation teaching to ESL learners (English as a Second Language, when English is acquired in an English-speaking country, e.g. Celce-Murcia *et al.*, 1996), as well as to ELF students (e.g. Walker, 2011), an important and highly controversial issue concerns selecting appropriate phonetic model(s) and pronunciation priorities for the largest group of learners, from the Expanding Circle, for whom English is a foreign language (EFL) and whose number is often estimated to be around 1.5 billion. The debate over this problem has been very heated (e.g. Dziubalska-Kołaczyk & Przedlacka, 2005) and is far from being settled, with many opposing views being expressed and different arguments presented.

This book is meant as a contribution to this discussion. It addresses the major theoretical issues relevant to contemporary English phonodidactics[1] approached from an EFL perspective and offers a novel approach to several fundamental problems such as, for instance, the choice of a pronunciation model for foreign learners, establishing teaching priorities for them and the 'segments versus suprasegmentals' debate concerning the salience of these two aspects of pronunciation for effective communication.

Moreover, it deals with numerous practical aspects of phonetic instruction and attempts to provide answers to many questions facing EFL teachers. For example, having a limited time at their disposal, how much attention should teachers devote to pronunciation? What realistic goals should be aimed at? Which aspects of English phonetics should be taught to foreign learners and which can be neglected with little loss to successful communication? How can pronunciation be taught in an interesting, effective and both teacher-friendly and learner-friendly way, in accordance with the latest scholarly and technological achievements? How should appropriate teaching materials be selected? These and many other practical issues are raised and addressed in this book with many new solutions offered within a holistic motor-cognitive multimodal approach to English phonodidactics, particularly suitable for EFL learners.

The present author is convinced that informed and non-arbitrary decisions concerning both theoretical issues as well as various details of pronunciation teaching can only be made on the basis of extensive empirical research which examines, on the one hand, the pronunciation problems of specific L1 learner groups and their acquisition of L2 phonetics, but also, on the other hand, the perception of foreign-accented English by native and non-native listeners. In other words, there is agreement with Derwing and Munro (2005: 379) that 'empirical studies are essential in improving our understanding of the relationship between foreign accent and pronunciation teaching'.

This book, with its meaningful subtitle, 'A Research-Based Approach', attempts to bridge the gap between relevant phonetic research and pronunciation teaching by drawing on the results of the author's and other scholars' empirical studies on EFL learners' acquisition of English pronunciation, its perception and production, as well as the efficacy of various instructional procedures and the usefulness of teaching materials. Since such research can only be carried out with specific participants, the discussion is supported by extensive experimental evidence provided mostly by Polish learners of English.

It should be added that within the last decade in Poland much empirical research has been done on various aspects of English pronunciation pedagogy (for a summary, see Szpyra-Kozłowska, 2008). Moreover, Poles appear to represent typical EFL students acquiring this language in a characteristic EFL context, i.e. in an instructed setting, in which language classes are monolingual and consist of the same L1 speakers who have a limited exposure to spoken English outside the classes, but a considerable exposure to written English and who are usually taught by non-native teachers trained to teach various aspects of English, including pronunciation. As English is taught and learnt in similar conditions all over the world, not only in Poland, empirical studies carried out in an EFL context appear to have broader didactic implications.[2]

To make the book both general and specific, global and local, as well as interesting to various readers and certainly not only to Polish readers, each chapter consists of two parts (Part A and Part B), the first of which provides a general theoretical discussion of a given issue while Part B contains a presentation of several experimental studies carried out by the author and meant to examine the problems raised in Part A empirically and to verify various theoretical claims. Thus, *Pronunciation in EFL Instruction* attempts to combine all the necessary ingredients for successful pronunciation instruction to EFL learners: phonetic theory, research and practice, all considered from both global as well as local perspectives.

The book does not provide a description of English phonetics; many other sources are available which supply the necessary information. Nor is it a pronunciation manual which contains sets of exercises to practise particular aspects of English phonetics although it does contain numerous practical hints and suggestions how to deal with specific problems.

The first two chapters are concerned with the issue of what should be taught to foreign learners pronunciation-wise: Chapter 1 deals with selecting an appropriate pronunciation model for instruction and Chapter 2 focuses on pronunciation priorities.

Chapter 1 starts with some necessary preliminaries, i.e. justifying the need to teach and learn the pronunciation of a foreign language, specifying the major reasons why L2 phonetic instruction often tends to be neglected and discussing various goals of pronunciation learning. The bulk of the chapter is devoted to the contentious and hotly debated issue of choosing an appropriate pronunciation model for foreign learners of English. Two approaches, traditional EFL (English as a Foreign Language) and a recent proposal known as ELF (English as a Lingua Franca) are examined and critically evaluated. Next put forward and developed is the concept of NELF (Native English as a Lingua Franca), meant to reconcile the previous two views by accepting the linguistic, but not the sociocultural aspects of native English and adopting native English pronunciation as a model, but not the goal of instruction, the latter being easy, intelligible communication with both native and non-native speakers. The major features of the three approaches to pronunciation teaching, i.e. EFL, ELF and NELF are juxtaposed and compared, with the superiority of NELF being argued in favour of. Subsequently, another important but frequently neglected distinction between EFL and ESL (English as a Second Language) is re-examined. It is claimed that regarding them as one phenomenon, as is currently the case, is detrimental to pronunciation instruction in EFL contexts and it is demonstrated that they differ too much to deserve a separate phonodidactic treatment. Finally, the major factors relevant to diagnosing the local educational context of EFL phonetic instruction are considered, as well as learner-dependent and teacher-dependent determinants of pronunciation teaching and learning.

Chapter 2 is devoted to the complex and controversial issue of establishing pronunciation priorities for EFL learners. First the major problems involved in this task are discussed with the focus on factors relevant for achieving comfortably intelligible pronunciation. Then we present and evaluate several recent proposals concerning pronunciation priorities, i.e. Jenkins' (2000) Lingua Franca Core, Cruttenden's (2008) Amalgam English and

International English, and Collins and Mees' (2003) pronunciation Error Ranking. An attempt is made to draw some generalizations from these concepts in order to formulate a set of general guidelines for foreign students of English. Next, a new suggestion, aimed specifically at EFL learners, is put forward, according to which phonetic instruction should focus on words prone to be notoriously mispronounced by foreign learners. It is argued and proved empirically that such lexical items hinder achieving comfortable intelligibility more than inaccurately produced sounds and prosodies, and should therefore be prioritized in EFL phonodidactics. The nature of phonetically problematic words and the major sources of their pronunciation difficulty are looked into. It is also demonstrated that, in view of the considerable impact of the written form of English on EFL learners' pronunciation, this issue ought to be placed among the top priorities in phonetic instruction.

In the remaining parts of this chapter the question, undertaken in the 'segmentals versus suprasegmentals' debate, whether these are sounds or prosodies that should be viewed as pronunciation priorities in EFL settings is addressed. It is shown that the answer cannot be universal, but must be provided for each L1 learner group by considering the phonetic distance between the L1 and L2, and evaluating the impact of specific segmental and prosodic departures from the L2 on intelligibility, established in the course of empirical research. This proposal is elaborated and exemplified with a set of pronunciation priorities formulated for Polish learners.

After a discussion of the complex problem of English pronunciation models and phonetic priorities for EFL learners, in Chapter 3 the issue of effective phonetic instruction is dealt with and a holistic multimodal approach to it is proposed. It is holistic as it concerns both the learner's body and mind. It is dubbed multimodal since it involves developing in learners appropriate motor habits needed in sound perception and production, employing cognitive mechanisms responsible for the formation of the L2 sound system in the learner's mind and appealing to different kinds of multisensory reinforcement. It is argued that these four aspects should all be combined and integrated in successful pronunciation training and some effective techniques which can be employed in it are suggested. A large part of Chapter 3 is devoted to the presentation of selected types of phonetic activities that are particularly useful for EFL learners. The necessity of pronunciation learning outside the language classroom and developing students' autonomy is also pointed to. The final section of Part A in Chapter 3 addresses an important, but frequently neglected issue of the critical assessment and appropriate choice of pronunciation teaching materials for EFL learners.

Finally, Chapter 4 sums up the major points made in the preceding parts of the book and highlights its most important claims.

The book is addressed to current and prospective EFL teachers and teacher trainers wishing to improve their teaching skills and pronunciation instruction in particular, in accordance with up-to-date theory and practice, as well as to pronunciation specialists, students of applied linguistics and anyone interested in English phonodidactics.

The author and publisher gratefully acknowledge permission from the following to quote from copyright materials:

Peter Lang Verlag for the extracts from "LFC, phonetic universals and the Polish context" by Jolanta Szpyra-Kozłowska, [In:] Dziubalska-Kołaczyk, K. and J. Przedlacka (eds) *English Pronunciation Models: A Changing Scene.* 2005, pp.151–176.

Springer-Verlag Berlin Heidelberg, for the extracts from "On the irrelevance of sounds and prosody in foreign-accented English" by Jolanta Szpyra-Kozłowska, [In:] Waniek-Klimczak, E. and L. Shockey (eds) *Teaching and Researching English Accents in Native and Non-native Speakers.* Second Language Learning and Teaching 2013, pp. 15–29. With kind permission of Springer Science+Business Media.

This study is an outcome of the author's several years of research as well as teaching experience which involved many people to whom I owe a great debt of gratitude. In particular I would like to thank very warmly Agnieszka Bryła-Cruz, Darek Bukowski, Iwona Czyżak, Wiktor Gonet, Marta Nowacka, Sławek Stasiak, Marek Radomski and Radek Święciński (listed here in alphabetical order) for being a great team of friends and colleagues whose contributions to this book are visible in many of its pages.

I dedicate this book to my daughter Iga.

Notes

(1) The term *phonodidactics* is used in this book as synonymous with *pronunciation pedagogy* or *pronunciation teaching.* It is preferred by the author due to its brevity, semantic transparency and combining the concepts of phonetics and phonology in one word.

(2) Furthermore, in recent years over 600,000 Poles have emigrated to the British Isles. This makes them a large and important group of learners and users of English.

1 English Pronunciation Teaching: Global Versus Local Contexts

This book starts with some necessary preliminaries. First a crucial question is posed concerning the need to teach and learn the pronunciation of a foreign language. It then proceeds to enquire why, in spite of the unquestionable importance of this aspect of language, it often tends to be neglected. Next the focus is on various goals of pronunciation teaching/learning and on a contentious and hotly debated issue of the choice of a model accent appropriate for foreign learners of English. The discussion centres around two approaches to ELT: the traditional idea of EFL (English as a Foreign Language) and a recent proposal known either as EIL (English as an International Language) or ELF (English as a Lingua Franca). They are characterized in some detail, and a critical evaluation of each is carried out before putting forward the concept of NELF (Native English as a Lingua Franca) as an approach to pronunciation instruction for foreign learners of English, meant to reconcile the two opposing views. The major features of EFL, ELF and NELF are juxtaposed and compared, with arguments provided for the superiority of the latter. Subsequently, another important but frequently neglected distinction between EFL and ESL (English as a Second Language) is re-examined. It is argued that treating them jointly as cases of learning a second language (L2) in the process of second language acquisition (SLA) is detrimental to EFL pronunciation instruction and demonstrate that they differ substantially and therefore deserve a separate treatment. Finally, the major factors relevant for diagnosing the local educational context of EFL instruction as well as learner-dependent and teacher-dependent determinants of pronunciation teaching and learning are briefly examined.

In Part B three studies are presented which provide empirical support for some of the claims made in Part A. More specifically, in order to prove the importance of good pronunciation in another language, an experiment devoted to foreign accent perception is related, demonstrating how accented speech affects listeners' judgements of personal characteristics ascribed to its users. Next, typical EFL learners' (i.e. Polish students') preferences concerning English pronunciation models are examined in a questionnaire study. Finally, an analysis of a cultural and educational context in which English is taught in Poland is presented, with the main focus on teachers' and students' attitudes to this language skill and the quality of phonetic instruction in schools.

Part A

A.1.1 Why Should Pronunciation Be Taught?

Suppose you are in a situation in which you have to speak a foreign language. It will take some time for the listeners to find out how well you know its grammar, how rich your vocabulary is. But it is enough if you utter just a few words for them to know how good (or bad) your pronunciation is. The first impression is formed and we all know how important first impressions are and how difficult it is to change those initial judgements.

But, of course, there is more to having good pronunciation than just creating a positive first impression. It is an important component of language without which no efficient oral communication is possible. Thus, phonetic errors may lead to misunderstandings and even communication breakdowns, as reported in many stories, like the one about a tourist asking in a London restaurant for *soup*, pronounced by him as *soap*, and being directed to the bathroom. Not long ago I had a conversation in English with a Polish student about her school experiences and she kept repeating how much she disliked *that [staf]*. I was quite confused as to whether she meant *the teaching staff* or *stuff*, i.e. school education in general, as in that particular context both items were just as likely to occur. Many similar stories, some jocular, some serious or even tragic, can be provided to prove the importance of clear and comprehensible pronunciation. Perhaps the most shocking of them concerns a collision of two aeroplanes with over 200 people dead in 1977 in Tenerife, attributed to a misunderstanding between the pilot and the air traffic controller due to the pilot's poor English pronunciation.[1]

Luckily, the consequences of phonetic errors are rarely so dramatic. In most cases misunderstandings can easily be explained. In other situations the linguistic and/or extralinguistic context will allow the listener to guess the meaning of an utterance. For example, if on a walk with your pet somebody asked you in Polish English: *Is this your [dok]¿*, you could guess without any major difficulty that the question concerns your dog rather than your physician. In another situation, if a person, using Polish-accented English, states that she has just bought a new [bek], you will easily identify this word as the highly probable *bag* and not as the totally unlikely *back*.

But can we be satisfied with having pronunciation that is just comprehensible? To answer this question, let us consider some of the consequences of heavily foreign accented speech which can, however, with some effort on the part of the listener, be understood. As various researchers have observed, pronunciation which puts too much strain on the listeners is very likely to cause them irritation and annoyance and, in consequence, discourage them from further contact with the foreign speaker. The effort that is required might simply be too much for our interlocutors. I have personally found myself in a situation of this kind. Some years ago I spent several months in the USA where I rented a flat in a university building for foreign visitors. It turned out that my upstairs neighbour was a girl student from China. I tried to talk to her a few times, but found her English so difficult to understand that I finally gave up. In consequence we never made friends and just exchanged greetings and polite smiles when we accidentally met.

Speakers with pronunciation problems often make, quite unconsciously and unintentionally, an unfavourable impression of their personality on their listeners. Kelly (2000), for instance, in his discussion of the role of English prosody, claims that German learners who use their native intonation patterns in English sound abrupt or impolite, while the Spanish who employ Spanish prosody in English might sometimes appear rather bored and disinterested. Other studies have demonstrated that listeners often judge people they have never met on their personality, intelligence and social status just from listening to the way they pronounce a few words. Needless to say, the less intelligible the foreigner's speech, the more critical such judgements are. In Part B a brief report is presented on the experiment which has been carried out to examine how native speakers of Polish perceive foreign-accented Polish and how the degree of accentedness affects the listeners' evaluation of the speakers' personal characteristics. It is shown that the better foreigners' Polish pronunciation is, the higher scores they receive on their alleged intelligence, education, reliability, pleasantness and trustworthiness. Of course, the opposite is also true; more heavily accented and less intelligible speech causes more critical assessments.

Further empirical evidence is also available to show that there are serious drawbacks to having poor English pronunciation. In one experiment the same lecture was delivered to two groups of students. In the first case it was presented with near-native pronunciation, in the other, a foreign-accented version. The students' judgements were very different; the first lecture was regarded as more interesting, more logical and better organized than the second, even though the content of both was exactly the same! In another study carried out in Sweden (Abelin & Boyd, 2000), students evaluated foreign teachers who taught various subjects in Swedish. In all instances teachers with good Swedish pronunciation were assessed as more competent and efficient than those with a strong foreign accent.

Negative perceptions of accented speech can have even more serious consequences and sometimes lead to foreigners' social stigmatization and discrimination (see Lippi-Green, 1997; Moyer, 2013). Munro (2003), for instance, discusses several cases of accent-based discrimination in Canada. One of them involved a Polish immigrant called Gajecki, who spoke fluent English but with a strong Polish accent. After a few years of a successful teaching career at school, Gajecki was denied employment because, according to the administrator, he 'did not speak English'. A court ruled that Gajecki was discriminated against on the basis of his accent and awarded him compensation.

Thus, no matter how good someone's general command of a foreign language is, if their pronunciation is poor, it might negatively influence the perception of such a person.[2] On the other hand, learners with good English pronunciation impress people favourably and often benefit from this asset. Some years ago a student of mine went to London for his summer holidays. He needed money to live on, but all he managed to find was a rather unattractive and poorly paid job of washing up in an expensive restaurant, which he did with two other foreigners. One day a waiter was taken ill and a replacement was needed. The manager decided to employ one of the three foreigners and chose the Polish student to be the new waiter (a considerably nicer and better paid job, with good tips from the customers) because of his good English pronunciation, much better than those of the other two candidates.

Finally, it should be pointed out that people with poor pronunciation often lack the confidence to speak up and try to say as little as possible. On the other hand, good pronunciation provides learners with the confidence to engage in conversations with other speakers of English, allows them to sound able and competent, and gives them a sense of achievement. It is an asset that cannot be underestimated.

I hope the above remarks make it clear why mastering the pronunciation of a foreign language is well worth both the teachers' and the learners' effort. As argued by Morley (1991), the question is not whether pronunciation should be taught, but rather what should be taught and how it should be done.

A.1.2 Why is Pronunciation Teaching Often Neglected?

In the preceding section we have pointed out the major advantages of having good English pronunciation as well as some negative consequences of poor pronunciation for language learners. A logical assumption based on the presented reasoning can be made that pronunciation instruction occupies an important place in ELT. Yet it is striking that many, if not most, books and articles devoted to pronunciation instruction begin in a similar fashion, i.e. with remarks concerning a general neglect of pronunciation teaching, often called the 'Cinderella' of ELT (e.g. Celce-Murcia *et al.*, 1996; Kelly, 2000). Hewings (2004: 11) maintains that, even if good pronunciation is important to many learners who are willing to work hard to achieve it, 'teaching does not always reflect this wish, and pronunciation is treated as a low priority area of study'. Derwing and Munro (2005: 382) also complain about 'the marginalization of pronunciation within applied linguistics'. This view is expressed by many authors in their assessment of the situation both in ESL and EFL teaching contexts, which indicates that this is a global rather than a local issue.

Thus, in spite of its undeniable importance, phonetic instruction tends to be neglected in ELT, which is a puzzle that requires some explanation. First of all, pronunciation is frequently regarded as the most difficult aspect of another language to master. Thus, numerous examples are often provided of language learners who achieve a high level of competence in grammar and vocabulary of the L2, but whose pronunciation leaves much to be desired.[3] In other words, different elements of language are learnt with varied success and in this respect pronunciation appears to be the most problematic area, particularly when native-like speech is seen as the goal of teaching and learning. Consequently, many teachers believe that since time and effort spent on pronunciation instruction usually brings unsatisfactory results, it should rather be devoted to those aspects of language which are teachable and learnable.

Secondly, as argued by Elliot (1995: 531), 'teachers tend to view pronunciation as the least useful of the basic language skills and therefore they generally sacrifice teaching pronunciation in order to spend valuable class time on other areas of the language'. This view is additionally reinforced in EFL contexts by predominantly written exams that learners must take, for example at the end of mandatory language courses in many countries, and for which teachers must prepare their students. It should be added that the teachers' professional reputation often depends on how well their students do in such tests. Also, many international language examinations (see Szpyra-Kozłowska, 2003) attach little importance to the examinees' English pronunciation in comparison with other language skills. If what is tested in language exams is primarily grammar and vocabulary, then intensive pronunciation training must be viewed by teachers and learners as a waste of precious class time. This is known as a 'washback effect'.

Furthermore, the negligence of pronunciation can be affected by the fact that frequently very little attention is given to it in general English course books as well as books preparing learners for different international examinations (see Section A.3.6. in Chapter 3 for more details). Many instructors, believing that course book authors are highly qualified specialists in ELT who know best how much attention should be given to various language components, follow the contents of such publications faithfully and tend to devote insufficient time to pronunciation training.

Little attention to practical phonetics stems also from the assumptions of the communicative approach, dominant in modern language teaching, in which, on the one hand, good pronunciation is viewed as essential for effective communication but, on the other hand, emphasis is placed on fluency rather than accuracy and pronunciation errors are tolerated. This, in consequence, means that pronunciation training tends to be fairly limited as 'communicatively adequate pronunciation is generally assumed to be a by-product of appropriate practice over a sufficient period of time' (Celce-Murcia *et al.*, 1996: 449).

Yet another reason for many non-native teachers' reluctance to teach practical phonetics more extensively is the poor quality of their own pronunciation and the resulting lack of confidence concerning this skill. It has been observed that the better the teachers' mastery of the English sound system is, the more attention they pay to their students' phonetic training. Of course the reverse is also true.

Finally, various researchers base many instructors' failure to teach pronunciation properly on their inadequate training which does not provide them with the necessary knowhow. This is particularly true of ESL contexts, in which only brief and often superficial courses are needed to obtain ELT qualifications. As pointed out by Celce-Murcia *et al.* (1996: 12), 'teachers can effectively address the pronunciation needs of their students only through comprehensive knowledge of the English sound system and through familiarity with a variety of pedagogical techniques, many of which should be communicatively oriented'. If prospective teachers are not properly trained in these issues, they are either likely to marginalize pronunciation training or do it ineffectively in their work.

A.1.3 Goals of Pronunciation Teaching/Learning

In Section A.1.2 we have provided many reasons why learners of English should strive to have good English pronunciation. The question that immediately arises is how good the student's pronunciation should actually be. In other words, what has to be decided is the goal of phonetic instruction.

The traditional answer was simple: the aim of the phonodidatic process was for learners to achieve either native or near-native pronunciation, the only important issue being the choice of a native accent model, which will be discussed in detail in Section A.1.5. This objective implies adopting native norms of linguistic correctness and granting native speakers a special status of being the ultimate authority on English language use.

With time, however, more and more researchers have arrived at the same conclusion: for the overwhelming majority of foreign learners, the goal of achieving native-like or even near-native pronunciation is simply unattainable. As mentioned in the preceding section, while a high level of proficiency or even mastery in grammar and vocabulary is not infrequent, pronunciation is different in that articulatory habits formed early in the process of L1 acquisition appear to be fairly resistant to change in learning the phonetics of the L2. Thus, although cases of foreign learners with native-like English pronunciation are sometimes reported, they are extremely rare, particularly when language learning takes place in the so-called instructed setting, i.e. in the classroom in a country where it is not spoken.

Nowacka (2008), for example, examined the ultimate phonetic attainment of 200 Polish university and college graduates in six different institutions of tertiary education, all specializing in English and about to become language teachers and interpreters. She recorded samples of their read and extemporaneous speech which were next evaluated by several native-speaker judges whose task was to decide how native a given speaker sounded. Of all the participants, only one of them was taken to be a native speaker of English. It should be added that the subjects can be considered highly motivated and talented learners, who received formal training in theoretical and practical English phonetics. In the study reported here, achieving native-like pronunciation has turned out to be impossible for all students but one, so attaining this goal seems to be even less likely in the case of other learners.

In modern phonodidactics it has long been suggested that a more achievable and realistic goal is 'intelligibility'. This rather vague and imprecise term has been understood, however, in a variety of ways (for a discussion, see Jenkins, 2000).

A distinction should be made between *basic* or *minimal intelligibility* which allows for rudimentary communication but puts a considerable strain on the listener and requires much effort on their part to understand the message, and *comfortable intelligibility*, to use Abercrombie's (1949) term, which puts little or no strain on the listener. While some learners need to achieve no more than basic intelligibility, such as tourists travelling abroad who need English to ask for directions, order a meal in a restaurant or pay a hotel bill (so-called 'survival English'), the majority of them need to be comfortably intelligible, which would allow them to use English in a variety of situations and for various purposes.

It is clear that these different goals have important consequences for phonetic instruction. When near-native pronunciation is aimed at, all phonetic details of the native model are important and should be practised and faithfully imitated. When the learner's objective is intelligible communication, some pronunciation areas must be prioritized while others can be neglected.

At this point another important but frequently confused and disregarded distinction must be made between a pronunciation model, which is a kind of idealized reference point, and the goal or target which learners try to achieve depending on their specific needs and abilities. This means that with one accent model different goals can be pursued, e.g. minimal intelligibility, comfortable intelligibility or native-like pronunciation. It can be likened to climbing mountains in order to admire a beautiful landscape. For some climbers the only imaginable and worthwhile aim might be conquering the highest peak, regardless of all the effort and hard work involved in getting there, while others will be quite satisfied with reaching some lower point from which the view is also nice, but does not require so much time and exhausting training.

While the majority of pronunciation specialists would agree that in most instances comfortable intelligibility is an appropriate goal, it is by no means clear how it can be achieved. What matters in particular is the adopted pronunciation model (discussed in the following sections) and the selection of phonetic features, mastery of which will ensure comfortable intelligibility (analyzed in Chapter 2). Another question concerns the participants of communication via English, i.e. native speakers or non-native speakers. In other words, the issue at stake is who learners' English should be intelligible to. We shall address it below.

A.1.4   EFL Versus ELF: English Pronunciation Models Debate

A starting point in English phonetic instruction to be considered even before it begins is the selection of a pronunciation model which will serve as a norm and a point of reference for foreign learners. In view of the global spread of English and a huge variety of native and non-native accents, however, this has become a very complex and highly controversial problem.

The spread and the use of English in the world is often expressed by Kachru's (1986) well-known model of concentric circles, with the Inner Circle, located in the middle of the drawing, representing those areas where English is spoken as a native language, e.g. the British Isles, the United States, Canada, Australia and New Zealand, the Outer Circle comprising postcolonial countries, such as India, parts of Africa and Asia, where English has an official or semi-official status and is used in education, administration, business and politics, and the Expanding Circle with those countries where English is learnt as a foreign language.

For years this division largely determined the type of English pronunciation adopted for teaching and learning purposes. Thus, those foreigners who settled in some Inner Circle countries naturally learnt the accent of their hosts (the phenomenon of ESL). In the Outer Circle, some firmly established local models of English, such as Indian English in India or Nigerian English in Nigeria, i.e. the so-called New Englishes, have been employed in teaching, alongside native pronunciation models, usually those of the former colonial empire. In the Expanding Circle, native models, usually RP or GA, have been adopted (EFL). The choice of an English variety, including pronunciation, for EFL learners has been dictated by geographical proximity as well as by the economic, political and cultural influences of an English-speaking country. Thus, in Europe British English and Received Pronunciation (RP) have traditionally been taught. In other parts of the world, for instance in South America and some Asiatic countries, it has been American English in its General American (GA) version that has been selected as appropriate for foreign learners. Other varieties, such as, for example, Australian English or South African English have also been employed in the regions where they are spoken. Nevertheless, RP and GA have undoubtedly dominated the English teaching scene worldwide.

After years of relative stability in the area of English pronunciation models, the last decade can be characterized as one of turmoil and debate. This change has been triggered by the growing realization that English, by becoming a global language, serves millions of non-native speakers of English as a means of communication with other non-native speakers of this language. Consequently, if native speakers are not involved in many international exchanges in English, why should their norms be valid in this kind of communication?[4] Moreover, if we assume that what matters in international contexts is mutual intelligibility of interlocutors, then certainly achieving native-like pronunciation is not necessary to attain this goal. Reasoning of this kind has been voiced in English for a long time in various publications (e.g. Abercrombie, 1949) and many attempts have been made to devise a simplified pronunciation agenda for foreign learners (e.g. Jenner, 1989). Nevertheless, it was the publication of Jenkins' (2000) book which introduced the idea of EIL or ELF that played a major role in the current changes in English phonodidactics.

In addition to these developments, another issue of importance to countries in which RP has been a traditionally accepted model of English pronunciation is a steady decline in the status of this accent observed within the last 40 years. Thus, all the sources dealing with this issue never fail to mention that only about 3% of the British population use RP. It is no longer BBC English as nowadays the BBC allows non-RP accents on its channels as well. It is not Oxford English as more and more Oxbridge graduates are proud to retain their local accents. Nor is it truly the Queen's English any more as even in aristocratic circles it is fashionable, particularly among the younger generations, to use other accents. Moreover, for many British people RP sounds posh, affected and unnatural, and its speakers are negatively evaluated as unfriendly, distant and arrogant. In brief, all these reasons suggest that RP is no longer suitable as a model of pronunciation for foreign learners.

These two trends, coupled with the changed goals of pronunciation instruction, have been the major reasons for questioning the tradition of employing native accent models as appropriate for the purposes of international communication by the proponents of ELF, who have undertaken severe criticism of, in their view, the old and outdated EFL approach, and contrasting it with the 'new' and 'progressive' concept of EFL. Thus, numerous books and articles on this topic have been published (e.g. Jenkins, 2000, 2006; Hülmbauer, 2010; Kaur, 2009; Seidlhofer, 2011; Walker, 2011). A number of international conferences have been devoted to these issues and De Gruyter Mouton started to publish the *Journal of English as a Lingua Franca,* concerned with international varieties of English.

It appears that there are two aspects of ELF research, one seeming less controversial and the other raising much discussion. The first of these is studying linguistic and cultural interactions between non-native speakers of English which, in our view, constitutes a fully legitimate object of study, just like any other form of human activity and creativity. This field, as evidenced by a growing number of publications, is developing rapidly, with various interdisciplinary tools of analysis being applied to the data, particularly those collected in several large ELF corpuses. The primary objective of these studies is to establish whether there are any regularities in such interactions and whether properties common to countless varieties of English as a lingua franca can be isolated at various levels of language: pronunciation, vocabulary, word formation, syntax and pragmatics.[5]

Another, far more controversial aspect of ELF concerns proposed modifications in the teaching of English. The proponents of ELF argue that native pronunciation models are both unrealistic and inappropriate for the majority of learners since, as has been already pointed out, very few learners are capable of achieving native-like pronunciation. Setting unrealistic goals can lead to both teachers' and learners' frustration, so only objectives that can be attained should be aimed at. Moreover, native pronunciation models are claimed to be inappropriate for international learners since they use English mainly in contacts with other non-native speakers, in which case native norms of correctness are irrelevant. What is needed is a kind of English pronunciation that would be intelligible to its users, even if it departs from traditional standards considerably. In other words, the success in ELF is measured by the effectiveness of communication and not by adherence to native norms of pronunciation (or grammar). As a matter of fact, for many ELF advocates the very concept of native speakers and their accents has become outdated. According to Setter (2010: 449), 'it has become unfashionable to assert that RP or GenAm should be used as a pronunciation model in this era of global English'. In other words, ELF advocates intend to put an end to what they call the 'tyranny of Inner Circle models' and 'linguistic imperialism'.

In order to achieve intelligibility, learners of ELF should master a set of phonetic priorities, formulated by Jenkins (2000) in her Lingua Franca Core

(LFC), the contents of which will be discussed in some detail in Chapter 2. The phonetic properties of English which remain outside the LFC are claimed not to be essential for intelligibility and even to be detrimental to it; the use of weak forms, different intonation patterns, rhythm and connected speech phenomena is argued to be harmful to intelligibility and should therefore be avoided in ELF contexts.

Giving up native speaker norms of pronunciation is supposed to be beneficial for international users of English for yet another reason; namely, by preserving a strong accent of their L1, they can express their national and personal identity, which is a vital issue in ELF. According to Walker (2011: 13), 'whatever accent we have, native speaker or non-native speaker, standard or regional, it is a part of our identity, and for some people losing their accent is the same as losing part of their identity'. It has even been suggested that imposing someone else's accent on learners is morally wrong and brings emotional harm to them.

Moreover, Jenkins (2006) argues that EFL, which she refers to as 'standard language ideology', creates an ideal and diminishes those who do not fit the model. According to her, it breeds prejudice, language insecurity and feelings of linguistic and social inferiority experienced by L2 English speakers. ELF, on the other hand, is democratic in that non-native users of English are free to do with it what they wish, i.e. simplify it or enrich it with various innovations, provided communicative efficiency is ensured. This, in consequence, means creating many new pidginized versions of English whose users are endowed with the power to establish new linguistic norms different from native standards. Evidently, ELF can be viewed as politically correct since with regard to the use of English it promotes democracy, equality and tolerance.

While ELF supporters generally claim that their proposal is intended only for those who want to use English in international contexts and is not meant to replace traditional EFL teaching with its native pronunciation norms, they imply that the latter type of learners constitute a true minority, which includes mainly prospective teachers and spies. Since this group is fairly small and therefore rather negligible, we should first of all cater for the needs of the overwhelming majority of international users of English who want to communicate intelligibly with each other. This, by implication, means that ELF is the most useful approach for almost all EFL learners.

Walker (2011) maintains that with regard to pronunciation instruction ELF brings several important benefits for both teachers and students, which are listed below.

(1) A lighter workload. The ELF pronunciation syllabus (based on the LFC) is considerably reduced in comparison with a typical EFL pronunciation syllabus. This means less work for both teachers and learners who can now concentrate on those aspects of English pronunciation that are directly relevant to intelligibility in international contexts.

(2)   Increased progress and achievability. According to Walker (2011: 63), many features of the traditional pronunciation syllabus are unteachable while 'most of the items in the LFC are teachable, with classroom teaching leading to learning'. This gives learners a sense of phonetic progress and achievement.

(3)   Accent addition instead of accent reduction. Learning EFL pronunciation means adding some phonetic features, i.e. those found in the LFC, to the learner's native pronunciation as opposed to accent reduction which implies that the learner's accent is wrong and should be modified.

(4)   Identity through accent. ELF allows learners to retain many features of their L1 pronunciation so that they can preserve their first-language identity. This, in turn, is supposed 'to increase their confidence as users of English'.

(5)   Mother tongue as friend. The L1 is not necessarily an obstacle to learning L2 pronunciation, but can be employed to help learners gain competence in the LFC, e.g. by reference to L1 sounds.

(6)   Non-native speakers as instructors. Non-native pronunciation teachers have a number of advantages over native instructors, such as their knowledge of both L1 and L2 sound systems, understanding learners' pronunciation difficulties through personal experience and as effective users of ELF.

Clearly, the approach sketched above departs radically from current teaching practice and its traditional assumptions. Moreover, in the light of its alleged advantages, it is worth considering as a viable alternative to the EFL tradition.

It should also be pointed out that ELF, which started as a proposal for pronunciation priorities in lingua franca settings, gradually extended its scope to include other areas of language instruction as well. As the main goal of ELF is intelligibility in international contexts, it is logical to assume that not all English vocabulary and grammatical structures need to be taught to achieve this objective. On the contrary, too complex grammar and too sophisticated words might be an obstacle to intelligibility. Therefore, proposals containing a set of grammatical and lexical priorities similar to the LFC in pronunciation are a natural consequence of adopting ELF.

As a matter of fact, various publications make it clear that ELF research is already heading in this direction. As argued by Jenkins and Seidlhofer (2001), various simplifications of English grammar (referred to by Seidlhofer, 2011, as a reduction of redundant linguistic features) cause no major disruptions in communication. They provide the following examples:

•   using the same form for all present tense verbs, as in *you look very sad* and *he look very sad*;

- not putting the definite or indefinite article in front of nouns, as in *our countries have signed agreement about this*;
- treating *who* and *which* as interchangeable relative pronouns, as in *the picture who* or *a person which*;
- using the verb stem in constructions such as *I look forward to see you tomorrow*;
- using *isn't it?* as a universal tag question, i.e. instead of *haven't they?* and *shouldn't he?* as in *They've finished their dinner, isn't it?*

They add a further comment, stating that 'what our analyses of ELF interactions suggest is that the time needed to teach and learn these constructions bears very little relationship to their actual usefulness as successful communication is obviously possible without them'. The implications are clear: there is no point in spending so much time and effort on practising such communicatively 'useless' features.[6]

It is interesting to note that certain elements of this approach are already being implemented by ELFers. In several volumes of papers from conferences on English as a lingua franca the editors refrained from meticulous copyediting, as stated in the introduction to Archibald *et al.* (2011: 5), 'The scope of this study is global and the contributions are from scholars around the world. We have therefore edited the contributions on the basis of their international communicative effectiveness and not according to their adherence to native English grammatical norms. (. . .) It would be hypocritical of us to insist that contributions adhere to a narrow local version of English', where 'a narrow local version of English' means Standard English used by several hundred million people all over the world, including the authors of the above words.

As many claims made by ELFers are highly controversial, they have triggered a lively discussion which has involved numerous general and applied linguists, teachers, teacher trainers and learners of English (see, for example, Dziubalska-Kołaczyk & Przedlacka, 2005). Since it is next to impossible to present here all the different viewpoints and opinions that have been voiced in connection with it, both in favour of and against the new approach (for a summary of some of the controversies surrounding ELF see Walker, 2011), in what follows the focus is on those aspects of ELF which appear to be particularly important for the EFL/ELF pronunciation debate. In other words, as prospective teachers and spies do not constitute particularly numerous groups of language learners, it is worthwhile considering whether we should perhaps give up teaching EFL and switch to ELF.

First of all, it must be pointed out that insufficient evidence has been provided for the validity of specific aspects of the LFC. Although Jenkins emphasizes that her proposal is empirically researched, she really alludes to the collected data rather than presenting and discussing it in any meaningful detail. She provides neither articulatory and acoustic measurements of learner speech nor statistical analysis of the data, customary in modern phonetic research. As pointed out by Nelson (2012), in his review of Jenkins' (2007) book:

> very importantly, the author refers at various points to 'my empirical data', 'my LFC research findings' and employs other such locutions which would lead a reader to believe that there exists somewhere a coherent body of evidence which could be examined to substantiate the claim of the existence of something called ELF. If fact, [...] Jenkins never presents any such data base and citations of the author's other publications are not persuasive in this regard.

This means that the LFC can only be viewed as tentative in nature and subject to further empirical verification and not as a firmly established and ready-to-use pronunciation teaching syllabus. While Jenkins herself seems to be aware of that,[7] her followers generally appear to regard her proposal as unquestionable and established beyond any reasonable doubt. Walker (2011), for example, whose book is based on the LFC, accepts this tentative proposal without any reservations and indications of the author's awareness that its various elements are highly disputable (see Chapter 2 for a detailed discussion of the contents of the LFC).

Let us now consider the validity of the arguments put forward by Walker (2011) concerning the alleged benefits of adopting an ELF approach to pronunciation teaching. It is true that due to its use the workload for both teachers and learners is diminished, as is always the case when a narrower syllabus is employed instead of a broader one. In other words, the less we teach, the less effort it requires. It is incorrect to assume, however, that in EFL every aspect of English pronunciation is taught and learnt because, first, it would be impossible within the time allotted to pronunciation instruction in an EFL teaching context and, secondly, because EFL teachers realize that not all elements of English phonetics are of equal importance and always focus on some of them while neglecting other features. To put it differently, good teachers never teach all they know.

Thus, typically, in phonetic instruction care has always been taken of phonemic distinctions, whereas allophony has been largely neglected as an issue regarded to be of secondary importance for communication. Moreover, in actual teaching practice approximations of target sounds have always been implicitly accepted because the exact imitation of many L2 segments is usually impossible to attain. For example, in Polish there are no palatoalveolar consonants (as in *shoe, pleasure, judge* and *chair*). Their closest equivalents are postalveolar segments, which are similar to the English palatoalveolars, but not identical. The difference is noticeable and an obvious sign of foreignness, but has no impact on intelligibility (see Chapter 2). Moreover, palatoalveolars are rather difficult to teach as Polish learners, even after phonetic training, quickly switch to the old articulatory habits and replace them with postalveolars. Polish teachers, realizing the learning difficulty of these sounds as well as the negligible consequences of such mispronunciations, usually give up teaching this aspect of English. In brief, simplifications of various kinds are nothing new in EFL pronunciation teaching and have always been made.

According to Walker, another benefit of adopting ELF is that due to it learners make much progress since they acquire only learnable pronunciation features. This claim, however, can be taken to be only an article of faith since, to our knowledge, no research has proved that all the core elements of the LFC are learnable by all students of different L1s and that those found outside it are not. Thus, the teachability/learnability argument should be approached with due caution, as what is teachable to some learners may be unteachable to others. As observed by Cunningham (2010: 5), 'teachability can only be considered within a given educational context', which includes a specific setting, teachers, learners and employed instructional procedures.

Walker's benefit 3, which refers to a change from 'accent reduction' to 'accent addition', can be viewed in terms of political correctness since its main function is to make learners feel better about their accented speech ('accent reduction' implies that something is wrong with the speaker's accent, which should be modified, whereas 'accent addition' means that some phonetic features must simply be added to one's phonetic repertoire). It seems that this idea underlies much of ELF proponents' reasoning since adopting their approach is supposed to improve both learners' and teachers' self-confidence and wellbeing as they are constantly reminded what a great asset speaking with a foreign accent is (without any mention of the evident drawbacks of a heavy foreign accent discussed in Section A.1.1). Of course it is nice when teachers can make their learners (and themselves) happy, but this is not what we see as their major task, which is to provide their students with a good command of the L2 and practical skills as to how to use it. The more proficient learners become, the better use they can make of their L2 competence, which will certainly make them happier and more self-confident.[8]

Benefit 4 concerns the preservation of L1 accent features which allows learners to retain and express their personal and national identity, an issue that has already been mentioned. It should be pointed out that this can also be achieved in EFL since in current practice, as argued earlier, not all aspects of English phonetics are taught (and learnt). This, coupled with the already discussed issue of a general inability of EFL learners to achieve a native-like accent means that the overwhelming majority of them speak with a distinct foreign accent, which in many cases tends to be quite heavy. The issue of expressing learners' national identity through their accent in the L2 is therefore not a problem; it is rather not revealing it that is far more difficult.[9]

The last two benefits of adopting ELF, according to Walker, concern the role of the learners' mother tongue and the non-native instructors who share it with them. We cannot agree more that they are indeed strong assets in the pronunciation teaching/learning process (more on that in Chapter 3), but this has nothing to do with ELF. In typical EFL settings, in which language classes are usually monolingual and teachers are non-native speakers of English, the use of the L1 as well as comparing L1 and L2 sound systems are commonplace and constitute no particular novelty. As a matter of fact, a frequent problem is an overuse of the L1 in foreign language classes in which both teachers and learners often tend to switch to their native language.

To sum up the above discussion, the majority of Walker's alleged benefits of an ELF approach to pronunciation instruction can also be ascribed to the current teaching of EFL phonetics. In other words, most of the ELFers' criticism levelled against EFL is misguided as it concerns its very conservative version which is rarely, if ever, employed in contemporary teaching practice.

Let us now consider several negative consequences of the proposal under consideration. According to its proponents, a decision must be made as to what goal learners want to achieve: intelligible communication with native speakers of English, in which case EFL offers proper phonetic training, or effective communication with non-native speakers, in which case ELF is more appropriate. The two types of communication are seen as entirely different phenomena which entail different didactic decisions not only in matters of pronunciation, but also grammar and vocabulary. The problem is, however, that many learners do not want to choose between these two options, but wish to learn a kind of English which will enable them to communicate both with native and non-native speakers, without excluding any of these two groups of potential interlocutors. For example, in a questionnaire study I carried out with Polish secondary school students, the respondents were confused by the question as to whom they want to converse with in English and clearly expressed their desire to learn 'good English' that would allow them to use this language with anybody who speaks it. In this case neither of the two possibilities, i.e. EFL or ELF, is fully adequate, which creates a dilemma for English teachers. Whatever their decision is, it will put learners at a disadvantage with one group of potential interlocutors.

An important issue concerns a pronunciation model in ELF. As argued convincingly by Walker (2011: 53), 'without a stable model, learners will have nothing to base their attempts at pronunciation', which is 'an unacceptable situation'. Since the LFC, as often emphasized by Jenkins, is not a model for imitation, the question arises as to what should it be like. According to Walker (2011: 54), 'if they wish, teachers can use one of the standard native-speaker accents as a model for features that are essential for ELF', adding that some of these properties are to be avoided as 'they have a negative impact on intelligibility in ELF'. This seems somewhat illogical since a partial imitation of a model must be very confusing for learners, particularly those who want to practise pronunciation on their own, since they need to be able to tell apart desirable from undesirable features. But a model, by definition, is a kind

of ideal and imitation involves faithful and mechanical repetition of the auditory input without having to decide what should be imitated and what
should not. What Walker is suggesting is a flawed ideal which uses both
features which are desirable and undesirable for intelligibility and its partial,
i.e. non-mechanical and therefore complex and perhaps even impossible imitation. Logically, for the same reasons, native teachers of English who cannot
suppress in their speech features regarded as detrimental to international
intelligibility are bad models. A possible option is to rely on non-native teachers' pronunciation, provided they are competent users of ELF. However, teachers who are trained to speak one of the standard varieties and are expected
(together with spies) to approximate to native pronunciation, even if not exactly
native speakers themselves, do use many prosodic and connected speech phenomena which are supposed to be undesirable for ELF learners. Again, the
latter are faced with the necessity of making a distinction between LFC features and the remaining ones, and the teacher using a native or near-native
accent is placed in an awkward position of being a flawed model forced to
tell learners that they must not imitate their pronunciation faithfully, but
only partially if they want to remain intelligible in international contexts.
As a matter of fact, a perfect ELF teacher would be a non-native speaker who,
while attending university or college courses for future teachers of English,
failed to learn many features of English pronunciation and preserved the
majority of L1 properties. In other words, it would be someone who was a
failure as a student of English. A more talented or more hardworking gradu-
ate would be far less desirable as an ELF teacher.

Moreover, English native speakers are in a particularly difficult position
because of the pronunciation requirements imposed on them. Walker (2011:
42), in his discussion of weak forms, states that 'native-speaker teachers
should not only avoid teaching weak forms, they should avoid using them,
too'. This seems a rather difficult if not an impossible task to accomplish as
it requires native speakers to change their lifelong speech habits which are
extremely difficult to control. The advice Walker (2011: 42) provides seems
of little help: 'in practice, this is basically a question of more careful enun-
ciation in class, which almost automatically leads to weak forms being
replaced with their strong form equivalents'. This reasoning appears to be
incorrect as the use of weak forms by native speakers has nothing to do with
the carefulness of speech, but is a feature that follows from the rhythmical
structure of English. Thus, in slower speech weak forms are also employed,
but content words are often lengthened. The use of weak forms resembles
vowel reduction; in over-careful speech native speakers do not replace schwa
with full vowels. The conclusion is that native speakers are totally inappropriate for teaching ELF pronunciation.

According to Walker (2011: 54), 'alternatively teachers can use competent
ELF speakers as a model'. Apart from the technical difficulty of finding
appropriate recordings, a more general question arises as to which ELF

accents learners should be given to imitate. Theoretically, all efficient ELF users can serve as phonetic models. Recall, however, that one of the ideas of ELF is the retention of many L1 features in order to express learners' national and personal identities. Suppose now that, say, Spanish learners are given samples of Japanese English to imitate. Clearly, they will learn to speak English with a Japanese accent (mixed with their native Spanish and English features), which will apparently make the learners' identity more difficult to express than in the case in which only L1 features are preserved.

As a matter of fact, this is not a hypothetical example. In the eastern part of Poland in smaller towns and villages there is a shortage of English teachers. Because of that, many schools started to employ language instructors from the Ukraine and Belarus, who usually speak English with a strong East Slavic accent. This has resulted in many Polish learners acquiring English pronunciation with a mixture of accents: Polish, English and East Slavic. Whether this fact is of relevance to their intelligibility remains to be tested, but there is no doubt that it influences the expression of their national identity through their accent in English. In other words, to Polish learners of English wishing to retain their native accent, having a Ukrainian or Belarus teacher as a model constitutes a threat to achieving this goal. The same consequences arise if ELF speakers will serve as pronunciation models.

A frequent criticism levelled at ELF concerns the impoverished nature of its pronunciation agenda and thus the limited use that can be made of it. Proponents of ELF maintain that by teaching it we do not do harm to its learners since after mastering ELF pronunciation, they can go on to acquire features of native English if they wish to do so. After all, the argument goes, they will have nothing to unlearn; they will only have to learn a few new things. But anyone who has been involved in language teaching knows perfectly well that, once formed, articulatory habits are very difficult to change. Suppose, for instance, that for several years someone was taught according to the LFC agenda, in which vowel quality is irrelevant and local substitutions are allowed. Then the learner decides to acquire native-like vowel qualities. The amount of time and hard work involved in modifying pronunciation habits would be enormous, in fact far larger than in the case of learning native-like vowels from the beginning. As is well known, phonetic fossilization is extremely difficult to eliminate. In other words, it is not a simple matter of adding something to one's speech; switching from ELF to EFL is not as painless as we are led to believe.

On the other hand, a change in the opposite direction is much more likely to happen, i.e. EFL learners with a good command of English pronunciation (but also grammar and vocabulary) can, with a small amount of effort, become competent ELF users. The key term in this approach, next to 'intelligibility', is 'accommodation'.[10] As is often argued, successful communication between speakers using different accents (but also between speakers representing different levels of language proficiency) is always connected to a need for accommodation. Generally, in such cases more proficient learners accommodate to the less proficient ones by simplifying their language in terms of grammar, vocabulary and pronunciation to make it more intelligible to their interlocutors.[11] The better the learners' English pronunciation is, the better they can phonetically accommodate to other speakers in terms of native accent features. In other words, less proficient speakers cannot do that. For instance, those users of English who employ connected speech phenomena, such as assimilations and elisions, can, with some effort, modify their speech in such a way as to avoid these features while talking to other foreigners, but less advanced learners are incapable of adjusting their speech to that of a more proficient interlocutor for the obvious reason of not being capable of using elements they have not mastered. While travelling abroad and using English as a lingua franca, I have often been in a situation where I have had to communicate in English with less proficient speakers than myself. In all cases I was the person who had to accommodate to my interlocutors as no matter how hard they tried, they were not able to do that and could not start speaking fluent English to accommodate to me.

These observations find support in the observations of several of my students in the English Department, advanced to proficient speakers of English, who have had a theoretical and practical training in RP. They spent five months studying at a university in Finland within the Erasmus exchange programme. I asked some of them to write down their observations concerning their use of English pronunciation in contacts with other students. Below, I present the relevant fragments of two such essays. This is what Andrzej wrote:[12]

> During my five month stay in Finland I was involved in numerous interactions with foreign exchange students from all around the world. It has to be mentioned that at that time there were some 560 exchange students, almost all of them non-native speakers of English with French, Spanish and Italian speakers dominating the statistics, and just a handful (two or three) native speakers of English from the USA. Naturally, such multitude of different language users calls for a common means of communication. Being the lingua franca of the world, English was the obvious choice. But what kind of English was it that I used throughout my stay?
>
> On the first couple of days after my arrival I strived very much to sound British, to sound RP and stood very strongly by what I had been taught over the years of my English language education. I must say, however, that this strategy worked only partially. People did understand me, albeit every now and then I had to paraphrase or repeat what I had said. What struck me as curious was that many people remarked that the way I spoke was somewhat different to what they were used to hearing and funny. At that time it got me thinking and paying attention to what

kind of English people were using. I learnt quickly that for a more successful communication to take place I had to succumb to at least some
degree of levelling and language accommodation that would make conversations with my foreign peers easier. To do that was not particularly
difficult as I believe I was well prepared to accommodate the required
changes and alterations to my language due to my solid and comprehensive knowledge of English. The only thing I had to bear in mind was that
for a person who has expert knowledge on the subject it is easy to tone
down while for a person with little or no knowledge it is not possible to
pretend to be an expert especially when it comes to language use. [*Here
Andrzej describes phonetic modifications he introduced in his speech.*]

To summarise, the stay in Finland gave me a fresh look on English.
Now I know that sometimes language has to be modified to meet the
needs of our interlocutors, a situation I never experienced at my university. Secondly, such modifications can only be possible if a person has
proficient knowledge of language which ensures they will resist bad language habits that can be commonplace in multinational setting.
Therefore, I believe that the aim of language teaching should always be
as high as possible, as the higher we aim, the higher the end result is and
one can be confident that learners will be able to use language in different settings whether it is a learned discourse with native speakers or a
chat with an intermediate learner of English from China.

And this is what Przemek wrote:

My five-month stay in Finland as an exchange student made me
realise that an overwhelming majority of talk exchanges done in English
is in fact done by non-native speakers communicating with other non-
natives. This lingua franca use of English brings about numerous changes
in the way the language is used. For instance, I found myself talking
differently to my American or Australian professors and to my fellow
exchange students coming from all over the world.

Being a student of English, I always tried to speak correctly, also in
terms of pronunciation. After some time, however, I realised that being
correct had a negative impact on my interlocutor's understanding of the
message I was trying to convey. Obviously, it was only the case with
those whose proficiency was not very high. [*Here Przemek describes the
changes he introduced into his pronunciation.*]

All these changes happened quite quickly and I became more
entrenched in them than I would have wanted. After some time I
realised, for instance, that my British-like, careful accent weakened even
in formal interactions with native speakers. Of course, I could come back
to it when I wanted to, but it took a great deal of attention and concentration on my part.

The two essays quoted above make it clear that these are more proficient learners doing the accommodating in terms of native English accent features and not lower-level students.[13]

Another argument which supports the above claim is indirectly provided by Hülmbauer *et al.* (2008: 28), who state that, 'it is possible for one person to be in position of an EFL user at one moment and of an EFL user at another moment, depending on who he or she is speaking to and for what purpose'. It should be noted that this can only be done by someone who is proficient enough in English to be able to switch from a more complex to a simpler variety of language. The reverse cannot be done. In other words, a person who has in their phonetic repertoire the interdental fricatives can try to modify their pronunciation and replace these segments with, for example, dental or alveolar /t, d/ to accommodate to the speech pattern of the interlocutor. The opposite is impossible, i.e. a speaker who cannot pronounce 'th' sounds will not be able to accommodate to those speakers who use them. This means that a fluent speaker of EFL can switch to ELF, but not the other way round.[14]

There are other disadvantages that ELFers are likely to face. Since the majority of English learners in the Expanding Circle already use English pronunciation based on some native model, EFL users might have problems not only communicating with native speakers, but also with non-native speakers. Moreover, they might have problems using dictionaries and other materials based on natural varieties of English since their pronunciation will often depart considerably from the dictionary versions.

The final issue to be addressed here concerns the learners' right to decide what type of English pronunciation they want to learn, which is frequently emphasized by ELF researchers as an argument in the EFL/ELF debate. For example, according to Jenkins (2009: 14), 'L2 English speakers should have a choice of what type of English they would like to learn'. Setter (2010: 449) also emphasizes this issue and states that, 'what the target accent is should be the choice of the individual' and that the teacher has no right to impose it on the learners since 'the imposition of any variety is akin to linguistic imperialism'. This means that learners should make a decision as to whether EFL or ELF should be employed in their language education.

So let us look somewhat closer at the issue of choosing an approach to pronunciation teaching/learning by foreign learners, which entails a decision concerning the adopted accent model. In many countries English is already taught in kindergarten and continues through primary and secondary school into tertiary and adult education. Two basic stages in this process and, consequently, two groups of learners can be isolated:

Group 1: Learners in the kindergarten, primary and secondary school (up to about 18 years), attending state as well as private schools, including language schools. We shall refer to them as Younger Learners.

Group 2: Learners in post-secondary education, which includes tertiary education (college and university) and courses for adults (general and specialized, e.g. for nurses, engineers, businessmen, etc.). We shall refer to them as Adult Learners.

Members of Group 2, which involves adults, learn English for some specific purposes as part of their professional training to become, for instance, flight attendants, missionaries or nurses and doctors planning to work in Third World countries, and language instruction should be adjusted to their needs. Such learners know well what they need English for and where and with whom they are most likely going to communicate in it, which should affect their teachers' decisions as to how much pronunciation practice they require. Thus, for example, prospective and current economists will need extra training in Business English, but will not usually need to master pronunciation beyond the level of comfortable intelligibility. It is usually assumed that language teachers and interpreters will need to acquire English pronunciation almost perfectly. An important feature of this group of learners is the fact that they are adults who have already decided what they want to do in their lives and can make informed decisions as to the type of English they want to learn. For many of them ELF might be appropriate; others might prefer traditional EFL.

On the other hand, Group 1, which comprises the majority of all EFL learners, is different. Children and adolescents who learn English at school cannot choose an approach to English pronunciation appropriate for them for a variety of reasons. First of all, they do not have sufficient knowledge about English accents to be able to make informed decisions in this respect. Secondly, and much more importantly, they do not know where and for what purposes they will need English in the future. Some of them might want to communicate with native speakers. Others might wish to communicate only with non-native speakers. Some will be satisfied with learning 'survival English' while others might become language teachers or spies, and will need to be proficient in various aspects of English. Since all these possibilities must remain open, they should be taught English in such a way as not to exclude any of these options. Any attempt at reducing the pronunciation syllabus might be regarded as an incomplete, flawed educational offer. We can liken the situation to teaching arithmetic. Suppose pupils were taught how to do addition and subtraction, but not multiplication and division, on the basis of an assumption that the majority of them will need only the former in their future lives. While this assumption might turn out to be true in some cases, in others depriving learners of an important portion of mathematical competence will be regarded as a wrong pedagogical decision and a grave error.

Finally, if pupils were, after all, allowed to choose an English accent they wanted to learn and the type of approach to their L2 education, this would lead to enormous additional problems, such as the need to offer different courses for those who have selected various options with competent instructors to teach them. Suppose now that some learners would opt for RP, some for GA and yet others for the ELF approach. It is extremely doubtful whether there are many schools that could satisfy these demands.

We should also take into account the teacher as a particularly important participant in the language teaching process. It seems that the old principle according to which the teacher can teach only what he/she knows is particularly valid for the present discussion. If the instructor has received training in a native accent model, this is what he/she is going to teach to learners. If the adopted approach is ELF, then an undesirable discrepancy will arise between the teacher's pronunciation and that required of the students.

In this section we have considered in some detail the issue of whether an ELF approach to pronunciation teaching is a viable alternative to the traditional native speaker based model in typical EFL contexts.[15] We have concluded that, in spite of its initial appeal, ELF suffers from significant shortcomings and cannot be employed in the teaching of the majority of foreign learners (Group 1) as its goals are too narrow and it has many negative consequences for its users. Moreover, many aspects of this proposal appear dubious and difficult or even impossible to implement. This is not to say, however, that the traditional EFL view of pronunciation instruction has no drawbacks. As pointed out by the ELF critics of EFL, it is unrealistic in its objectives and its excessive reliance on native speakers. Furthermore, it fails to cater for international learners' needs as well as neglects the role of English as a global lingua franca (for other arguments against EFL, see Section A.1.5).

To sum up, it appears that neither of the two approaches is fully acceptable in typical EFL settings as they are too extreme: EFL in its insistence on strict adherence to native accent models and native speaker norms and ELF in its highly restricted, anti-native speaker phonetic agenda. In this context it seems that some middle ground should be sought.

A.1.5 EFL, ELF or NELF?

As argued above, neither ELF nor the traditional EFL, as two rather extreme approaches to pronunciation teaching/learning, can be viewed as fully adequate for contemporary foreign learners. This means that some alternative and more satisfying solutions are needed.

What we would like to suggest here is an approach to pronunciation teaching termed NELF (Native English as a Lingua Franca), which combines some ideas of ELF and EFL, and can be viewed as a kind of compromise between them. It is intended for foreign learners who wish to learn English in order to communicate in it with other speakers of this language, both native and non-native, without excluding any of these two groups of potential interlocutors. As shown earlier, most learners do not want to make a choice as to who they want to communicate with and need to acquire the type of pronunciation that will enable them to use English in a variety of contexts and with different speakers. However, instead of proposing an artificially created pronunciation syllabus, such as the LFC, which is a mixture of RP, GA and learners' L1 phonetic features (see Chapter 2 for details), we suggest that use should be made of native English accents, such as RP or GA, but in a modified fashion, specified in this section. A logical and fully justified assumption is that the closer foreign learners approximate to these models, the easier it is for them to communicate, both in contacts with native and non-native speakers.

The novelty of this approach might be questioned since native varieties have traditionally been employed in the role of a lingua franca. In NELF, however, we propose that native English accents should be adopted not because of their alleged historical, cultural or social superiority but simply as valuable and effective tools of linguistic communication. To put it differently, we opt for native models of pronunciation not because of special admiration and reverence for their speakers and their culture, but because native English serves a useful communicative function. As it is impossible to learn English without some pronunciation model, already existing, natural and ready-to-use native accents are an obvious choice. What I mean is that ideological arguments should be put aside and replaced with pragmatic considerations.

RP is a case in point: since there are very few native speakers of RP, the selection of this accent as a British English pronunciation model cannot stem exclusively from the wish to communicate with the speakers of this particular accent (the chances of EFL learners' meeting such speakers are slight), but follows from various practical reasons, such as the wide intelligibility of this accent, the easy availability of phonodidactic materials and dictionaries, and the teaching tradition in various parts of the world, such as Europe. Paradoxically, the fact that RP has so few native speakers might even work to its advantage; rather than singling out a particular national or geographical variety and causing accusations of favouritism towards some nationality, a geographically neutral, non-localizable but still socially prestigious and traditionally accepted accent can be employed for the purposes of foreign language instruction.

We can draw here on experiences of other languages which are spoken in more than one country, such as German, used in Germany, Austria, Switzerland, Liechtenstein and Luxembourg. A largely artificially created and codified variety, known as High German, which originated as a written language (based mostly on High German dialects) with its phonetics stemming to a large extent from Low German accents and heavily influenced by German 'stage pronunciation', is employed in the media, in formal situations (e.g. in schools and various other institutions) and in communication with people from different regions of Germany and other German-speaking countries.[16] It is also regarded as an appropriate model for foreign learners, even if in everyday situations, when talking to neighbours, friends and family, Germans usually use some local dialect. This observation is supported by Trask (1995: 175), who observes that:

> the regional dialects of German differ so greatly that speakers from, say, Berlin and Bonn cannot understand each other at all if they use their local vernaculars. Consequently, German speakers use their local variety when talking to others from their area and standard German when talking to everybody else: that is, German-speakers are typically bidialectal.

Thus, High German has the function of a lingua franca both for native and non-native speakers of German and its somewhat artificial character apparently constitutes no obstacle to this role. No-one considers any local dialect as a viable model for foreign learners as pragmatic reasons suggest that High German is the best choice for them.

Let us examine further aspects of pronunciation in EFL, ELF and NELF. In both EFL and NELF native (standard) models are employed, which means evident advantages in terms of both clarity as to the reference point and ample resources for teaching and learning in the form of theoretical descriptions and practice materials. As shown in Section A.1.4, the issue of a pronunciation model in ELF is beset with numerous problems. It can be assumed, however, that an efficient ELF user's pronunciation can be considered an appropriate accent model.

The three approaches under discussion differ in the goals they set: in (traditional) EFL learners strive to achieve near-native pronunciation, which in most cases is unattainable and therefore frustrating; in ELF the objective of effective communication with other non-native speakers requires intelligible pronunciation in international contexts; while in NELF comfortable intelligibility in contacts with both native and non-native speakers is aimed at. As NELF caters for the needs of all participants of communication via English, this approach should be regarded as most universal and therefore most appropriate for the majority of learners.

In order to achieve their objectives, EFL, ELF and NELF establish different pronunciation priorities. In the traditional EFL approach all phonetic features of a native model should be mastered since a departure from any of them leads to the rise of a foreign accent, viewed as an undesirable phenomenon which should be eliminated as much as possible.[17] In ELF crucial phonetic properties are specified in the LFC and their mastery is supposed to safeguard the mutual intelligibility of international users of English while the remaining features are considered either of secondary importance or even harmful. We would like to suggest that in NELF pronunciation priorities should be established in a non-arbitrary fashion on the basis of empirical evidence as to which phonetic features learners of a given L1 background should acquire in order to be comfortably intelligible to other speakers of English. This means different priorities for specific L1 learners (see Chapter 2 for details). A consequence of these three approaches is that their respective phonetic syllabi are of different sizes; the most restricted one is that of ELF and the most elaborated that of EFL. A NELF syllabus occupies an intermediate position between these two options.

In both EFL and NELF native norms of correctness are employed, which means that a learner's phonetic performance is compared to that of a native speaker model and assessed in terms of the differences between them. Nevertheless, while in the former case all departures from the native norm are viewed as errors to be eradicated, in NELF only those that hinder comfortable intelligibility should be eliminated. Thus, generally, NELF is more permissive than EFL, but not as much as ELF. Adopting native norms of correctness in NELF refers also to the use of grammar and vocabulary, like in EFL.

What follows from the above examination of the three approaches to English phonodidactics is that they take a different stance with regard to the retention of the learners' L1 accent in English. In EFL a foreign accent is undesirable as a sign of a failure to master the L2 sound system while in ELF it is elevated to the status of a virtue and argued to be essential for preserving learners' national and personal identity. In NELF a foreign accent is accepted as a natural phenomenon and an unavoidable feature of learning an L2 in an instructed setting, but what matters is how strong it is and how much it hinders achieving comfortable intelligibility. In other words, in NELF an important difference is made between heavily accented speech, which usually constitutes an obstacle to comfortable intelligibility, and a moderate or slight foreign accent which does not have this detrimental effect on successful communication and is therefore acceptable.

In the traditional EFL instruction learners are exposed to the native model(s) of pronunciation, usually in the form of recordings, both for comprehension and imitation. In ELF it is advocated that learners are exposed mainly to non-native accents, while in NELF they are exposed to a variety of accents for the sake of intelligibility, but to a native model of pronunciation for the purposes of imitation. In practice, however, EFL/NELF teachers are usually non-native speakers of English and it is their pronunciation, based on native English but containing elements of their L1, that serves as a major phonetic model for learners.

In ELF special attention is paid to practising accommodation skills, which involve adapting the speakers' pronunciation and way of speaking to that of their interlocutors. This concept does not appear in EFL, but should be incorporated in NELF as an important factor in achieving the mutual intelligibility of its users. In this respect the ELF and NELF are generally in agreement.

As pronunciation is only one aspect of ELT, it should also be added that various approaches differ significantly in the way culture-related issues are supposed to be treated in instructional materials. The traditional EFL textbooks are typically oriented towards native speaker culture(s). Those devoted to teaching British English contain, for example, descriptions of Big Ben or the Houses of Parliament, stories of Guy Fawkes and the British monarchy. ELF supporters, with their anti-native speaker agenda, are in favour of materials concerning various non-native cultures. In NELF a compromise position can again be advocated between these two extremes, with a mixture of various cultural elements, both native and non-native. For instance, stories about the Statue of Liberty or Windsor Castle can be intertwined with descriptions of interesting Japanese or Brazilian customs and the architecture of Kuala Lumpur.

At this point it is worth quoting Lamb's (2004: 3) comment about typical EFL students' attitudes towards English and the culture behind it: 'In the minds of learners, English may not be associated with particular geographical or cultural communities but with a spreading international culture incorporating (inter alia) business, technological innovation, consumer values, democracy, world travel, and the multifarious icons of fashion, sport and music.' This means that many learners develop a 'bicultural' identity 'which includes being a competent speaker of English while retaining one's L1 and the L1 culture', very much like the use of High German for official purposes and local dialects in local contexts.

Table 1.1 summarizes the major aspects of EFL, ELF and NELF approaches to pronunciation teaching/learning. The table demonstrates that NELF shares some features with EFL, others with ELF, and has some properties of its own. NELF can be viewed as a compromise between these two perspectives or as a modified version of traditional EFL which takes into account the present-day role of English as a global language and its international learners' needs.

The NELF approach advocated here is, in fact, intuitively adopted by an overwhelming majority of EFL teachers who, being predominantly non-native speakers of English and speaking it with some degree of a foreign accent, in their pronunciation instruction take a native phonetic model as a reference point, but focus on selected features of English which they consider particularly important for successful communication. They do not require their students to master every phonetic detail as they know very well that in this respect perfection is impossible to achieve. It should also be noted that most of the contemporary English course books, apart from culture-specific texts, usually include passages of general interest, for example devoted to ecological or demographic issues. In other words, NELF can be viewed as consistent with prevailing current teaching practice. A similar opinion is

Table 1.1 Comparison of EFL, ELF and NELF approaches to pronunciation teaching

(Traditional) EFL	ELF	NELF
Prepares foreign learners to communicate mainly with native speakers	Prepares foreign learners to communicate with other non-native speakers[a]	Prepares foreign learners to communicate with both native and non-native speakers
Adopts a native (standard) model of pronunciation	An efficient ELF user's pronunciation as a model	A native model of pronunciation
Traditional goal: native or near-native pronunciation	Goal: (basic) intelligibility in international contexts	Goal: comfortable intelligibility in contacts with both native and non-native speakers
Tries to eliminate L1 accent features	L1 accent features preserved on condition they do not hinder intelligibility; pronunciation priorities listed in the LFC	Selected native accent features allowed, with pronunciation priorities established for L1 speakers in intelligibility research
Exposure to and imitation of native models	Exposure mainly to non-native varieties	Exposure to both native and non-native varieties for comprehension, but imitation/ approximation of native models
No mention of accommodation skills	Acquiring accommodation skills of critical importance	Acquiring accommodation skills of some importance
Native linguistic norms of correctness (pronunciation, grammar, vocabulary, pragmatics)	Native linguistic norms of correctness unimportant; non-native users establish their own norms in communication with other non-native speakers	Native linguistic norms of correctness
Native sociocultural norms adopted and presented in instructional materials	Native sociocultural norms unimportant; instructional materials concern mostly non-native cultures	Includes both native and non-native sociocultural norms, native and non-native cultural elements in instructional materials

Note: [a]Under criticism for excluding native speakers from ELF, some more recent versions of this approach attempt to include them as well. Seidlhofer (2011: 7), for instance, defines ELF as 'any use of English among speakers of different first languages for whom English is a communicative medium of choice'.

expressed by Trudgill (2005: 93), who claims that, 'the sensible, pragmatic course is to continue, as before, employing ENL models [...] with the understanding that in most cases phonetic accuracy is unlikely to be achieved'.

Moreover, further evidence that NELF is not only a hypothetical construct but something already in existence is provided by its many users. Take, for instance, various officials of different nationalities in the European Union authorities who are fluent and efficient speakers of English, which they use to communicate with both native and non-native speakers, but whose pronunciation, while based on native English, retains various phonetic features of their L1. Thus, NELF emerges as a viable alternative both to traditional EFL and the new proposal of ELF. It must be added, however, that, for the sake of tradition and avoiding unnecessary confusion, in the remaining parts of this book we will continue to employ the term EFL in its new, modified meaning expressed by NELF.

Finally, it should be pointed out that numerous studies on the accent preferences of international learners of English, carried out in various parts of the world, e.g. in Europe (Henderson *et al.*, 2012), Japan (Matsuda, 2003), China and Singapore (Goh, 2009), Argentina (Friedrich, 2003) and 45 different countries (Timmis, 2002) show that the majority of them opt for native speaker pronunciation models. In Section B.1.2 we present a questionnaire study carried out among Polish teenagers in which this general tendency finds full support.

A.1.6 Which Native Pronunciation Model?

Since in the approach advocated here a native model of pronunciation and the native norms of correctness are generally adopted, the question that arises is which particular variety of English should be selected for foreign learners. Evidently, no simple answer to this can be provided.

It is clear that, in view of numerous varieties of English used in the world, no single native type of pronunciation can serve as a model for all learners. As a matter of fact, there is no native version of English pronunciation that would fulfil everyone's possible communicative needs.[18] This means that, whatever choice is made, it will always have some drawbacks and the desire of many learners to 'speak good English' is difficult to realize as, in terms of pronunciation, there are many 'good Englishes' and no obvious ways of making the right decision.

At this point it should be mentioned that now and again various suggestions are made as to the best native accent model for EFL phonodidactics. Crystal (1995), for example, has argued that Scottish English is a good alternative to RP since it has a smaller vowel inventory and is therefore simpler to learn. Other scholars have proposed Estuary English as a replacement for RP.

It seems that such proposals cannot be regarded as realistic as they fail to recognize the fact that a model accent should satisfy a number of important criteria which are provided below.

- It should be a standard variety. Non-standard accents are restricted to specific groups of users (regional or social) and are often unintelligible to other speakers of English. Some of them might also be socially stigmatized (e.g. Liverpool English, Glaswegian English). Moreover, usually only standard types of pronunciation enjoy high social prestige and provide their learners with considerable benefits.
- It should be intelligible to many users of English, both in a given country and outside it. This means many standard varieties which are, however, generally unfamiliar outside their regions or countries, such as Scottish English, Welsh English or New Zealand English, are not good candidates.
- The model accent should provide learners with increased chances of an educational and professional career, both in their own country and outside it. It is doubtful whether this requirement can be satisfied by non-standard or regional varieties.
- It should be a variety for which teaching resources (textbooks, learner dictionaries, recordings) are easily available. Clearly, EFL teachers need appropriate materials for their instruction and their availability is of primary importance to them.
- It should be an accent which EFL teachers use (or which they try to approximate). It is rather obvious that we can teach only what we know and it would be unrealistic to expect instructors to do otherwise.

The above arguments should make it clear that there are very few varieties of English which fulfil the above conditions. Scottish English and Estuary English certainly do not. As a matter of fact, only two of them appear to do so in the European context, namely RP and GA.

RP[19] has become internationally known due to the BBC channels and because of its use as a pronunciation model in EFL in many countries, particularly in Europe, which has close traditional cultural and economic ties with Great Britain. This makes it intelligible to numerous users of English not only in the British Isles, but also outside them. In spite of the recent decline in its status, RP is still very often positively associated with good education, prestigious professions and economic success. Many EFL learners are interested in British culture and wish to visit this country or study/work there and communicate with British citizens (see Section B.1.2 and Polish learners' comments). Moreover, as frequently pointed out, RP is the most thoroughly described English accent, with a large variety of theoretical descriptions and available teaching materials, including learner dictionaries.

Finally, many teachers have received training in RP and try to approximate this accent. As observed by Trudgill and Hannah (1994: 9):

> First, while RP originated in the south-east of England, it is now a genuinely regionless accent within Britain; if speakers have an RP accent, you cannot tell which area of Britain they come from, which is not the case for any other type of British accent. This means that this accent is likely to be encountered and understood throughout the country. Second, RP is the accent which is used most often in radio and television broadcasts in England, so a student will have many opportunities to listen to it.

This is not to say that RP is an ideal choice and many arguments have been levelled against it. Let us consider them in some detail, taking as a point of reference Rogerson-Revell's (2011: 7) list of the most problematic aspects of this accent.

- 'RP is a minority accent which perpetuates the norms of an elite minority which few L2 speakers are likely to encounter.' This argument is based on the incorrect assumption that foreigners learn English in order to communicate with some small group of people. This is wrong as their purpose is usually to achieve their individual educational and professional goals as well as to communicate effectively with any speakers of English (native and non-native) and RP is employed as a tool to do so. Moreover, foreign learners are usually not aware of the social associations with RP that British people have so this accent is neutral for them in this respect. An objection to perpetuating the norms of an elite minority is thus of some importance to the British, but irrelevant for EFL learners.
- 'RP is far from the easiest accent to learn because it contains a large number of vowels and diphthongs, weak forms and is non-rhotic.' Anybody who undertakes the effort of learning another language must be prepared for some difficulties with its pronunciation, grammar and vocabulary. Choosing a phonetically easier accent (such as Scottish English) which is, however, intelligible only to a limited number of its users does not seem to be sufficiently justified.
- 'RP has changed considerably over time' so 'many feel it is old-fashioned'. A simple counterargument is that if the model accent changes, so must its teaching, which should follow these modifications. This is, in fact, what happens with descriptions of RP (e.g. Gimson's *English Pronunciation*, systematically updated by Cruttenden). It should be added that changes in pronunciation are commonplace and concern all accents, not just RP, which means that whatever native accent is adopted as a model, changes in its pronunciation must be taken into account. RP sounding old-fashioned is another argument of some relevance to the British, but not to foreign learners.

• 'Adopting an "alien" accent involves loss or threat to identity' and 'assuming a NS accent is an intrusion into a speech community that the NNS is not qualified to join'. These arguments clearly have nothing to do with RP, but concern any native accent that a learner might want to acquire. Besides, as argued in the preceding sections, learners of a foreign language usually retain a considerable degree of their native accent which allows them to preserve their national identity and saves them from accusations of being intruders into the native speakers' community.

To complete this discussion, many sources point out (e.g. Hudson, 1980) that speakers of other accents perceive RP in a dual fashion. On the one hand, they associate it with many positive features such as intelligence, good education, professional competence and diligence, i.e. values necessary to achieve socio-economic success. On the other hand, RP speakers are perceived as having various negative traits, as being distant, unfriendly and arrogant. It is not clear, however, whether EFL learners attempting to approximate RP, but retaining some degree of their native accent, as is usually the case, and therefore being recognized by native speakers of British English as foreigners, are judged in the same fashion. According to the reports of my colleagues and students (in the English Department where RP is used as a pronunciation model and whose graduates usually become language teachers or interpreters), they are often complimented on their pronunciation, seen by many British people in terms of a considerable achievement, in positive contrast to the hardly intelligible pronunciation of many other foreigners.

Let us now consider some advantages of employing GA pronunciation as a model accent for EFL purposes. It certainly satisfies most of the conditions specified in the previous pages. Thus, GA has been made popular in the world through music, films, the internet and other media, which means that it is widely used and therefore intelligible to many EFL learners. What is more, it enjoys high international prestige due to the economic and political power of the country of its native speakers. Learning it can certainly be beneficial for those people who intend to communicate with American and Canadian speakers as well as learners from many regions of the world (such as South America and some parts of Asia) in which this accent is used for EFL purposes.[20] Furthermore, there are numerous GA teaching resources (in Europe RP materials prevail). Its sound system is somewhat simpler than that of RP since, due to rhoticity, it is closer to spelling and lacks central diphthongs. To sum up, as an EFL pronunciation model, GA appears to have at least as many assets as RP and even some additional advantages by not having the negative connotations of social elitism that RP does and by having millions of native speakers. In Szpyra-Kozłowska and Stasiak (2004) we report on an experiment in which the comprehension of RP and GA by Polish intermediate learners of English was examined. Interestingly, the GA version of a diagnostic passage has turned out to be easier for the listeners to understand than the RP recording in spite of the fact that RP is the accent taught to them. This suggests that GA might be a better choice for many learners.

The arguments provided above in favour of RP and GA as appropriate pronunciation models for EFL purposes should also be considered from the perspective of a specific local educational situation (see Section A.1.8), as it might turn out that in non-European contexts some other English accents fulfil the presented criteria more adequately than the two varieties discussed here.

A.1.7 EFL Versus ESL

Another important issue that should be addressed is a distinction between two concepts: English as a Foreign Language (EFL) and English as a Second Language (ESL), as well as the consequences of adopting each of these perspectives in pronunciation teaching and of combining them into a single approach.

Until the 1990s, EFL and ESL were systematically distinguished, as in the first case English is learnt in the country in which learners are native speakers of some other language(s), while the latter concerned immigrants learning English in an English-speaking country. An assumption was made that EFL involves language learning (in an educational setting) and ESL language acquisition (in a naturalistic setting, as in the case of first language acquisition). Further research has shown, however, that both processes, although taking place in different contexts, share many features and should be viewed as two facets of the same phenomenon, now jointly referred to as second language acquisition (SLA). It has been argued, for instance, that various grammatical structures are learnt in a similar order by both EFL and ESL learners. Thus, in current studies the term SLA refers to learning another, i.e. second language (and also the third, the fourth, etc.), often also called an additional language, regardless of the place where it occurs. This is frequently reflected in the joint or interchangeable use of both abbreviations: EFL/ESL[21] or through a general reference to L2 (and L3, L4, etc.).[22]

In what follows we intend to argue that an approach which fails to recognize the specificity of EFL and ESL, and subsumes them under one rubric of SLA, is a retrograde step in pronunciation teaching which proceeds along markedly different lines in the two cases under examination. Let us thus consider the major differences between EFL and ESL phonodidactic issues in some detail.

As shown in the preceding sections, in EFL contexts the pronunciation model is usually imposed on learners by the teacher, most frequently on the basis of the educational tradition of a given country and the instructor's accent preferences. Of course, sometimes more model accents are employed, for example RP and GA, as is the case in some European countries such as Holland. In ESL the pronunciation model is naturally provided by native speakers of the English-speaking country where teaching/learning takes place. Here the choice is usually limited to the standard accent or the regional variety, where the former is often encouraged by government policy and the latter is enforced by communication with local native speakers. This means that the present chapter with its focus on the pronunciation models debate is relevant only in EFL, but not in ESL contexts.

Similarly, establishing pronunciation priorities, dealt with in Chapter 2, in the course of intelligibility research has to address the issue of L2 learners' potential interlocutors, i.e. the question of 'intelligibility to whom'. In the case of ESL students the answer is simple; they have to be intelligible primarily to the inhabitants of the English-speaking country/region where they have decided to live. In EFL settings the problem, as argued earlier, is more complex; potential interlocutors can be native speakers (of a specified or an unspecified nationality), non-native international learners or both.

The setting and way in which another language, pronunciation included, is taught and learnt is also different. In the EFL contexts it takes place in an instructed setting, i.e. in the classroom, whereas in ESL situations learning usually occurs in a naturalistic setting, i.e. in contacts with native speakers. Moreover, the former case involves explicit (formal) teaching while the latter involves informal (implicit) learning.

There are several significant consequences that follow from learning English in two different types of settings. First of all, EFL learners have limited or no exposure to spoken English outside the classroom. This means that their contact with the L2 is often restricted to a few hours of English classes a week, in which most of the time is usually devoted to vocabulary and grammar practice and not pronunciation. In other words, L2 auditory input, crucial for the acquisition of its sound system (see Section A.3.2.2) is severely limited. When English is learnt in a country where it is spoken, learners have many opportunities to hear and use it in a variety of everyday situations.[23]

In an instructed setting, pronunciation is learnt through exposure to the teacher's (and other learners') English as well as to different recordings, films and music, through explicit instruction, pronunciation activities and feedback provided by the teacher. As observed by Muñoz (2008), this means that target language input is limited in source (mainly the teacher), quantity (many teachers frequently use their L1 to communicate with learners) and quality (there is a large variability in teachers' oral fluency and general proficiency). In a naturalistic setting pronunciation learning takes place mainly through exposure to many varieties of spoken English and possible (though infrequent) feedback from native interlocutors.

EFL learners communicate in English mostly with other non-native speakers, i.e. the teacher and other classmates representing a similar level of foreign language proficiency. Occasionally, outside the classroom, they might use English as a lingua franca with other non-native speakers. ESL learners communicate in English predominantly with native speakers. Thus, in both cases the quantity and quality of phonetic input learners receive as well as the amount and type of communicative situations they are involved in differ strikingly.

EFL learners' motivation is predominantly instrumental, that is, they learn English to communicate in it with other speakers of this language (both native and non-native) and in order to achieve their personal goals (such as obtaining good marks at school, passing examinations, improving their professional qualifications, getting a job promotion, etc.). While many ESL learners' motivation is also instrumental, in numerous cases integrative (assimilative) motivation, i.e. the wish to integrate socially and culturally with the target language community, is very high. This is important since integrative motivation, which entails a desire to become linguistically indistinguishable from the community whose membership the learner aspires to, is claimed to be usually stronger than instrumental motivation.[24] Nevertheless, what matters is not only the type of motivation but also its strength. Thus, high instrumental motivation might lead to better results in L2 learning than low integrative motivation.

A significant difference in the type of exposure to English in the two contexts under discussion should be pointed out. For the reasons specified above, EFL learners are more frequently exposed to written than to spoken English. This means that orthography (of both English and the L1) tends to exert a powerful impact on their English pronunciation, as will amply be demonstrated in Chapter 2. ESL learners are also exposed to written English, but spoken input tends to be more dominant.

It should be added that ESL learners sometimes attend language courses in an English-speaking country in which they live (the so-called mixed setting). They differ, however, from EFL training in several important respects. First of all, EFL classes are almost always monolingual, i.e. learners have the same linguistic and cultural background, while ESL classes are usually multilingual. Secondly, in the former case language teachers are mostly of the same nationality as the learners (native speakers are sometimes employed, but rather infrequently) while in the latter instructors are predominantly native speakers of English who are generally unfamiliar with the learners' mother tongues and their sound systems.

In these two contexts, teachers also differ in terms of their professional qualifications. In order to teach English, EFL instructors are generally required to study English for several years at teacher training colleges and/or university L2 philology departments. Their linguistic education in most cases involves theoretical and practical English phonetics, but also contrastive phonetics of the L1 and L2, as well as pedagogical, psychological and didactic preparation for teaching English to different types of EFL learners. ESL teachers usually get their qualifications at ELT courses of a short duration in which English phonetics and phonodidactics are rather limited and frequently neglected.[25] As argued by Walker (2001: 4): 'NNS teachers often have a formal university background in both L1 and English phonology. Too many native speakers, sadly, have received very limited training in the phonetics and phonology of English and have even less knowledge of their learners' L1.' He adds that NNS teachers are better equipped to help learners than native speakers 'who may in practice be limited to providing a model for imitation'. Walker concludes that, in fact, NNS teachers are better suited to teach monolingual groups particularly since, being also learners of a foreign language, they can understand their students' difficulties in acquiring L2 pronunciation which a NS teacher may fail to comprehend.

Finally, the phonetic competence and the quality of teachers' English pronunciation is different; non-native instructor's pronunciation is not always very good, but strives to approximate to some standard model, whereas native teacher's pronunciation is perfect, but often departs from the standard variety adopted for teaching purposes. This, on the one hand, provides non-native teachers with some advantage. On the other hand, non-native, i.e. limited L2 competence usually means diminished confidence in the correctness of one's judgements in many aspects of language matters and, consequently, some teachers' unwillingness to engage in learners' intensive phonetic training. Native teachers can act as pronunciation models with more confidence,[26] which can, however, be somewhat undermined by their insufficient phonodidactic qualifications. Table 1.2 summarizes the major differences in pronunciation teaching/learning in EFL and ESL contexts.

The above discussion should make it clear that pronunciation teaching/ learning in EFL and ESL contexts displays a whole set of quantitative and qualitative differences concerning learners, teachers, the type and amount of L2 input and use, many aspects of the teaching/learning process and the conditions in which it takes place. These differences cannot be ignored as they have a significant impact on various elements of phonetic training, such as the choice of an accent model, discussed in this chapter, establishing pronunciation priorities for a given group of learners (see Chapter 2), and the selection of appropriate pronunciation practice materials as well as effective instructional techniques which must be suited to a specific instructed setting (see Chapter 3).

Thus, many further arguments in favour of separating ESL and EFL approaches to pronunciation teaching will be provided in the remaining parts of this book. At this point we shall only consider some consequences of the failure to make this distinction in many (most?) general books devoted to pronunciation instruction. The majority of them (e.g. Avery & Ehrlich, 1992; Celce-Murcia *et al.*, 1996; Rogerson-Revell, 2011) discuss the factors relevant for the acquisition of L2 phonetics, such as age, exposure to the target language, aptitude, attitude, motivation, the role of the L1, etc. When we examine, however, the amount of attention devoted to these issues, it is

Table 1.2 Comparison of pronunciation teaching/learning in EFL and ESL contexts

EFL pronunciation teaching/learning	ESL pronunciation teaching/learning
The pronunciation model (usually some standard accent) imposed on learners by the teacher	The pronunciation model(s) provided by native speakers, inhabitants of a given country/region
Teaching/learning takes place in an instructed setting, i.e. in the classroom in a limited amount of time	Teaching/learning takes place mostly in a naturalistic setting (only sometimes in a mixed setting)
Learners have a limited or no exposure to spoken English outside the classroom	Learners usually have an unlimited (massive) exposure to spoken English in a variety of everyday situations (learning through immersion in the L2 environment)
The teacher serves as the major (and often the only) pronunciation model (input limited both qualitatively and quantitatively)	Learners have many native pronunciation models (input neither qualitatively nor quantitatively limited)
Learning pronunciation mainly through exposure to teacher's English, recordings and explicit instruction	Learning pronunciation mainly through exposure to native English (implicit learning)
Communication in English mostly with other non-native speakers (the teacher and other learners), little or no opportunity to use English in natural communication situations	Learners communicate in English mostly with native speakers in natural communication situations
Predominantly instrumental motivation in learning English	Both instrumental and integrative motivation
Greater exposure to written than to spoken English; powerful impact of orthography on learners' pronunciation	Greater exposure to spoken than to written English
Usually monolingual language classes with learners of the same linguistic and cultural background	In instructed setting: usually multilingual classes with learners of different linguistic and cultural backgrounds
Teachers usually of the same L1 as learners	Teachers usually of a different L1 from learners
Teachers usually with college or university qualifications to teach English	Teachers usually with qualifications obtained at ELT courses of a short duration
Non-native teacher's imperfect English pronunciation which strives to approach a standard model	Native teacher's perfect English pronunciation which often departs from a standard model

clear that the focus is predominantly on ESL, but not EFL contexts, which makes them of little use to EFL teachers and learners. For example, the most frequently and extensively discussed problem is that of age, which refers to the beginning of exposure to the L2. It is usually referred to as AoA, i.e. the age of a learner's arrival in an English-speaking country. Clearly, this concept has no application to an EFL setting, similarly to LoR, i.e. the length of residence in the country of immigration.[27] The most important idea, however, is that of a critical period after which achieving native-like pronunciation is next to impossible. Numerous studies are devoted to this issue which is of much relevance to language acquisition in a naturalistic ESL setting, but not in an educational EFL context. Muñoz (2008: 586), based on the relevant research, concludes that, 'the CPH (Critical Period Hypothesis – J.Sz-K) is irrelevant to formal language acquisition'.

Thus, a common practice in many SLA studies consists of extending many claims based on research in ESL contexts to EFL learners. One such theory maintains that younger starters have an advantage over older starters in terms of their ultimate attainment in an L2. Muñoz (2008: 581) points out, however, that 'no evidence has yet been found that the generalization of the higher eventual attainment of younger starters in naturalistic settings can be automatically extended to foreign language settings'. In her discussion of symmetries and asymmetries between second language learning in naturalistic and foreign instructed settings, she criticizes equating ESL with EFL as follows (Muñoz, 2008: 591), 'for a number of years now in the field of SLA there has been a tacit acceptance of sweeping generalizations of findings from natural settings to classroom settings that have not been upheld by research into the latter' and adds that 'an inferential leap has been made in the assumption that learning age will have the same effect on learners in an immersion setting as on students of a foreign language, when the latter are exposed to only one speaker of that language (the teacher) in only one setting (the classroom) and for only limited amounts of time'. She concludes that the approach under discussion has negative effects on EFL instruction since 'not only have findings been generalized: the aims and priorities of research in naturalistic settings have also been extended to research in classroom settings'.

On the other hand, the role of the learner's native language, of primary importance to EFL instruction, is apparently downplayed by many authors.[28] A frequent argument is that among the speakers of the same L1 one can find very successful L2 learners as well as many who fail to get further than the basics. As any EFL teacher will agree, however, it is the L1 that plays the major role in shaping the pronunciation of the L2 as the phonetic difficulties of learners sharing the same language background are largely predictable. In other words, although other factors are relevant for achieving success and not all features of learner language can be accounted for by contrastive analysis, the transfer of L1 phonetic features to the L2 is responsible for the overwhelming majority of pronunciation problems.

This does not mean, of course, that the role of the L1 is not recognized at all, as is shown by the fact that many books devoted to L2 pronunciation instruction include separate chapters on the major phonetic difficulties encountered by different groups of L1 learners. In other words, the suggestion seems to be that English pronunciation can be taught in basically the same fashion to all learners, with additional phonetic tasks addressed to specific L1 speakers. One of the problems that arises in connection with this assumption is that such authors are not and cannot be specialists in the phonetic systems of all languages and therefore have to rely on other sources whose quality they are unable to evaluate. In consequence, many descriptions of the pronunciation difficulties of specific L1 learners contain numerous errors and are of little help to teachers. This issue is discussed in some detail in Section A.3.7.

Formal instruction in pronunciation, crucial to EFL learners but less important in ESL contexts, is given little attention in the majority of sources under discussion, which, again, proves that they focus on ESL rather than EFL contexts. It should be made clear that the effect of pronunciation instruction in ESL settings is a matter of much controversy, with some researchers, such as Purcell and Suter (1980) arguing that it plays a marginal role in achieving phonetic success and other specialists, such as Pennington (1987), Morley (1991) and Derwing *et al.* (1997), maintaining that it should be an important component of ESL learners' language training. On the other hand, within EFL settings no doubts appear to have been raised with regard to the usefulness and absolute necessity of formal pronunciation teaching. On the contrary, various authors (e.g. Cenoz & Garcia-Lecumberri, 1999; Kendrick, 1997; MacDonald *et al.*, 1994) have proved empirically that it brings positive results and substantially increases EFL learners' phonetic proficiency. It is rather a question of choosing effective phonodidactic techniques, as discussed in Chapter 3, that can and should be debated.

A.1.8 Diagnosing the Local Teaching Context. Learner-related and Teacher-related Determinants of Pronunciation Instruction

As argued by Celce-Murcia *et al.* (1996), in order to make informed decisions concerning various aspects of L2 pronunciation instruction, it is necessary for the teacher to become familiar with the most important factors relevant to the participants of the teaching/learning process and the specific conditions in which it takes place. In other words, it is useful for language instructors to prepare a general diagnosis of the local teaching context. Below we briefly present the major elements affecting EFL pronunciation instruction, dividing them into the teaching context and the learner- and teacher-related factors, following Celce-Murcia *et al.* (1996).

- **EFL educational context** refers to language teachers' and learners' educational situation. It includes the following issues:
  - **National language policy:** importance attached in a given country to the teaching/learning of foreign languages and English in particular, reflected, for example, in regulations concerning the age at which English instruction begins, the mandatory or optional nature of English classes, the duration of courses and the number of hours of instruction, the size of language classes, education authorities' role in determining the shape of the curriculum and the selection of teaching materials, types of language examinations and their requirements with regard to speaking skills and pronunciation in particular;
  - **Teacher preparation:** establishing the necessary qualifications for language teachers, the development of language teacher training institutions and concern for the quality of teacher preparation;
  - **Curriculum, materials and teaching/learning facilities:** the place of oral skills and pronunciation in the curriculum, the availability of appropriate teaching materials and the technical facilities in a given teaching institution, for instance, recording and playback equipment, language or computer laboratory and access to the internet.

The factors listed above are almost all beyond the teacher's control who should, however, take them into consideration while planning the phonetic training for their students since they determine, to a large extent, the amount of time that can be devoted to work on different components of an L2 including pronunciation as well as technical facilities-dependent and teaching materials-dependent instructional procedures which can be employed in the classroom. The size of language classes should be singled out as particularly important as effective phonetic training cannot be carried out with very large groups. As a matter of fact, the smaller the learner group, the more intensive pronunciation practice can be and the more opportunities there are for catering for individual learners' phonetic problems.

As to the national language policies, with the global spread of English and its recognized importance in international communication, the education authorities in many countries make a great effort to facilitate and intensify English language teaching and learning. This is certainly true of the majority of European countries, including Poland, where there is a very positive social and educational climate for the teaching of English, a good command of which is seen as a necessary condition for achieving professional and economic success in many areas, a view shared by various relevant decision makers as well as large sections of the society. This is reflected in the fact that in Poland, as well as in many other countries, mandatory English classes begin in elementary schools (at the age of 6–7) and last for several years (in primary, secondary and post-secondary education). The popularity of English is evident in the fact that numerous private language schools offer courses in this language, some of them accepting even small babies. In brief, EFL teachers are nowadays in a comfortable position teaching the language that everybody wants to know.[29]

Let us turn now to the participants in the process, i.e. teachers and learners, with a brief presentation of the most important factors concerning them that are relevant to EFL pronunciation teaching and learning. We start with the well-known and frequently discussed EFL learner-related determinants which are listed below (for more details concerning ESL learners see, for example, Celce-Murcia *et al.*, 1996; Flege *et al.*, 1995; Moyer, 2004, 2013; Rogerson-Revell, 2011).

- **EFL learner-related factors** concern such features of learners as:
    - L1;
    - Language aptitude (including phonetic and analytic abilities);
    - Motivation;
    - Goals, expectations, needs and preferences;
    - Involvement in pronunciation practice (also outside the classroom);
    - Exposure to English outside the classroom;
    - The amount and type of prior pronunciation instruction;
    - Cognitive and learning styles;
    - Sociocultural factors (cultural identity and attitude toward the target language and its speakers)
    - Age;
    - Personality.

As mentioned earlier, in a typical EFL context with learners of the same L1, some of these factors, such as learners' linguistic and cultural backgrounds, are usually the same. This simplifies the teaching process as students' pronunciation problems, stemming mainly from the phonetic and phonological transfer from L1 to L2, are largely predictable and well known to the instructor who shares an L1 with them.[30] In the case of mandatory language classes in schools, the learners' ages are the same and appropriate phonodidactic methods, suitable for a given age group, can be employed.

Learners differ, however, in terms of the remaining features, which are specific for each individual. These differences concern first of all language aptitude or language talent (see Jilka, 2009), which includes phonetic and analytic abilities. The former, commonly referred to as 'an ear for language', involves a talent for mimicry, i.e. reproducing the sounds of the L2 faithfully from auditory input; the latter refers to the phonemic coding ability, which is 'the capacity to discriminate and code foreign sounds such that they can be recalled' (Celce-Murcia *et al.*, 1996: 17). Differences in phonetic aptitude mean that teachers cannot 'expect all learners to achieve the same level of success in the same amount of time'. A word of warning is in order here: teachers who are convinced that only language talent determines the quality of their students' L2 pronunciation might tend to neglect phonetic training. Therefore they should be reminded that there are also other important learner-related factors (listed above) which play an important role in achieving good L2 pronunciation.

Phonodidactic specialists emphasize the importance of motivation and attitude toward the target language and its speakers as the major driving forces behind learners' efforts to achieve a good command of another language, particularly its pronunciation. They are closely tied in with their personal goals of learning the L2, expectations and accent preferences which, in turn, affect the students' involvement in pronunciation activities both inside and outside the classroom. It should be added that these factors are relevant in the case of teenagers and adults who approach their language education consciously and often critically, as opposed to children who have not yet developed any specific views in this regard. Teachers should be aware of these issues and should try to obtain some knowledge about their students' approach to learning an L2 in general and its pronunciation in particular, in open discussions or, preferably, through brief anonymous (and therefore more reliable) questionnaires, such as those presented in Sections B.1.2 and B.1.3.

Ideally, the teacher should also examine individual learners' pronunciation problems, their phonetic aptitude, personality and cognitive and learning styles which, particularly with large groups, is not an easy task to accomplish as it requires not only a substantial amount of time, but also the necessary knowhow. What the instructor can do, however, is to get some feedback from students on various aspects of phonetic training, for instance, their evaluation of the amount and quality of pronunciation practice as well as of the effectiveness and attractiveness of different types of phonetic activities. In Sections B.1.3 and B.3.2 we present some questionnaire studies which aim to elicit learners' opinions on such issues. Information obtained in this fashion can provide enormous help to instructors in developing a more individual approach to students and in improving their teaching skills considerably. Needless to say, they should work on the learners' motivation, particularly on developing their concern for good pronunciation and showing the consequences of heavily accented speech. The more attention is devoted to phonetic training and the greater the instructor's involvement in it, the better the results and the more ingrained in learners will be the conviction about the importance of pronunciation and the need to improve it. We return to these problems in Chapter 3.

The major teacher-related factors which have a strong impact on pronunciation instruction are as follows:

- **EFL teacher-related factors**:
  - Teacher preparation: training in English theoretical and practical phonetics, familiarity with the sound systems of the L1 and L2, and phonetic transfer phenomena;
  - Teaching skills concerning, for example, diagnosing learners' pronunciation difficulties, designing appropriate activities to remedy these problems, familiarity with different pronunciation teaching techniques and activities;
  - Teacher's experience as a language learner;
  - Teacher's attitude to the role of pronunciation;
  - Quality of teacher's English pronunciation;
  - Teacher's involvement in instruction (e.g. sensitivity to learners' phonetic needs and their individual pronunciation problems, and the amount of time the teacher is willing to devote to them).

It is clear that teachers' approaches to pronunciation instruction are largely shaped by their own professional education as well as their learning and teaching experience. If, in the course of teacher training, they acquire sufficient phonodidactic knowledge concerning the L1 and L2 sound systems, phonetic and phonological transfer from L1 to L2 and various pronunciation teaching techniques, then they are likely to develop this language skill in their students effectively and with confidence. Otherwise, they will have to rely on their own experience as, first, L2 learners (teachers often tend to teach the way they have themselves been taught) and then as language instructors. Much also depends on the quality of teachers' pronunciation as those with a good mastery of the English sound system usually pay more attention to teaching it while those whose pronunciation is poor tend to neglect this aspect of language. Finally, instructors differ with regard to their involvement in the teaching process. Those who are more sensitive to their learners' pronunciation problems and are willing to devote some extra time to them will certainly get better results than their colleagues who do not go beyond what is basically required of them. It is also important to point out that what matters is good teamwork among the language teaching staff in a given educational institution whose members should plan together and discuss various aspects of the teaching process and share their professional experiences with beginner teachers.

Conscientious pronunciation instructors, who want to improve their teaching skills and be professionally successful, should self-inspect their teaching practices and the results obtained. In order to do that, they should attempt to provide answers to several important questions, such as, for instance, those given below:

- Do I pay sufficient attention to my students' pronunciation?
- Am I well aware of their major pronunciation problems?

- Do I know what these problems stem from and how they can be dealt with?
- Do I strengthen my students' motivation to work on their English pronunciation?
- Do I devote enough time to their phonetic training (given course requirements and other pressures)?
- Do I employ effective pronunciation teaching techniques?
- Are the phonetic activities I use in the classroom interesting, attractive and motivating for my students?
- Do I pay sufficient attention to the choice of appropriate pronunciation teaching materials?

While answers to some of the above questions should not be difficult, others may be more problematic and require either consultation with other teachers or students. All of them, however, can help to clarify the major issue expressed by the following general query, i.e. *Am I a good pronunciation teacher?* Thus, what we recommend is the instructors' self-examination and self-evaluation of their phonodidactic approach which can be the first step towards its improvement.

In analyzing various determinants of pronunciation teaching and learning, it is useful to make a distinction between those factors over which the learner/teacher have no control and those which can be externally manipulated by the participants (Pawlak, 2010). The first group comprises the following issues: transfer from the L1, learners' age, language aptitude, cognitive and learning styles, group membership and identity, educational context, the operation of language universals and developmental sequences, and markedness of phonological features. While these factors are beyond the teachers' control, they should be aware of their effect on the process of pronunciation teaching/learning. The second set, which contains those aspects of the process in question that can be shaped or modified by the instructor are as follows: goals, expectations, needs and preferences, motivation, the amount of in- and out-of-class exposure to the L2, awareness of pronunciation issues, selection of targeted pronunciation features, choice of instructional techniques, materials and resources, application of effective learning strategies and adoption of an autonomous approach. Thus, while adult learners might have specific goals in learning the L2, teachers should make sure that they are realistic and attainable. Students' needs and expectations as well as their motivation can also be shaped to some extent by the instructor, particularly in the case of younger learners whose views on pronunciation are not yet fixed and can be influenced. Nevertheless, what seems to matter most is the instructor's expertise in phonetics and the effectiveness of their pronunciation training coupled with genuine care for the quality of the learners' pronunciation.

As the local educational context as well as learner-dependent and teacher-dependent determinants of EFL pronunciation teaching and learning discussed in this section have a direct bearing on the shape and outcome of phonetic instruction, teachers should be familiar with them and aware of their consequences. In Section B.1.3 we provide an attempt at diagnosing selected aspects of English pronunciation teaching in Poland which can help EFL teachers in other countries either to design similar studies or at least offer them guidance as to what issues should be taken into account in analyzing the current state and local context of English phonodidactics.

Part B

In this part we shall focus on presenting some empirical evidence concerning various points raised in Part A. First, in Section B.1.1 an attempt is made to prove the importance of good pronunciation by showing how accented speech affects Polish listeners' judgements concerning the personal characteristics of foreign speakers of Polish, i.e. their alleged education, intelligence, reliability, pleasantness and trustworthiness (based on Radomski & Szpyra-Kozłowska, 2014). Next, we address the EFL versus ELF debate, i.e. the issue of choosing an appropriate English pronunciation model for EFL learners by examining Polish teenagers' accent preferences, expressed in a questionnaire study carried out by Szpyra-Kozłowska (2004). Finally, Section B.1.3 presents an attempt at diagnosing the major aspects of English pronunciation teaching in Poland on the basis of a questionnaire administered to 200 secondary school pupils and aimed at arriving at an English pronunciation profile of an average Polish secondary school learner and a pronunciation teaching profile of an average Polish school teacher of English.[31]

B.1.1 Attitudes to Accented Speech and its Users

Munro *et al.* (2006: 67–68) point out that: 'a foreign accent is a common, normal aspect of the speech of those who acquire their L2 after early childhood. Even linguistically unsophisticated listeners are highly sensitive to accent differences and readily perceive the speech of L2 learners as accented.' The perception of accented speech frequently entails its, usually unconscious, assessment in terms of various communicative, linguistic and aesthetic features such as comprehensibility, foreign-accentedness and acceptability, but might also involve other types of judgements concerning the speaker's education and intelligence as well as personality traits.

As noted by several scholars (e.g. Lindemann, 2002; Lippi-Green, 1997), such assessments generally tend to be negative. According to Munro *et al.* (2006: 68), 'one of the potential consequences of speaking differently from other members of a community is negative social evaluation. In fact, minority accents are often disparaged or held to be signs of ignorance or lack of sophis-tication.' The reason why people with a foreign accent may be perceived negatively is usually seen in the stereotypes and prejudices since 'when lis-teners are exposed to accented speech, pre-existing stereotypes associated with that particular accent may be invoked' (Munro *et al.*, 2006: 71). Furthermore, it has been suggested (e.g. Munro & Derwing, 1995) that in the case of foreign accents extra processing time is needed to gain understanding and that these processing difficulties might be responsible for the rise of prejudices towards accented speech.

Thus, it has often been noted (e.g. Lev-Ari & Keysar, 2010; Said, 2006) that native speakers of English respond more positively towards those who speak like them than to those who speak with a different accent. The more accented a foreigner's speech is, the more negatively he/she is rated by native speakers in terms of features related to competence, integrity and social attractiveness such as credibility, intelligence, education, responsibility, friend-liness, sincerity, kindness, sense of humour and many others. This is expressed in the telling title of Lev-Ari and Keysar's (2010) paper, 'Why don't we believe non-native speakers? The influence of accent on credibility', which deals with the lower credibility ratings ascribed by native English listeners to speakers with a foreign accent.

Moreover, accent evaluations play a crucial role in the assessors' attribu-tion of status and professional competence to foreigners. Kalin and Rayko (1978) show, for example, that native speakers of English judged non-native speakers to be less suitable for high-status jobs and more suitable for low-status jobs than native speakers. Abelin and Boyd (2000) demonstrate that Swedish students assigned more positive scores for teaching skills to Swedish university teachers than to foreign staff speaking accented Swedish. Many other studies, which usually employ a matched-guise technique with the same speech delivered by the same person using two or more accents, have proved native speakers often perceive accented speech as deviant and flawed, and its users as in many ways deficient and inferior.

Such negative perceptions can, in turn, influence the way foreigners are treated and sometimes even lead to their discrimination. The most detailed account of accent-related cases of disadvantage in employment and educa-tional institutions in the United States has been provided by Lippi-Green (1997) and Moyer (2013). The latter author discusses the phenomenon of 'linguistic profiling', seen in the fact that 'landlords determine how they will treat potential occupants and employers decide whether to interview and hire those with a foreign accent' (Moyer, 2013: 6). Lev-Ari and Keysar (2010) also conclude that accent might reduce the credibility of non-native job seek-ers, eyewitnesses, reporters or people taking calls in foreign call centres.

The attitudes to foreign accents discussed above have been studied pri-marily in immigrant-receiving countries, such as Great Britain, the United States, Canada and Australia, where the in-flow of immigrants has a long tradition and a powerful social, economic and cultural impact. In contemporary Poland, however, the presence of a growing number of Polish-speaking foreigners, who study and work in the country and who appear in the Polish media with increasing frequency, is a fairly new phenomenon. Thus, it seems that no particular accent-related attitudes have had a chance to develop yet, although several nationality-related stereotypes do exist.

Below, we report on an empirical study in which 40 Polish students assessed 11 samples of foreign-accented Polish (produced by American, French, Italian, Russian, British, Ukrainian, Spanish, Hungarian, Romanian, German and Turkish learners) both in terms of accent features and personality traits ascribed to the speakers. Below we focus only on the relationship between the degree of accentedness and Polish listeners' evaluation of the speakers' personal characteristics.

The 11 samples were evaluated by 40 students in the English Department of Maria Curie-Skłodowska University in Lublin, aged 22–24. In one part of the experiment, the participants were required to listen to the recordings of foreign-accented Polish and to evaluate them with respect to three criteria: comprehensibility, the degree of foreign accent and pleasantness. In each case, five options were provided, which were assigned numerical values from 1 to 5, where 1 = very negative evaluation and 5 = very positive evaluation. The students were not informed about the speakers' nationalities.

In the next part of the experiment, the participants ascribed personal characteristics to 11 foreign speakers on the basis of their Polish speech samples using five bipolar adjectives, which fall into three types: those related to social attractiveness: (not) nice, competence: (un)intelligent, (un)educated, and personal integrity: (ir)responsible, (un)trustworthy. The students were asked to indicate on a 5-point scale (where 1 = very negative evaluation and 5 = very positive evaluation) the degree to which the recorded speakers are likely to display the provided personal characteristics on the basis of their accents.

Table 1.3 shows the average ratings of the samples' comprehensibility, foreign-accentedness and pleasantness. Pearson correlation coefficients computed between pairs of the features under examination demonstrate that there is a consistent relationship between them. Thus, a favourable assessment of comprehensibility positively correlates with higher scores assigned to both foreign-accentedness ($r = 0.64$) and pleasantness ($r = 0.70$). Also high ratings of foreign-accentedness correspond to positive evaluations of pleasantness ($r = 0.54$). These findings are in accordance with a common observation that heavily accented speech tends to be perceived as incomprehensible and unpleasant, whereas a decreasing degree of foreign accent results in less harsh judgements regarding other aspects of accented speech (e.g. Fayer & Krasinski, 1987).[32] Table 1.4 contains average scores for five personal characteristics assessed in the experiment.

Let us now move on to examining the relationship between the two sets of results presented in the tables below. The Pearson correlation between the

Table 1.3 Average ratings of three accent features of experimental samples

	Speakers	Comprehensibility	Foreign-accentedness	Pleasantness	Average
1	S1	3.25	2.05	2.45	2.58
2	S2	2.65	1.50	2.65	2.26
3	S3	3.35	2.10	2.95	2.80
4	S4	4.80	3.85	4.45	4.36
5	S5	3.10	2.10	2.45	2.55
6	S6	3.95	2.65	3.70	3.43
7	S7	4.10	2.70	3.50	3.43
8	S8	2.20	1.70	2.05	1.98
9	S9	4.40	4.10	3.85	4.11
10	S10	4.10	3.40	3.65	3.71
11	S11	3.55	2.15	2.65	2.78

Table 1.4 Average ratings of five personal characteristics ascribed to speech samples

	Speakers	Intelligent	Responsible	Nice	Educated	Trustworthy	Average
1	S1	3.85	3.35	3.30	3.65	3.45	3.52
2	S2	3.35	3.05	4.15	3.55	3.40	3.5
3	S3	3.40	3.30	3.35	3.45	3.30	3.36
4	S4	4.25	3.85	4.20	4.20	3.85	4.07
5	S5	3.45	3.35	2.75	3.40	3.20	3.23
6	S6	4.00	3.70	4.40	4.05	3.90	4.01
7	S7	3.60	3.35	4.00	3.75	3.50	3.64
8	S8	2.95	3.00	3.25	2.85	2.90	2.99
9	S9	4.10	3.80	3.90	4.05	3.90	3.95
10	S10	3.50	3.30	3.60	3.30	3.15	3.37
11	S11	3.05	3.10	3.60	3.10	3.10	3.19

evaluation of accent features and the assessment of personal characteristics calculated for both groups indicates that there is a positive correlation between these two factors ($r = 0.40$). In other words, the respondents' ratings of foreign speakers' personal characteristics coincide with foreign accent features in that a more favourable evaluation of accented speech also implies a more positive perception of the speaker's personality. The opposite is true as well; the heavier someone's accent is and the less comprehensible his/her pronunciation, the less positive features are ascribed to this speaker. This finding supports a common observation made in accent studies (e.g. Lev-Ari & Keysar, 2010; Said, 2006) that native speakers react more positively to foreigners with mildly accented speech than to those with heavy accents. Moreover, our research suggests that accentedness plays a greater role in the listeners' attribution of personal integrity and competence (status) to speakers than of social attractiveness, expressed by the feature of pleasantness.

The conclusion is straightforward; good pronunciation in an L2 is an important asset as it positively affects our interlocutors' judgements of what kind of person we are. The opposite is, of course, also true; poor pronunciation may result in the foreign speaker's negative evaluation by native listeners.

B.1.2 Native Accent Models or ELF? A Questionnaire Study

In view of the pronunciation models debate reported in Sections A.1.4 and A.1.5, an important part of diagnosing the sociocultural context of teaching English in a given country involves examining learners' accent preferences. In this section we present a summary of Szpyra-Kozłowska's (2004) questionnaire study administered to secondary school students, all intermediate learners of English, the aim of which was to find answers to the following questions:

• If the participants had a choice, what English accent would they choose to learn?
• Would it be a natural variety, such as RP or GA, or rather ELF?
• Which accents would they not want to learn?
• What arguments are provided by the respondents to justify their views?
• What phonodidactic implications follow from this study?

A total of 134 pupils attending two senior secondary schools in two Polish towns (one in Lublin and one in Stalowa Wola) aged 16–17, of both sexes, were asked to complete an anonymous questionnaire. As argued in Part A, children and teenagers constitute the largest group of foreign language learners in Poland and in many other countries. Secondary school pupils are particularly important in the sense that they have been learning English and other languages for some years and are intellectually mature enough to provide meaningful and justified answers to our questions. Moreover, they have a variety of interests and needs, and are about to make decisions concerning their further education and professional careers.

The reported study consisted of two parts. In Part 1 the English teachers who carried it out presented a 15-minute talk on different varieties of English and their pronunciation. The major English accents were illustrated with several examples. The pupils were also informed about the concept of ELF, meant for international communication between non-native speakers, and its pronunciation priorities found in Jenkins' (2000) LFC. Much care was taken to make the presentations as objective as possible, restricted to basic facts without any evaluative comments. Then, if any questions were raised, they were answered by the teachers until they were sure the pupils clearly understood the issues under discussion.

Next, the students were asked to provide answers to the following question:

If you had a choice, which accent of English would you like to learn at school?

The provided list included eight options:

(a)   standard British pronunciation (RP)
(b)   standard American pronunciation (GA)
(c)   non-standard British or American pronunciation
(d)   standard Scottish English pronunciation
(e)   standard Welsh English pronunciation
(f)   standard Irish English pronunciation
(g)   standard Australian pronunciation
(h)   ELF pronunciation

The following results were obtained concerning the respondents' accent preferences:

- standard British pronunciation (RP) – 40.2%
- standard American pronunciation (GA) – 32.8%
- ELF pronunciation – 13.4%
- non-standard British or American pronunciation – 8.9%
- standard Irish English pronunciation – 2.9%
- standard Scottish English pronunciation – 1.1%
- standard Australian pronunciation – 0.7%
- standard Welsh English pronunciation – 0.0%

Thus, the winner was RP, followed by GA. It should be noted that these two accents were selected by 73% of the respondents. Only 13.4% of them opted for ELF pronunciation, in spite of its expected appeal for teenage learners. About 9% wanted to learn non-standard British or American accents. The remaining options were chosen by a negligible number of the participants.

Let us now examine some typical comments made by pupils in justification of their choice of either RP or GA.

RP:
- *it is a universal variety, it is understood by all speakers of English, many people in Poland and abroad learn it;*
- *other foreigners also learn it, so it is very useful, you can communicate with it everywhere;*

- *it is taught in Poland and you have to know it for various exams, if you use a different variety during exams, this might be considered an error;*
- *it sounds nice, I like it best;*
- *I'm interested in British culture; I'm planning a trip to England.*

GA:

- *American pronunciation, of course, because there are more Americans than British people;*
- *many people use it, it is popular all over the world, you can communicate with it everywhere;*
- *many people know it from films, songs and TV, many radio and television channels use it, I can hear it more often than other varieties;*
- *I like it, it's cool;*
- *it is easier than British pronunciation, it is easier to understand than British pronunciation in which words are often lumped together and difficult to tell apart;*
- *I'm going to study/to work/to visit relatives in the USA;*
- *the USA is a powerful country so it is useful to learn American English;*
- *I'm fascinated by this country, it is more democratic than Great Britain, with no big differences between social classes.*

As shown by these quotations, in both cases the provided arguments are very similar and predominantly pragmatic in nature. Thus, the respondents point out the international spread of both varieties, their wide intelligibility, easy access to them (through the media) and the usefulness of employing RP or GA in contacts with other foreigners who also speak them. They also emphasize the importance of these two accents in their future lives (travelling abroad, visiting relatives, studying or working in the USA or Britain). Another group of comments reflects subjective evaluations of aesthetic values the participants attribute to specific accents, i.e. their alleged beauty, but also the perceived degree of the ease/difficulty involved in learning them. Finally, some arguments are political or cultural in nature and refer to the position of the US and Great Britain in the world or the pupils' interest in or even fascination with a given culture. Many of the presented opinions concern not so much specific accents as dialects of English as it is apparently difficult for the respondents to keep these two notions apart.

Let us now pass on to the presentation of arguments provided in favour of learning ELF pronunciation. A selection of typical answers is given below:

ELF pronunciation:

- *you can use it all over the world, in many countries and continents, it is universal;*
- *English is an international language and it should have an international pronunciation;*

> – *it would simplify learning English, not everybody has a gift for languages,*
> *every person could learn it without worrying of using the wrong accent;*
> – *I'm planning trips to many countries and this type of pronunciation would*
> *allow me to communicate in English everywhere.*

These opinions resemble arguments used by the proponents of ELF and emphasize the utilitarian aspects of this proposal: its lingua franca character, usefulness in international communication via English and – something that is crucial for many learners – its assumed simplicity and ease of learning. For obvious reasons, the choice of ELF pronunciation is not supported by any aesthetic and culture-related arguments, amply provided in the case of natural varieties.

Several participants expressed the wish to learn non-standard British or American pronunciation for the following reasons:

Non-standard British or American pronunciation:
– *more people use non-standard than standard pronunciation;*
– *such pronunciation appears in the majority of songs and films, I like hip-hop*
  in which there is lots of slang and non-standard pronunciation;
– *it is more useful in contacts with ordinary people, it is less formal;*
– *such pronunciation is cool, standard is for nerds, it is more natural, standard*
  pronunciation is artificial.

The above comments indicate that these are mainly cultural factors which underlie the respondents' choice of non-standard accents, i.e. teenagers' interest in popular (American) culture embodied mostly by films and music. Moreover, non-standard accents are perceived by young people as more natural and less formal (*they are cool*) whereas standard varieties are associated by them with formality and artificiality which they generally dislike (*they are for nerds*). It should be pointed out, however, that such arguments show pupils' desire to communicate mainly with native speakers of English rather than international learners.

The least popular accents turned out to be Irish English and Scottish English pronunciation (nobody opted for Welsh English pronunciation). As in both cases similar arguments were provided, they are presented jointly:

Standard Irish English or Scottish English pronunciation:
– *because of the unique Scottish/Irish culture;*
– *because of fascinating Scottish/Irish history;*
– *I like Sean Connery, I know a few Scotsmen and like them;*
– *not many foreigners know this accent.*

It is obvious that the authors of these comments were guided by their cultural interests, but also by the wish to be original and different from the others, in a fashion typical of their age group. Clearly, in the case of these students no pragmatic reasoning could be found.

In the second part of the questionnaire we asked the respondents to make a negative choice and indicate those English accents which they would not want to learn. The same list of options was provided as in the first part. We obtained the following results:

- standard Irish English/Scottish English/Welsh English/Australian pronunciation – 59%
- non-standard British or American pronunciation – 18%
- ELF pronunciation – 17%
- RP or GA – 6%

As expected, the results of this part of our study are exact reversals of the data obtained in its first part, with the least frequently chosen options in the former case now occupying the first place. Thus, varieties restricted to some regions/countries have generally been rejected for learning purposes.[33] They are followed by non-standard accents and ELF pronunciation. RP and GA have the fewest critics (6%).

Below we present typical arguments employed by Polish learners to justify their negative opinions.

Standard Irish English/Scottish English/Welsh English/Australian pronunciation:
- *this kind of pronunciation is local and is used only in a given country/region, it would be difficult to communicate in it with other people, not many people would be able to understand me;*
- *I don't think I will ever go to Australia, I have no plans to go to these countries.*

The above comments reflect the respondents' belief that learning language varieties limited to particular regions or countries which might not be understood outside them is impractical. Moreover, they adopt a personal perspective and eliminate as potential pronunciation models those accents which they think will play no role in their future lives.

The opponents of non-standard accents argue against learning them as follows:

Non-standard British or American pronunciation:
- *such pronunciation is unintelligible to many people, it is used by some speakers only, it is not useful in international communication and in contacts with educated people;*
- *it is commonly associated with lower, uneducated classes, I don't want to be taken for an uneducated person, many people dislike such pronunciation and try to get rid of it.*

The participants regard non-standard accents as inappropriate for communication with both non-native and native speakers of English, regarding them as largely unintelligible, socially stigmatized and as indicators of membership of the lower classes and lack of education. Apparently, in international contacts young Polish people want to speak English with an accent that will win them respect and their interlocutors' positive opinion.

Many critical comments on ELF pronunciation have also been expressed by the participants. A representative selection is given below.

ELF pronunciation:
- *I want to learn English in all its beauty and richness, and not some kind of a simplified version to talk to foreigners, I don't want to learn a simplified, artificial pronunciation, I prefer a real one;*
- *an unnatural, artificial accent can't sound nice, it must be uglier than standard British or American pronunciation;*
- *in an English-speaking country such an accent would not be well-received, for many English and American people such pronunciation could be irritating, it would make communication with native speakers more difficult;*
- *I don't like artificial languages – who wants to learn them?, Esperanto has shown that artificial languages don't attract many people.*

Many pupils take a critical view of international English pronunciation and do not consider it as a simplification of the learning process, but rather as making communication, particularly with native speakers, more difficult. They frequently use terms such as 'artificial' and 'unnatural', negatively assessing its aesthetic value. It should be pointed out that the participants appear to attach much importance to contacts with native speakers of English, with British and American people in the first place, and do not seem to be much concerned with communication with other non-native speakers.

The fewest objections have been levelled against the winners of our study, i.e. RP and GA, with only four respondents providing critical comments on them.

RP or GA:
- *I don't like American pronunciation, it sounds sloppy and careless to me;*
- *I don't like British pronunciation because it sounds unnatural to me;*
- *I don't like Americans because of the wars they are involved in, I don't like American foreign policy and don't want to go to the States.*

These opinions are fairly emotional and reflect some respondents' (negative) attitude to English-speaking countries and have nothing to do with pronunciation. Other comments express pupils' subjective aesthetic judgements on the way these accents sound to them.

Let us sum up the results of this study. If Polish secondary school pupils were allowed to decide which English accent they should learn, most of them (73%) would choose either RP or GA, for pragmatic reasons such as the use of these varieties by numerous both native and non-native speakers, their international intelligibility or learners' personal plans to visit specific countries, but also for cultural and aesthetic reasons, such as young peoples' interest in these countries' history and culture (films and music in particular) as well as their ideas of which accents sound nice or ugly. It should be emphasized that many comments express the participants' wish to interact with native speakers of English and to be perceived by them as well educated and cultured. ELF pronunciation, although easier to learn and claimed to be more useful in international communication, has turned out to be of very limited appeal to Polish teenagers, mainly because of its lack of specific cultural background, artificial character and a significantly diminished role of native speakers. In other words, the respondents hold a traditional view of English as a language learnt by foreigners mainly in order to communicate with its native speakers. The role of English as the international lingua franca is apparently secondary to them.

It should be added that our results coincide with those obtained in other studies carried out with Polish participants (e.g. Janicka *et al.*, 2005; Waniek-Klimczak, 1997a), but also with learners from other European countries (e.g. Henderson *et al.*, 2012). The results of such investigations are unanimous – the majority of respondents opt for one of the two standard accents, i.e. RP or GA, with the former being an unquestionable winner in all European studies.

B.1.3 Diagnosing the Pronunciation Teaching Context in Poland

As argued in Part A, it is very useful for EFL teachers to examine the local conditions in which pronunciation teaching and learning take place and the major factors which affect them. It is equally important to analyze and evaluate various aspects of the current phonodidactic practice, its strengths and weaknesses, as well as its outcome in order to devise and carry out necessary improvements. In this section we undertake an attempt at characterizing and assessing the teaching of English pronunciation in Polish schools from the perspective of secondary school pupils. The collected data will then be used to construct an English pronunciation profile of an average Polish teenage learner as well as a pronunciation teaching profile of an average Polish teacher of English.

Various aspects of English pronunciation teaching in Poland have been discussed in a number of publications which deal with the analysis and evaluation of phonetic instruction in Polish schools of various types, including secondary schools, teacher training colleges and university English departments (e.g. Baran-Łucarz, 2006; Majer, 2002; Nowacka, 2003; Porzuczek, 2002). All researchers are highly critical of the quality of pronunciation teaching in primary and secondary schools, maintaining that this aspect of language instruction is largely neglected, with emphasis being put on grammar and vocabulary. Thus, only a few selected features of English phonetics are occasionally practised, with the use of a small repertoire of traditional techniques, mostly of the 'listen and repeat' type, based on limited teaching resources.

Many researchers point out that this undesirable situation is also a result of a 'washback effect' – a low priority of pronunciation skills in language examinations of various kinds, starting with the Polish school-leaving exam and the English language contests, and ending with the international Cambridge English Examinations, American TOEFL and TSE tests (Szpyra-Kozłowska, 2003). In all of them communicative skills are more highly valued than phonetic accuracy, which leads to further neglect of pronunciation training by both language teachers and learners. As a result, secondary school graduates usually show no concern for good pronunciation and no awareness of the importance of this aspect of language and are, consequently, characterized by low phonetic competence.

Below we present selected (unpublished) results of a questionnaire in which 200 secondary school pupils (aged 18–19), all intermediate learners of English[34] about to finish their secondary education, were asked to provide answers concerning various aspects of the phonetic training they received in school. The participants attend several state upper-level secondary schools in eight different Polish towns, which allowed us to obtain fairly representative data. The choice of the respondents was motivated by the fact that these are all experienced language learners who have learnt English for several years and have been taught by several English teachers, and are in a position to sum up and evaluate their language education.

The questionnaires were fully anonymous. They were administered to the respondents in the schools they attend, but not by their English teachers in order to avoid any possible direct influence of the instructors on the provided answers. In each class the first 10 pupils from an alphabetically ordered list took part in the study, the assumption being that such randomly selected groups will include both very good, medium and poor learners of English. Thus, the respondents come from 20 classes, taught by 20 different teachers in eight Polish towns (in the eastern and central parts of Poland).

The first set of questions concerned the pupils' attitude to English pronunciation and its teaching/learning. Below we provide the questions, together with the percentage of pupils who selected a given answer.

(1) *English pronunciation is, according to you:*
    (a)   easy – 19%
    (b)   not very difficult – 56.5%

    (c)   rather difficult – 22.5%
    (d)   very difficult – 0.5%
    (e)   I don't know – 1.5%

Thus, as many as three-quarters (75.5%) of the respondents consider English pronunciation either easy or not very difficult and only 23% think it is rather difficult or very difficult. The high percentage of the former views can be attributed to the respondents' poor awareness of their pronunciation problems which, in turn, probably stems from an insufficient feedback on their phonetic performance they receive from their teachers.

    The next question was open, with no prompts as to possible answers.

(2) *List three aspects of English pronunciation which you find particularly difficult:*
    (a)   the same letters pronounced differently in different words – 27%
    (b)   word stress – 21%
    (c)   long words – 7%
    (d)   difference between long and short vowels – 6.5%
    (e)   the interdental fricatives – 3.5%
    (f)   final devoicing of obstruents – 3%
    (g)   I don't know – 30%

There are several interesting issues that arise in connection with the above answers. First of all, 30% of the pupils were unable to specify any problematic aspects of English pronunciation. As in the previous case, this result points to the participants' low level of awareness of their phonetic handicaps and insufficient phonetic training. Secondly, answers (a) and (c) deserve to be singled out as they do not concern typical phonetic issues; the former refers to the lack of one-to-one correspondence between English letters and sounds, regarded by the respondents particularly problematic, and the latter to the difficulty of pronouncing long words, which issue generally fails to be addressed in pronunciation manuals. It is also interesting that vowel length and the interdentals, usually considered to be the major problems for Poles, do appear in the above list, but not at the top of it. The second place of word stress also deserves mention in view of a recent discussion concerning the importance and (un)teachability of this prosodic issue (e.g. Jenkins, 2000; Walker, 2011; see also Chapter 2 in which all the phonetic problems listed by the respondents are found among pronunciation priorities for Polish EFL learners).

    The next question dealt with the participants' views on the factors relevant for achieving good English pronunciation. In this case several options were provided and the pupils were to choose three of them.[35]

(3) *What does, in your opinion, achieving good English pronunciation mostly depend on?*
    (a)   frequent listening to English recordings, watching films and TV programmes in English – 65%

(b)   learner's own work on pronunciation – 60%
(c)   frequent use of English in conversations with foreign speakers of English – 52.5%
(d)   frequent stays in English-speaking countries – 51%
(e)   learner's linguistic talent – 36%
(f)   teacher's good English pronunciation – 34%
(g)   phonetic training during English classes – 29.5%

What is striking in these answers is the fact that, on the one hand, the most frequently selected options (in (a), (b) and (c)) all require pupils' active involvement in the process of learning pronunciation and, on the other hand, very little appears to depend on the teacher. Thus, according to the participants, the quality of the teacher's English pronunciation and phonetic training during the classes occupy the lowest position among the factors responsible for learners' phonetic success (answers (f) and (g)). In other words, the respondents believe that achieving good English pronunciation is in their own and not their teachers' hands. These results can be taken to point to the poor quality and ineffectiveness of the phonetic training offered in schools; since it brings unsatisfactory results, learners conclude that other ways of learning English pronunciation must be superior to it. Nevertheless, their conviction that it is up to them to improve their phonetic skills has a positive side as it provides an excellent opportunity to develop learner autonomy (see Chapter 3).

Our further enquiry concerned pupils' assessment of the quality of their English pronunciation.

(4)   *How good is your English pronunciation in your opinion?*
(a)   very good/good – 58.%
(b)   poor – 34%
(c)   very poor – 2.5%
(d)   I don't know – 5.5%

These responses demonstrate that almost 60% of the participants consider their pronunciation either as good or as very good and over 36% as poor or very poor. Interestingly, over 5% of them were unable to answer this question, which proves our earlier conclusion concerning the insufficient amount of feedback learners receive from their teachers.

An interesting issue concerns the grounds on which pupils assess the quality of their English pronunciation. It appears that their judgements are based on the general marks they receive in English, as shown by the correlation between these two factors. Thus, the best opinion on their pronunciation was given by pupils with top marks (75%), then those with medium marks (63%) and finally those with poor marks (18%).

The next group of questions examined learners' attitude towards the English pronunciation training they received at school and its evaluation.

(5) *What is your attitude to pronunciation practice activities?*
    (a) I like them/I like them very much – 47%
    (b) I neither like them nor dislike them – 33%
    (c) I don't like them – 15%
    (d) I don't know – 5%

According to these responses, almost half of the students are positively inclined to pronunciation activities, one-third is indifferent to them and only a minority of 15% dislike them. Such results mean a positive ground for phonetic training that teachers should make good use of.

As in the previously discussed case, there is a clear correlation between pupils' marks and their attitude to pronunciation activities: they are enjoyed by 84% of good students, by 62% of medium students and by 18% of the poor ones. The reverse is also true: they are disliked by 75% of poor students, by 26% of medium learners and by 15% of high achievers.

We also wanted to know what the respondents think about the amount of time allotted to pronunciation activities.

(6) *What do you think about the amount of pronunciation practice during the English lessons?*
    (a) there are too many pronunciation activities – 1%
    (b) there are enough pronunciation activities – 42%
    (c) there are too few pronunciation activities – 46%
    (d) there are no pronunciation activities at all – 2%
    (e) I don't know – 9%

The participants' generally positive attitude towards pronunciation practice finds further support in answers to the above question which show that almost half of them are not satisfied with its amount and would like to have more of it. It is also important that only a negligible 1% of the respondents complain of too many pronunciation activities. It should be pointed out, however, that a large group of students (42%) think they are offered sufficient phonetic training. These differences of opinion can be attributed to the fact that English teachers vary in the amount of time they devote to pronunciation instruction and this fact is reflected in the provided responses.

Let us sum up this part of the study by sketching an English pronunciation profile of an average Polish secondary school student that emerges from the questionnaire. Point (6) refers to answers to Question (9) which are discussed later.

An English pronunciation profile of an average Polish secondary school learner:

(1) An average student thinks that English pronunciation is either easy or not very difficult (75%).

(2) They assess their English pronunciation as either good or very good (60%).

(3) They have either a positive or neutral attitude towards phonetic training (80%).

(4) They think that the most effective ways to learn English pronunciation are through frequent watching of English-language films, TV programmes and recordings (65%), through their own work (60%), conversations in English with foreigners (52%) and trips to English-speaking countries (51%).

(5) Their major phonetic problems concern relations between English spelling and pronunciation, word stress and the pronunciation of long words.

(6) More or less the same number of learners think they receive a sufficient (42%) or an insufficient (48%) amount of phonetic practice at school.

(7) They have a positive attitude to the use of phonetic transcription (76%).

The second part of the questionnaire dealt with the students' assessment of their pronunciation instruction. Question (6) asked the respondents to evaluate their English teacher's attitude to pupils' pronunciation:

(6) *What is your teacher's attitude to the pupils' English pronunciation?*
   (a) He/she pays much attention to it – 49%
   (b) He/she pays some attention to it, but not much – 42%
   (c) He/she pays no attention to it – 9%

The above answers seem to indicate that teachers can be equally divided into those who are concerned with their pupils' English pronunciation and those who do not pay particular attention to it. This result confirms the observations made in connection with the preceding question.

Our next enquiry was into the pronunciation teaching techniques employed by the teacher. Here several prompts were given to choose from and the pupils' task was to mark all that were used in the classroom:

(7) *What pronunciation teaching techniques are used by your English teacher?*[36]
   (a) correcting pupils' pronunciation – 94.5%
   (b) listening to English recordings – 81.5%
   (c) explaining rules of correct pronunciation – 52%
   (d) repeating words/phrases after the teacher – 50%
   (e) repeating words/phrases after the recording – 26.5%
   (f) watching English language films and TV programmes – 21.5%

(g)   explaining phonetic differences between English and Polish – 18.5%
(h)   reciting poems and acting out plays, singing songs – 13.5%
(i)   other – 0%

According to the respondents, the two most frequent pronunciation teaching strategies employed by over 80% of their English teachers are the correction of phonetic errors and making pupils listen to English recordings. About 50% of the instructors provide rules of correct pronunciation and use imitation tasks (repeating words and phrases after the teacher). The remaining techniques are employed by fewer than 30% of teachers. What is particularly striking is the relatively infrequent use of what seems to be a basic type of pronunciation practice activity, i.e. imitation of a recording provided by a native speaker, which comes as a surprise in view of the fact that all the teachers in this study are Polish and are therefore not ideal pronunciation models for their learners. It is also worth pointing out that routine-breaking activities which are particularly attractive to teenage learners, i.e. singing songs, reciting poems and acting out plays, very rarely find their way into the language classroom.

The next two questions examine the use of phonemic transcription:

(8)   *Is phonemic transcription used during your English lessons?*
(a)   very frequently – 9%
(b)   rather frequently – 24%
(c)   infrequently – 48.5%
(d)   never – 18.5%

Thus, 67% of English teachers either do not use phonemic transcription in the classroom at all or do it infrequently. Only one-third of them employ this important tool of phonetic instruction regularly. It should be pointed out that, as argued in Chapter 3, an occasional use of the phonemic script cannot be effective.

Let us now examine what learners themselves think of the usefulness of this technique.

(9)   *What do you think about the role of phonemic transcription in learning English pronunciation?*
(a)   it is useful – 55.5%
(b)   it is absolutely necessary – 20.5%
(c)   it is of little usefulness – 15%
(d)   it is useless – 4%
(e)   I don't know – 5.5%

The above data indicate that the majority of the respondents (76%) regard phonemic transcription either as useful or indispensable in learning English pronunciation and only 19% express a negative opinion about its usefulness. This result has clear teaching implications: the phonemic script should be more frequently employed in language instruction.

The last question concerning teachers' involvement in pronunciation teaching was the following:

(10) *Does your English teacher work individually with pupils who have pronunciation problems?*
    (a)   no – 77%
    (b)   yes, but infrequently – 20.5%
    (c)   yes, very frequently – 2.5%

The obtained figures are self-evident – the majority of teachers do not devote attention to individual learner's pronunciation problems at all and about 20% do it infrequently. Instructors who do it on a regular basis constitute a rarity (2.5%). As we argue in Chapter 3, in many cases it is only approaching learners individually that can improve their pronunciation skills.

In another study (Frankiewicz *et al.*, 2002), we asked 100 secondary school teachers of English about the phonetic issues they focus on, depending on the learners' level of language proficiency. According to the obtained data, Polish teachers devote most time and attention to the phonetic instruction of beginners, less to intermediate learners and the least to advanced learners. In the first case the focus is on segmental phonetics and such issues as the pronunciation of the interdentals, the inflectional endings, the -ing suffix and English monophthongs, in the second case on some aspects of prosody (mainly intonation, word stress, stress in compounds, sentence stress), and in third case on other suprasegmental problems and phonostylistic changes (strong and weak forms, consonant elisions in fast speech, palatalization and consonant assimilations in phrases). Unfortunately, those phonetic elements that have already been introduced at some stage tend to be neglected in further linguistic education. This means that segmental phonetics is practised at the beginning but not later on, and that learners who do not reach more advanced levels of proficiency do not have a chance to get acquainted with various suprasegmental issues. Moreover, many different aspects of English phonetics are either never or very rarely taught. They include both segmentals (e.g. pronunciation of diphthongs, dark and clear 'l', palatoalveolar consonants, syllabic consonants, smoothing of triphthongs) and suprasegmentals (e.g. rhythmic stress shift, schwa elision in fast speech).

Below we summarize the relevant results of both studies which allow us to characterize the pronunciation teaching profile of an average Polish teacher of English.

The pronunciation teaching profile of an average Polish teacher of English:

(1) Only half of the teachers are concerned with their students' English pronunciation. The remaining ones tend to neglect their phonetic training.
(2) They teach pronunciation mainly through correcting pupils' pronunciation (94%), giving them English recordings to listen to (81%), comparing English and Polish sounds (52%) and making students repeat words/phrases after the teacher (50%).
(3) 67% of English teachers either do not use phonetic transcription in the language classroom or do it infrequently.
(4) The majority of teachers (97%) do not devote attention to individual learners' pronunciation problems or do it only occasionally.
(5) Teachers devote most time to the pronunciation instruction of beginners, less to intermediate learners and the least to advanced students.
(6) First they teach segmentals (to beginners), then suprasegmentals, i.e. stress and intonation (to intermediate students), and finally connected speech phenomena (to advanced learners).
(7) Teachers tend to focus on selected phonetic issues (such as the pronunciation of 'th', inflectional endings, -ing, long and short vowels) and neglect many others.

The results of the studies presented above lead to an overall pessimistic conclusion concerning a general neglect of pronunciation teaching in Polish schools. There are several reasons for this situation. First of all, teachers complain of various pressures they are subject to and a notorious lack of time for pronunciation practice. The exams they prepare their students for are predominantly written and require a focus on grammar and vocabulary. Moreover, what is emphasized in communicative language teaching is developing in learners the ability to communicate, often at the cost of accuracy and correctness. Finally, the poor quality of teacher preparation that fails to provide them with proper tools for pronunciation instruction can be blamed for the problem under discussion which fails to provide them with proper tools for pronunciation instruction. As pointed out by Celce-Murcia *et al.* (1996), 'To be adequately prepared to teach pronunciation, teachers must have at their disposal a working knowledge of articulatory phonetics, theories of second-language phonological acquisition and an up-to-date command of techniques and procedures to use in the classroom'. Unfortunately, not all these requirements are met by teacher training courses.

Notes

(1) According to Crystal (1997), in just the years 1982–1991, 11% of fatal aeroplane crashes were due to pilot–controller miscommunication. For this reason very strict regulations have been introduced in the English pronunciation that can be used in

aviation. In 'Airspeak', for instance, no interdental fricatives are allowed so that *three* must be pronounced as *tree*.

(2) As pointed out by some researchers (e.g. Derwing & Munro, 2005), a positive side of speaking with a foreign accent is that it signals to a native interlocutor that the speaker is non-native and may require modified input.

(3) This is often referred to as the 'Joseph Conrad phenomenon', since the writer's Polish-accented speech was extremely difficult to understand and contrasted sharply with his mastery of written English.

(4) Graddol (1999) refers to this phenomenon as the decline of the native speaker.

(5) The major controversy concerns the question of whether ELF can be regarded as a variety in its own right as it is extremely heterogeneous and characterized by considerable fluidity and variability.

(6) Several proposals for simplifying English grammar for foreign learners have been put forward, e.g. Globish, Nuclear English and Basic English. Seidlhofer (2011) argues that these are theoretical constructs which are prescriptive in character while ELF is descriptive and based on real data. It is difficult to agree with this reasoning as Jenkins' LFC, although claimed to be grounded in empirical research, is evidently prescriptive.

(7) Seidlhofer (2011) refers to the LFC as a partly empirical and partly artificial construct.

(8) Some exaggeration with respect to political correctness can be seen in the fact that even the use of the term 'learner' is criticized in ELF as derogatory and as breeding a feeling of inferiority (e.g. Seidlhofer, 2011). Therefore a more neutral label of 'language user' is suggested.

(9) As a matter of fact, as shown by various questionnaire studies, many learners are actually proud of achieving a level of pronunciation proficiency which does not allow listeners to identify their nationality.

(10) Accommodation is usually understood as the ability to adjust one's speech and other aspects of spoken communication so that they become more like that of one's interlocutors.

(11) It should be added that other kinds of accommodation require the active participation of both interlocutors, particularly in the use of pragmatic strategies in which they show a willingness to accept the linguistic and cultural differences of other speakers (see Archibald *et al.*, 2011).

(12) I have not influenced or modified the contents of these essays. I have only shortened them by removing those parts which are not directly relevant to the discussion.

(13) It is doubtful whether other forms of accommodation, e.g. changing the tempo of speech or using other strategies, can successfully compensate for incorrectly realized native accent features.

(14) It should be added that it seems easier for EFL learners to accommodate to ELF users than for native speakers since the former have gone through various stages of language learning and know which structures, words and sounds are easier and which are more difficult. Therefore they can simplify the language they use. Native speakers do not have this kind of knowledge and often try to help foreign interlocutors by speaking louder and more slowly without, however, modifying their grammar or pronunciation. According to Jenkins (2000), in the future native speakers who wish to communicate with ELF users will have to attend special courses to acquire accommodation skills. For a criticism of this idea see Trudgill (2005).

(15) In our presentation of the major assumptions of ELF we attempt to reproduce Jenkins' and her followers' reasoning as closely as possible. It is worth pointing out, however, that in many publications devoted to ELF she keeps accusing her critics of bias and of misunderstanding her ideas. It seems that, if so many researchers fail to

understand Jenkins' reasoning, maybe the fault lies not with the readers but with the clarity of her argumentation.

(16) This does not mean that High German is monolithic and some regional differences can be noted. For instance, Austrian High German is known for its 'singsong' pronunciation.

(17) As mentioned earlier, in the actual teaching practice, however, in EFL some phonetic features have been prioritized by teachers more or less in an arbitrary fashion, mostly on the basis of their intuition and experience.

(18) As a matter of fact, according to various authors, mutual intelligibility of all speakers of English is a myth.

(19) For the reasons stated in the previous sections, many scholars attempt to avoid using the term 'RP' and replace it with, for example, 'BBC pronunciation', 'BBC English', 'non-regional pronunciation', 'educated southern English' and 'standard southern English'. As these are all largely equivalent terms, in this book we will continue to use the traditional and well-known label, i.e. RP.

(20) It has to be admitted, though, that in some parts of the world an American accent (taken as a sign of being an American citizen) might meet with hostility.

(21) This is done, for example, by Celce-Murcia *et al.* (1996), who in the preface to their excellent book on pronunciation teaching address it to ESL/EFL teachers and frequently refer to ESL/EFL learners.

(22) The term 'second language' is ambiguous. The discussion in this section focuses on comparing the acquisition of pronunciation in EFL and ESL settings, where the latter is understood as the process which takes place in the country where the L2 is spoken.

(23) As pointed out by various researchers, many immigrants do not make full use of these opportunities and tend to live, work and socialize with people from their country of origin. As noted by Celce-Murcia *et al.* (1996: 18): 'even in ESL settings, where the learners are surrounded by the English-speaking world, many learners live in linguistic "islands" with relatively little exposure to native speakers of the target language in their homes and even in their worksites.' This means that there are frequent cases of immigrants who, after having spent many years in another country, can hardly communicate in its language.

(24) Some scholars (e.g. Lamb, 2004; Ushioda, 2006) argue that in many EFL contexts integrative and instrumental motivation are often indistinguishable, particularly when the former is understood as a desire to integrate not with a particular Anglophone culture, but with an international, global community of English language users. According to Ushioda, in places such as Europe the notion of integrativeness should be expanded to cover both intercultural friendship and vocational interests. Moreover, it should be noted that different types of motivation may be involved at various stages of the learning process.

(25) The awareness of this fact is probably the major reason why many authors of books devoted to pronunciation instruction (e.g. Avery & Ehrlich, 1992; Celce-Murcia *et al.*, 1996; Kenworthy, 1987; Rogerson-Revell, 2011) feel it necessary to include lengthy presentations of the English sound system even if there are many sources which deal with such issues.

(26) As a matter of fact, as observed by some researchers (e.g. Steinbrich, 2014), native teachers of English frequently modify their pronunciation when teaching in EFL contexts and try to make it closer to a standard accent.

(27) Muñoz (2008) argues against the attempts to equate AoA with the age when language instruction began as well as against equating LoR with the number of hours of instruction. In the former case a distinction must be made between the initial age of learning and the beginning of significant exposure to L2, which takes place when learners 'are able to carry out a variety of speech acts over a wide range of

situations and topics, and to participate in social settings effectively dominated by the L2' (Muñoz, 2008: 582). She concludes that 'initial age of foreign language learning may be equated with the age at which insignificant exposure begins' (Muñoz, 2008: 582). The number of instruction hours is not always indicative of the amount of exposure to L2, as frequently the learners' native language appears to dominate in EFL classes.

(28) For example, Rogerson-Revell (2011) discusses the role of the L1 as the last factor which influences pronunciation achievement and does not mention the role of formal instruction at all.

(29) In Europe there are countries in which English is used extensively (e.g. The Netherlands, Sweden), moderately (e.g. Greece) and rarely (e.g. Spain).

(30) This generalization is false in the case of multilingual societies in which EFL learners may have different cultural and linguistic backgrounds.

(31) The descriptions of the experiments presented in this book, for reasons of space and clarity, are largely simplified and devoid of many technical details which could be cumbersome to many readers.

(32) It should be noted, however, that, as observed by some scholars (e.g. Munro & Derwing, 1999), even heavily accented speech can be comprehensible, particularly in the case of listeners' frequent exposure to accented speech. Polish participants' negative comprehensibility ratings of heavily accented speech might thus be attributed to their limited experience with foreign versions of Polish.

(33) It should be added that many respondents enumerated all these varieties as the ones they do not want to learn and provided very similar arguments. Therefore, they are presented jointly.

(34) The participants have all been learning English for at least eight years and, according to their teachers, represent all types of intermediate learners, from pre-intermediate to upper intermediate.

(35) This means that the provided percentages do not sum to 100.

(36) Some types of activities listed in (7), i.e. listening to English recordings and watching English language films and television programmes are, in fact, listening comprehension tasks which, however, can be seen as part of phonetic training since they provide learners with authentic auditory input (see Section A.3.2.2.). For this reason they are included here.

2 Global and Local Pronunciation Priorities

The choice of an appropriate pronunciation model, which serves as a general point of reference for teachers and learners of English, constitutes only the first step in the process of deciding what to teach pronunciation-wise. Its selection, however, as demonstrated in the preceding chapter, does not imply the need to master each phonetic feature, since this is both unrealistic and unnecessary for the majority of EFL learners whose aim is to achieve comfortable intelligibility in communication with other speakers of English. While this goal of phonetic instruction is frequently accepted, there is no agreement as to how it can be attained and what role specific aspects of English pronunciation play in safeguarding (or hindering) the intelligibility of foreign learners' speech. Thus, as argued by Field (2005: 399), 'the most pressing issue in L2 pronunciation research today is the quest to identify the factors that most contribute to speaker intelligibility'. In other words, what should be addressed is a complex and controversial issue of pronunciation priorities for EFL learners. This chapter is devoted to this problem.

In Part A first the major aspects of pronunciation priorities research concerning those factors which affect intelligibility are discussed. Then we present and evaluate several recent proposals concerning this issue, namely Jenkins' (2000) Lingua Franca Core, Cruttenden's (2008) Amalgam English and International English, and Collins and Mees' (2003) pronunciation Error Ranking. On the basis of these three approaches, a generalized set of EFL phonetic priorities is formulated.

Next a new proposal, meant to complement the previous ones and aimed specifically at EFL learners, is put forward, according to which individual sounds and prosodies should not be the focus of phonetic instruction, but rather whole words prone to be notoriously mispronounced by foreign learners. It is argued and proved empirically that such lexical items hinder achieving comfortable intelligibility more than inaccurately produced segments and/or prosodic patterns and should therefore be prioritized. We also enquire into the nature of phonetically problematic words and the major sources of their pronunciation difficulty. Subsequently, it is argued that in view of the fact that EFL learners are more frequently exposed to the written form of English than to authentic English speech, sound and spelling correspondence should also constitute a phonodidactic priority.

In the remaining parts of this chapter we examine the communicative importance of two main aspects of English phonetics, i.e. sounds and prosody, an issue often referred to as the 'segmentals versus suprasegmentals' controversy. A solution to this problem is offered based on the principle of a phonetic distance between the L1 and L2, coupled with a hierarchy of pronunciation errors which, as we shall argue, should be established empirically on a language-specific basis.

In Part B several studies supporting some of the claims made in Part A are presented. First we deal with phonologically deviant words, known as local errors, and prove experimentally that they hinder intelligibility and lead to listener irritation far more than global errors, the reduction of which is the major concern of current pronunciation pedagogy. Next we look a bit more closely at phonetically difficult words and the factors which make them problematic. Finally, a study aimed at identifying pronunciation priorities for Polish learners of English is summarized.

Part A

A.2.1 How to Establish Pronunciation Priorities

While the need to establish pronunciation priorities for EFL learners is generally acknowledged, it is neither obvious nor uncontroversial how this could actually be done. Thus, many often contradictory suggestions have been put forward which usually reflect differences in the authors' theoretical stance and various ways of determining pronunciation priorities. In this section we first discuss the different criteria employed in search of phonetic priorities and then focus on the factors which are responsible for the (un)intelligibility of foreigners' speech.

A.2.1.1 Criteria for determining priorities

According to Rogerson-Revell (2011: 246): 'learners may well be aware of their pronunciation difficulties but they will not be able to tell how important they are. It is therefore the teacher's role to decide (...) which areas of pronunciation to prioritize and which to leave well alone.' The problem is that placing this burden entirely on teachers does not seem to be justified as they may either have insufficient knowledge to decide what is important and what is not, or may be guided by their intuition[1] which is not always reliable and often leads to contradictory didactic decisions. Take, for instance, the question of teaching the English interdental fricatives, a notorious pronunciation difficulty for many EFL learners. Some instructors attach much importance to practising this aspect of English; others tend to neglect it. Note that consulting various written sources is of no help since conflicting views can be found regarding this problem. Moreover, we should also keep in mind that non-native teachers who share a mother tongue with their monolingual classes, as is usually the case in EFL settings, are poor judges of their students' intelligibility since after years of hearing the same mispronunciations, they can understand their learners' speech,[2] no matter how far it departs from the adopted accent model. In brief, teachers need help from pronunciation specialists to provide them with the necessary guidelines for selecting pronunciation priorities appropriate for their students.[3]

Let us examine the issue in question as it relates to achieving the goal of comfortable intelligibility or listener-friendly pronunciation. Collins and Mees (2003: 186) argue that 'a realistic aim is to speak in a way which is clearly intelligible to your listeners and which does not distract, irritate or confuse them'. In order to accomplish this task, a hierarchy of error must be established which must take into account listeners' reactions to them. They isolate three types of errors:

(1)   errors which lead to a breakdown of intelligibility;
(2)   errors which give rise to irritation or amusement;
(3)   errors which provoke few such reactions and may even pass unnoticed.

Obviously, the first type of errors is of crucial importance since without intelligible pronunciation there can be no communication at all. The second category is also relevant because, if a speaker's pronunciation is intelligible but irritates listeners or causes their amusement, it distracts them from following the message and diminishes the ease of communication. The third type of errors is of negligible importance and can be omitted in the phonetic training of those who do not aim for native-like pronunciation. The major difficulty lies in determining which pronunciation errors made by learners belong to each of these three categories.

Rogerson-Revell (2011) proposes a set of five criteria for establishing pronunciation teaching priorities which include intelligibility, functional load, degree of tolerance, return on investment and end-purpose. Intelligibility corresponds to the first type of errors specified by Collins and Mees (2003), that is, those which may cause communication breakdown. The degree of tolerance refers to the second category of errors which are a source of irritation/amusement for the listener. The remaining three criteria require some explanation.

The concept of functional load, which has been present in linguistics for a long time, refers to the frequency of occurrence of minimal pair contrasts (Brown, 1988; Levis & Cortes, 2008). Thus, for example, the phonemes /l/

and /r/ serve to distinguish many word pairs, such as, for example, *light – right, late – rate, fly – fry*, so this distinction has a high functional load in English, while /ʃ/ and /ʒ/ do not differentiate many items, which means that this contrast has a low functional load. According to pronunciation specialists, contrasts with a high functional load should constitute a teaching priority while those with a low functional load are of secondary importance.

The criterion of return on investment concerns a comparison of the amount of work needed by the learner to acquire a given aspect of pronunciation and the obtained results. Rogerson-Revell suggests that if the effort involved merits the achieved result, then a phonetic feature should be given high priority. When the effort is greater than the 'return', then we are dealing with a low priority area. This criterion bears a close resemblance to the notion of teachability/learnability (e.g. Dalton & Seidlhofer, 1994) since some aspects of L2 pronunciation are easy to learn, some are more difficult and yet other features are almost impossible to master for students of a given L1.

The final criterion proposed by Rogerson-Revell concerns learners' end purpose for studying English, i.e. the level of linguistic competence they want to achieve. Evidently, a different degree of phonetic proficiency is required for those who want to pass for native speakers and for tourists who need to know 'survival English'. Consequently, pronunciation priorities cannot be the same for all learners.

An analysis of Rogerson-Revell's (2011) criteria for deciding pronunciation priorities as well as the error types isolated by Collins and Mees (2003) indicates that, apart from functional load which can be studied for English in general (or for different varieties of English), the remaining issues cannot be established in an a priori fashion, but must be research based. In other words, justified phonodidactic decisions can only be made on the basis of empirical evidence as to the impact of various features of accented pronunciation on communication with other speakers of the L2.

It should also be noted that the employment of various criteria for evaluating the role of particular phonetic features often produces contradictory results. Take again the issue as to whether to teach the interdental fricatives to foreign learners. It has been argued (e.g. Jenkins, 2000) that they are irrelevant to intelligibility in international contexts as they are absent in various native English accents. Moreover, these consonants, not occurring in many languages, are very difficult to learn so they represent a poor return on investment. On the other hand, they have a medium functional load and, according to Collins and Mees (2003), their replacements trigger irritation and/or amusement (low degree of tolerance). This is supported by empirical evidence provided by some studies (Bryła-Cruz, 2013; van den Doel, 2006). Table 2.1 summarises these results and demonstrates that, depending on the adopted criterion, the interdental fricatives can be regarded as a low or high priority area.

Table 2.1 Priority evaluation of 'th' according to four criteria

Criterion	Priority evaluation
Intelligibility	Low
Functional load	Low
Degree of tolerance	High
Return on investment (teachability/learnability)	Low
End-purpose	Minimal intelligibility – low Comfortable intelligibility – high

A.2.1.2 Pronunciation and intelligibility

All specialists in phonodidactics are likely to agree with the claim that intelligibility constitutes the most important criterion when establishing pronunciation priorities. As argued by Munro (2011: 12): 'intelligibility is the simple most important aspect of all communication. If there is no intelligibility, communication has failed'. What remains to be done is to establish in an non-arbitrary, i.e. empirical, fashion which elements of the English sound system are crucial for safeguarding intelligibility and should therefore be prioritized.

There are two major ways of approaching this issue. The first of them is an observation of real-life interactions in English and an analysis of cases in which communication breakdown occurs due to learners' pronunciation. The second option is to carry out experiments designed to examine the communicative impact of various elements of English phonetics. Thus, intelligibility can be studied in real-world and experimental settings. None of these approaches, however, is devoid of its problems due to the complex interplay of intelligibility-affecting factors.

While evidence from real-life interactions is undoubtedly valuable, it is not only difficult to obtain, but cannot be viewed as fully reliable[4] since the reported cases are usually anecdotal in nature and insufficient to allow for meaningful and significant generalization. Moreover, in many instances it is not easy to determine what exactly is responsible for the comprehension problem.

Take, for example, an amusing conversational exchange quoted by Gilbert (2008: 5), between a student and a teacher, provided to prove that incorrect stress placement may cause communication breakdown.

Student: Mrs Stiebel, can you help me with comedy?
Teacher: Comedy?
Student: Yes, comedy is big problem.
Teacher: I don't quite follow.
Student: (Patiently) Problem – this is worry.
Teacher: Yes, a worry. Um ... you mean a problem with comedy on TV?

Student: TV⸮ (Trying again). The boss put me on department comedy. Everybody on comedy, all the time argue.
Teacher: Oh, you mean <u>committee</u>!
Student: Yes, what I told you, comedy.

Apparently, the cause of the above misunderstanding is the incorrect placement of stress (on the initial syllable) in the word *committee* by the foreign student, coupled with some segmental inaccuracies, due to which this item sounded to the teacher more like *comedy*. Observe also that another important factor at work here is the existence of the word *comedy* which, in terms of prosody, forms a near-minimal pair with *committee*. The claim, based on this particular case, concerning the crucial impact of word stress placement on intelligibility is only partly justified since many other examples can be provided to show that mis-stressed items can be comprehended without any major problems. Suppose, for instance, that a learner stresses the initial syllable of the word *'computer'*, which is frequently done by Poles. As there seems to be no similar English trisyllabic word with initial stress, no confusion arises and it can be interpreted properly. Thus, misplaced stress does not always have the same communicative consequences.

Consider another example of a real-life communication breakdown, reported by a colleague of mine. Two men, a Pole and a Spaniard, were conversing in English about their families. One of them asked the other about his wife's job. He answered: 'She works in a lab. She does food tests', pronouncing *food* as [fut]. The listener accepted this answer without any comment or sign that he failed to understand the message, but later asked my colleague if he knew how legs are tested in a lab. Clearly, the major culprit of this misunderstanding was the devoicing of the final plosive in *food*, accompanied by an inappropriate vowel quality and length as well as the occurrence of a minimal pair *food – foot*. Note that if other words had been used, for instance, *wood* or *blood*, which have no counterparts ending in voiceless obstruents (*woot, *bloot), no communication breakdown would have occurred.[5] In other words, the devoicing of word-final obstruents, which is common among, for example, German, Dutch and Polish learners, sometimes has serious consequences for intelligibility, but in other cases is of negligible importance.

The instances of communication breakdown reported here demonstrate that it is usually not a single phonetic feature that is responsible for it, but a set of pronunciation inaccuracies, frequently coupled with semantic and grammatical factors as well as the existence of minimal pairs whose members can potentially be employed in the same context. If more than one pronunciation errors are involved, it is not clear which of them causes misunderstanding or whether it is a joint effect of several inaccuracies.

It should be added that the occurrence of minimal pairs does not necessarily imply that their mispronunciation will result in communication problems.

As argued by Levis and Cortes (2008), if two words belong to different grammatical categories, they are not likely to be confused. For example, the members of the minimal pair *eat/it*, where the first item is a verb and the second is a pronoun, appear in entirely different grammatical contexts, allowing the listener to identify the word intended by the speaker.

The role of the semantic and pragmatic context in the intelligibility issue should also be brought up. In some instances a phonetically inaccurate message can be understood perfectly well since in a specific situation only one interpretation makes sense. For example, a sentence *In court a judge wears a black robe*, with the final noun pronounced with a devoiced plosive as *rope*, is not in much danger of being misinterpreted as it is more likely for judges to wear robes than ropes at work. However, in a crowded bus a similar type of substitution in *Watch your bag* will result in the just as likely, but quite different in meaning, *Watch your back*. Thus, the existence of a minimal pair and a substitution of one of its members with another sometimes affects intelligibility, but not always. Levis and Cortes (2008) conclude that minimal pairs might lead to miscommunication if they fulfil the following conditions: both members are the same parts of speech, both are equally likely to occur in the same linguistic context and both are semantically plausible, and add that such requirements are not met by the majority of minimal pairs in English. Moreover, if one member of the pair is a frequent word and the other is very rare, e.g. *thigh/thy*, *should/shoed*, then the listener is more likely to decide that the speaker used the more common item.

Consider one more frequently quoted example involving the mispronunciation of 'th', employed in a video advertisement for a language school. A distress call comes over the radio:

Voice: Mayday, Mayday! Hello. Can you hear us? Can—you—hear us? Can you [static]? Over. We are sinking! We are—sink–!
Young man: Hallo, zis is ze German Coastguard.
Voice: We're sinking! We're sinking!
Young man: What are you sinking [thinking] about?

The humorous effect is undeniable but, as pointed out by Levis and Cortes (2008), this kind of miscommunication is completely implausible as in the context of a dramatic 'mayday' message sent to the coastguard only one interpretation is possible.

The provided examples involve cases of real or potential confusion in which the message was misunderstood by the listener due to various phonetic distortions. There are also situations in which an utterance is not so much misunderstood as it fails to be comprehended completely. It seems that such cases are not always easy to observe since not all listeners signal their lack of understanding of a given message for various reasons, e.g. embarrassment, shyness and a wish not to upset the speaker or simply because they are not aware that they have failed to comprehend what has been said. Thus, a distinction should be made between confusion, i.e. a listener's misunderstanding of an utterance and taking it to mean something else than intended by the speaker and a total communication breakdown in which the listener fails to understand a message completely. Evidently intelligibility is a scalar phenomenon. Moreover, in the latter type of situation no minimal pairs have to be involved and other types of mispronunciations might play a crucial role. This means that in studying intelligibility it is incorrect to focus on minimal pairs only, as is often done.

To conclude, a rich variety of factors affect intelligibility, several of which might be involved in a single communicative situation. We present the major determinants in Table 2.2, isolating speaker-related, listener-related and context-related factors.

While most of the contents of Table 2.2 has already been explained, some additional comments are in order. Thus, certain factors appear both in the speaker's and listener's columns. They include familiarity of the interlocutors, which is viewed as an important aid in comprehending each other, and the amount of effort and involvement invested by both parties in an interaction. The latter refers to how much they are determined to communicate successfully and are willing to accommodate to each other, for example, by raising the volume of their voices in noisy conditions[6] and when talking to elderly people whose hearing is often weaker[7] or by slowing down the tempo of speech when the listener's lack of understanding becomes apparent. Much also depends on various temporary factors, such as the speaker's and/or the listener's mood, state of health, tiredness, concentration, emotional state or alcohol consumption, all of which might affect the clarity of speech and its perception. All foreign learners have probably experienced good and bad days of L2 use, i.e. the ease of speaking the L2 on one occasion and doing it with much difficulty on another.

Finally, learners' phonetic ability can be considered not only in terms of sound articulation, but also of speech perception. This means that, just as some of us are more successful as L2 speakers than others, listeners, both native and non-native, may differ in their aptitude for comprehending accented speech. As argued by Munro (2011: 11): 'successful communication depends on the abilities and efforts of both speaker and listener. Listeners with certain experience, background, and perhaps aptitude may be more successful than others at comprehending L2 speech.' If this assumption is true, maybe we should take the literal meaning of the phrase 'to have an ear for languages' more seriously. Those with a good ear require less processing time to understand accented speech than other listeners.

The discussion above has demonstrated that, in view of the complexity of factors which affect intelligibility, generalizations concerning the impact of individual phonetic features are difficult to draw. Moreover, conclusions based on isolated cases of miscommunication have to be approached with

Table 2.2 Major factors affecting intelligibility

Speaker-related factors	Listener-related factors	Context-related factors
• general language proficiency (grammatical correctness, appropriate choice of vocabulary and idiom); • degree of foreign accent (number of phonological and phonetic departures from the native model); • fluency, number of pauses, hesitations, self-corrections and fillers; • frequency of phonetic errors; • amount of effort and involvement invested in an interaction; • speaking volume (ability to adapt it to the conditions in which an interaction takes place); • speech rate; • enunciation (quality of vocal projection) and speaking techniques; • familiarity with the listener; • speaker's temporary characteristics (mood, state of health, level of stress, tiredness and concentration, emotional state, alcohol and drug consumption).	• exposure to accented speech; • familiarity with foreign languages; • listener's native accent; • degree of tolerance for accented speech; • age, sex, education, place of living, occupation; • attitude towards speaker's cultural background and accent; • familiarity with the speaker; • attitude towards the speaker (speaker likeability); • amount of effort and involvement invested in an interaction; • aptitude for comprehending accented speech; • listener's temporary characteristics (mood, state of health, level of stress, tiredness and concentration, emotional state, alcohol and drug consumption).	• grammatical, lexical, syntactic, semantic and pragmatic context (co-text and context); • the number of minimal and near-minimal pairs a word is a member of; • topic of conversation (speaker's and listener's familiarity with it); • conditions in which an interaction takes place, particularly noise level; • type of communicative situation (formal versus informal); • place in which communication occurs (at workplace, at home, in a shop, in a pub).

caution as in other situations similar errors have no such consequences. Therefore, what we need is more solid and unambiguous evidence, supplied by experiments specially designed to measure the impact of various elements of English phonetics on intelligibility. Throughout this chapter some empirical studies devoted to the intelligibility of EFL learners' speech will be discussed.

So far we have focused on the issue of pronunciation and intelligibility. In foreign accent research, however, three phonetic aspects of learner speech are usually isolated: accentedness (degree of foreign accent), intelligibility (ease of understanding the speaker) and acceptability (amount of irritation caused by a given accent).[8] Evidently, these three factors are closely connected in that these are foreign accent features which affect both intelligibility and annoyance. Moreover, the more unintelligible someone's speech is, the more irritation it may trigger in the listener. It is important to point out that, as is frequently emphasized, a foreign accent does not always impede intelligibility. This means that even heavily accented speech may be intelligible. For example, French and German learners often replace English /r/ with a uvular trill which, although an indicator of a strong foreign accent, is of no consequence for intelligibility.

Another important aspect of foreign accent relevant to successful communication is its acceptability by listeners, i.e. the degree of annoyance (irritation) it triggers in them. It seems that in this case similar factors are at work as those listed in Table 2.2, although acceptability seems to be more subjective and listener dependent than intelligibility. However, as argued by van den Doel (2006): 'it is difficult to separate the effects of unintelligibility and irritation. This is why we shouldn't concentrate only on those errors which are likely to cause intelligibility breakdown. The degree of native speakers' irritation with strongly accented speech may be partly dependent on their ability or inability to understand the message.' We can conclude that comfortable intelligibility of accented speech depends first of all on its comprehensibility, but also on its acceptability by listeners.

A.2.2 Selected Proposals for English Pronunciation Priorities

The search for pronunciation priorities for EFL learners is not a new phenomenon and has been present in phonetic studies for a long time. For example, Jenner (1989) attempted to isolate those phonetic features which are shared by all native English accents and suggested that since native speakers are usually mutually intelligible, these properties should be taught to foreign learners.

In this section we look at some recent proposals concerning pronunciation priorities for EFL learners, at their strengths and weaknesses, starting with perhaps the most influential – Jenkins' (2000) LFC – which we discuss in some detail. Next we juxtapose and compare this concept with Cruttenden's (2008) Amalgam English and International English as well as Collins and Mees' (2003) Error Ranking. This is done in order to find out whether these suggestions provide teachers with reliable guidance in deciding on pronunciation priorities for their students.

A.2.2.1 The Lingua Franca Core

As pointed out in Chapter 1, the best known, but also fairly controversial proposal of pronunciation priorities has been put forward by Jenkins (2000). While the LFC is meant to be a set of phonetic properties of English to ensure mutual intelligibility in the international communication of non-native speakers and is not intended for EFL learners, it might be possible that it is also sufficient to safeguard the intelligibility of foreign-accented speech both in native and non-native contexts. For this reason Jenkins' proposal merits our special attention.

In Chapter 1 we dealt with the major assumptions of ELF without, however, examining the actual contents of the LFC. In this section we intend to analyse this proposal in some detail, focusing on the empirical justification of its various elements. A fuller discussion is found in Szpyra-Kozłowska (2005a). The following features characterize the LFC:

Consonants:
- approximations of consonants allowed
- /r/ pronounced whenever spelt as a retroflex approximant
- no dental fricatives
- no substitutions of the glottal fricative
- aspiration of /p, t, k/
- no dark [ɫ]
- no tapping of intervocalic /t/
- initial consonant clusters preserved; medial and final clusters can be simplified
- preservation of the velar nasal

Vowels:
- preserving vowel quantity (inherent and context dependent)
- permissive approach to vowel quality
- [ɜː] preserved

Suprasegmentals:
- Nuclear stress essential
- Division into word groups important
- Some rules of word stress
- Articulatory setting[9]

- No weak forms
- No features of connected speech
- No rhythm
- No intonation

Consonants

According to Jenkins (2000: 143), the consonantal inventory of English should generally be taught with the proviso that 'the LFC learners should approximate rather than imitate exactly the RP and GA consonant sounds'. In this case she follows many other linguists who regard consonants as a more stable aspect of the English sound system than vowels which display much variability in native English accents. Thus, the need to preserve a distinction between consonantal phonemes of English seems largely uncontroversial.

The problem concerns the term 'approximation', as it is not clear which learner versions of English consonants can be regarded as acceptable and which as unacceptable. For example, is the replacement of English bilabial plosives by bilabial fricatives frequent in Spanish English an acceptable departure from native English or not? The question is non-trivial as although learners are required only to approximate and not to imitate the English consonants, there are certain exceptions to this rule.

One of the substitutions which is disallowed by Jenkins is the replacement of the glottal fricative /h/, as in *house*, with its velar counterpart /x/. This ban is problematic for those learners whose native language contains the velar consonant, but no glottal sounds at all. It should be added that the two segments in question are very similar from the auditory point of view, which suggests that the substitution of one with another should not cause intelligibility problems, contrary to what Jenkins claims. This point is explicitly made by Sobkowiak (1996: 79), who maintains that since in English there is no other fricative than /h/ in the back region of the vocal tract, the use of /x/ instead of /h/ can cause no misunderstanding and is only an indication of foreign accent. He also adds that for speakers of languages which have no glottal sounds, /h/ is very difficult to learn because the vocal cords are harder to control consciously than other articulators. Thus, what seems to matter is the presence of the back fricative in learner speech rather than its exact quality. This example indicates that the concept of 'approximation' should be sharpened and more clearly defined.

International English, in Jenkins' view, should be rhotic with the grapheme <r> pronounced whenever it is spelt since it is easier for learners to use pronunciation which is closer to spelling. This assumption seems to find firm empirical support in other studies as well, which prove that r-less pronunciation in non-prevocalic positions is problematic for many learners, not only because of the spelling, but also due to the lack of a similar phonotactic constraint in their L1s.

The troublesome point is the advocated pronunciation of the consonant in question; in Jenkins' opinion it should be a retroflex approximant of GA since this variant 'is simpler for both production (...) and for reception' (Jenkins, 2000: 139). It should be pointed out that many international users of English may encounter some difficulty in learning to pronounce the approximant since, as observed by Ladefoged and Maddieson (1996: 215), 'the most prototypical members of the class of rhotics are trills made with the tip or blade of the tongue'. Trills are later referred to as 'central members of the class'. This is confirmed by Laver (1994: 299), who maintains that 'a sound type that is fairly rare in the languages of the world is the voiced retroflex (...) approximant, which is used as a pronunciation of /r/ in a number of American accents of English and of rhotic accents of southwestern England'. Thus, the insistence on the use of this particular consonant in the LFC finds no justification in phonetic universals. In other words, the LFC postulates a segment problematic for many international learners of English. Moreover, Jenkins provides no evidence to prove that the use of a retroflex approximant guarantees international intelligibility of the words with this segment while other substitutions of this consonant will have an adverse effect on communication.

According to Jenkins, the interdental fricatives do not belong to the LFC as they are difficult to learn and are frequently absent from the consonantal inventories of various English accents (e.g. Cockney or Caribbean English). Moreover, she argues, substitutions of these consonants do not cause unintelligibility.

This is certainly good news for many learners, including the French, Italians, Germans and Poles, who find these segments very difficult to pronounce since they are absent in their L1 inventories. A somewhat worrying aspect of excluding these segments from phonodidactic priorities is the fact that, as Jenkins (2000: 138) herself admits, substitutions of these consonants are stigmatized in most communities of English native speakers, which puts learners who fail to use the sounds in question at a disadvantage in communication with them. Interestingly, even native listeners in whose speech these consonants are not found also appear to be critical of foreign accents in which they fail to occur. This has been proved experimentally by van den Doel (2006) for Dutch-accented English and by Szpyra-Kozłowska (2004), Gonet and Pietroń (2005) as well as Bryła-Cruz (2013) for Polish-accented English. Van den Doel (2006: 16) attempts to account for this phenomenon as follows: 'certain dialectal markers may be perfectly acceptable when coming from a native speaker, but be quite offensive when spoken by a foreigner'.

Another problem is that of possible substitutes of 'th'. These can, in Jenkins' view, be any 'close approximations' of the consonants in question: the plosives /t/ and /d/, the fricatives /f/ and /v/ or /s/ and /z/, provided they are used consistently. Nevertheless, the latter requirement is problematic for many learners. Take Poles as an example. Although they use all three kinds of substitutions, they do not do it consistently. For instance, the voiceless word-initial 'th' tends to be pronounced as /t/ in *Thacher* [tačer] or as /f/ in *think* [fⁱiŋk], while the word-final spirant is often realized as /s/ in *Smith* [smⁱis] and /f/ in *bath* [baf]. It should be added that any attempt to 'regularize' these pronunciations as [sačer], [sⁱiŋk], [smⁱis] or [tačer], [tⁱiŋk], [smⁱit] or [fačer], [fⁱiŋk], [smⁱif][10] is doomed to failure as it creates many forms which sound very unnatural and artificial to the Polish ear. Put simply, in a specific context some substitutions seem 'better' than others. As demonstrated by Gonet and Pietroń (2005), Polish learners tend to replace interdentals with plosives word-initially, with fricatives word-finally, while in other contexts no regularities have been detected.

If the interdental fricatives do not belong to the LFC and Polish learners are not consistent in their replacements of these segments, the question arises as to what didactic decision should be made in this situation. Should the teacher impose the use of one type of replacement? If so, which one should it be? Jenkins does not provide any guidelines for instructors as to what to do in such cases.

As the articulation of dark /l/ is problematic for many learners of English, the LFC eliminates this segment and allows for its substitution with either clear /l/ or /u/, with the second option being particularly strongly recommended as the one found in various accents of native English. While the lack of dark /l/ is, indeed, unlikely to lead to intelligibility problems, substituting dark [ɫ] with a back vowel might cause miscommunication as in a number of cases the two segments are carriers of a phonemic contrast, e.g. in the following minimal pairs in which the lateral is present in the second member of each pair, but not in the first member: *go – goal, so – soul, dough – dole, mow – mole, row – role, bow – bowl, how – howl.*

Furthermore, although vocalic realizations of the dark lateral are found in some English accents (e.g. Cockney, Estuary English), they are, as observed by Jenkins herself, stigmatized in standard varieties and unintelligible to speakers of American English and other accents in which they are absent. This is of no relevance to ELF, but is important for EFL learners. Moreover, such vocalizations considerably depart from the orthographic forms which Jenkins tends to follow in other cases. For these reasons, this option seems to be ill advised for international users of English whose pronunciation is largely spelling based. Thus, Jenkins is not consistent in insisting on rhotic pronunciation because <r> is present in spelling and proposing a vocalized pronunciation of the dark lateral which departs from orthography considerably.

In Jenkins' view, the aspiration of initial fortis plosives in stressed syllables is one of the most important aspects of English phonetics to be learnt by foreigners, since without it a listener finds it difficult to identify a given consonant as voiceless. In other words, 'an unaspirated /p/ may be mistaken for /b/, a /t/ for /d/, and a /k/ for /g/' (Jenkins, 2000: 140).

This proposal is very problematic for those learners in whose mother tongue aspiration is absent. For example, since it is not a property of Polish, even very proficient learners generally fail to employ it (Nowacka, 2008). The major source of difficulty is not so much articulatory in nature (adding an extra puff of air is not particularly hard) as mental; aspiration in English is an allophonic not a phonemic feature and, as such, it is viewed by most learners as unimportant and of no consequence to the meaning of words, particularly because the voicing distinction between initial consonants is usually retained.

Furthermore, it seems that Jenkins' worry about the difficulty of identifying pairs of fortis and lenis plosives when the former are devoid of aspiration is based on the relevance of this feature for native English listeners. As Roach (1991: 32) states, 'if English speakers hear a voiceless unaspirated plosive they will hear that as one of **b, d, g,** because it is aspiration, not voicing which distinguishes initial **p, t, k** from **b, d, g**'. He adds that the importance of aspiration in the speech perception of native speakers of English has been proved experimentally. In other languages, such as Polish, Hungarian or French, however, from which aspiration is absent, the voiced/voiceless distinction is of primary relevance in distinguishing /p/ from /b/ or /t/ from /d/. Suppose, for instance, that speakers of such languages communicate in English. As in their languages aspiration does not occur, it cannot play any role in their mutual intelligibility. Thus, lack of aspiration might be problematic for native speakers of English, but not for its numerous international users. Let us recall that ELF, for which the LFC has been devised, is not concerned with the former but only with the latter learners and their communicative needs.

It should also be added that, as observed by Jenner (1989) and Wells (1982), aspiration does not appear in all native varieties of English. As Wells (1982: 74) maintains, 'there are accents in the north of England and in Scotland where /p, t, k/ are never aspirated'. This means that for the speakers of these varieties aspiration is not crucial for making a distinction between /p, t, k/ and /b, d, g/. Wells adds that accents which do have aspiration of voiceless plosives differ as to the amount of it in different contexts. In other words, aspiration is a scalar rather than an absolute phenomenon. Note that in other cases Jenkins argues that if some feature is not found in all native varieties of English, like 'th' and dark 'l', it is not necessary in international communication. In insisting on aspiration she is evidently not consistent with her other decisions concerning the content of the LFC.

Finally, according to the LFC, initial consonant clusters must be preserved while medial and final clusters can be simplified in the same way as in native English. This claim is generally supported by other researchers, as shown in the following sections, but is inconsistent with other aspects of the LFC in its reference to native cluster reductions which increase the gap between spelling and pronunciation.

Vowels

We shall now proceed to comment on the LFC approach to English vowels which is characterized by strict requirements with regard to their quantity and high permissiveness in respect of their quality. According to Jenkins, preservation of appropriate vowel length is the most important feature of the vocalic system of the LFC. This should be understood in two ways: first as the maintenance of the phonemic contrast between long and short vowels, e.g. /iː/ and /ɪ/ or /uː/ and /ʊ/. Secondly, what is meant is the allophonic adjustment of vowel length to the presence of the following fortis and lenis obstruents (the so-called pre-fortis clipping). Preserving inherent and context-dependent vowel length is claimed to be crucial for international intelligibility.

Both requirements are difficult to fulfil by those learners whose native tongue makes neither phonemic nor allophonic use of vowel quantity. Thus, maintaining the length contrast between *ship* and *sheep* or *come* and *calm* constitutes a very serious learning problem while modifying vowel quantity in relation to the fortis/lenis distinction is next to impossible for the majority of them. This has been amply demonstrated by Nowacka (2008).

A more general question which emerges in connection with contextual modifications of vowel length is their alleged relevance for international intelligibility. It seems that, as in the case of aspiration, Jenkins' approach is biased by her mother tongue and reflects a typically English way of processing auditory input. Roach (1991: 34), for instance, claims that 'the vowel length difference before final voiceless consonants (. . .), **which is very slight in most languages**, (emphasis mine) in English has become exaggerated so that it has become the most important factor in distinguishing between final **p, t, k** and **b, d, g**'. Laver (1994: 446) also agrees that 'the (small – J. Sz.-K.) size of this difference is more likely to be typical of the general majority of languages than the rather extreme differences which typify English'. Clearly, allophonic length differences, very rare in languages of the world, cannot be important for international communication via English.

Jenkins observes that varieties of English differ considerably in the number and quality of the vowels they employ, yet they are mutually intelligible. She draws a conclusion that this aspect of English phonetics is largely overrated in the traditional approaches to pronunciation teaching. Consequently, the LFC allows for different L2 vowel qualities on condition that they are used consistently and incorporate vowel length contrasts.

There are, however, certain important problems with this proposal. The first concerns an inconsistent use of vowel qualities when one sound is perceived differently by various learners. A case in point is the Polish English pronunciation of ash as either /e/ or /a/ as Polish lacks an open front vowel which could be used to replace /æ/. Such substitutions, however, occur with no apparent consistency with regard to the target vowel, which is clearly seen in the Polish versions of English loan words which originally contain ash and are sometimes polonized with /e/ and sometimes with /a/, e.g.[11]

/e/   *flesz* 'flash', *czempion* 'champion', *dżez* 'jazz', *mecz* 'match'
/a/   *fan, gadget, basket, tramping, rap, panel*

As in the case of 'th', it is not clear what in this situation the recommended course of action for the teachers and learners of the LFC should be.

Interestingly enough, Jenkins singles out one particular vowel, i.e. /ɜ:/ (the so-called long schwa), whose quality should be learnt by ELF users. This vowel is often substituted with /a:/ by speakers of many Asiatic languages, which frequently causes intelligibility problems. Clearly such learners require special phonetic training in the articulation of the long schwa, but it is doubtful whether this requirement should be extended to all international learners of English since this is the least frequent monophthong in English (Gimson, 1994). Moreover, as noted by Gibbon (2005), in rhotic accents – and the LFC is rhotic – this vowel is absent.

Suprasegmentals

One of the most controversial claims made by Jenkins is that, apart from nuclear stress and division of speech into word groups, the remaining prosodic features are not only irrelevant for international intelligibility, but are detrimental to it. In other words, by teaching them, we are doing a disfavour to learners by diminishing their chances of successful communication with other non-native speakers. Consequently, the LFC does not include rhythm, intonation and connected speech phenomena. Word stress is considered important but also unteachable and therefore remains outside the list of pronunciation priorities.

This stance is particularly striking in view of recent research which points in the opposite direction and emphasizes the crucial role of suprasegmentals in communication via English. We discuss this issue in more detail in Section A.2.5. At this point it should be noted that, in Jenkins' view, many aspects of English sentence phonetics, such as strong and weak forms as well as various connected speech phenomena must be learnt receptively since without familiarity with them understanding native speakers of English might become very difficult. This means putting teachers in a somewhat awkward position in having to teach their students about suprasegmentals, employed by the instructors themselves, and at the same time discouraging learners from using such features, alleged to be harmful for intelligibility. Moreover, a mismatch between what learners hear and what they are told to articulate adds to the learning difficulty.

Let us sum up the above analysis of the LFC. The most striking feature of this proposal is the importance it attaches to the preservation of consonantal contrasts, coupled with a liberal approach to vowel quality (but not quantity) and an almost total negligence of prosody (except nuclear stress). As shown above, the approach under discussion lacks consistency. Thus,

Jenkins postulates several features for ELF learners which, in spite of the claims concerning their importance in international contexts, are in fact of relevance to native speakers only, i.e. aspiration and pre-fortis clipping. There is no consistency either with regard to her treatment of spelling and sound relations. The general assumption is that pronunciation features reflected in spelling should be preserved in the LFC as foreign learners are frequently exposed to written forms. Nevertheless, while ELF is rhotic because /r/ appears in spelling and an untapped pronunciation of intervocalic /t/ is proposed for the same reason, a vocalic realization of /l/ is advocated even if it departs from spelling rather drastically. The insistence on the accurate pronunciation of one consonant (the glottal fricative) and one vowel (the long schwa) does not seem to be justified either, as substituting the former with a velar fricative does not affect intelligibility and there is insufficient evidence for the crucial role in comprehension of the least frequently occurring English vowel.[12] The concept of 'consistent approximations' also raises some doubts as it is not always evident which approximations are and which are not acceptable in ELF. It is not clear either what should be done with cases of inconsistent substitutions.

The above critical comments show that the LFC is not a fully consistent and phonetically justified proposal. Many of its elements are only tentative in nature and have not been supported by sufficient empirical evidence. Yet, as pointed out in Chapter 1, in ELF literature the correctness of the LFC is generally taken for granted and approached uncritically, with the majority of ELF studies focusing on the grammar and the lexicon since their authors believe that its phonological/phonetic aspects have been firmly established. In other words, in spite of several years having passed since the publication of Jenkins' (2000) book, very few attempts have been made to verify the validity of the LFC contents.

A.2.2.2 Amalgam English and International English

The LFC is not the only proposal to determine pronunciation priorities for learners of English. Cruttenden (2008) puts forward the concepts of Amalgam English and International English, which are presented briefly and compared with the LFC in this section.

First of all, it should be pointed out that the properties specified in both Amalgam English and International English are not based on any empirical evidence, but are speculative in character. This is admitted by Cruttenden (2008: 330), who states that 'this whole section is in the nature of a hypothesis about what constitutes the characteristics of such a model'. Moreover, he also states (Cruttenden, 2008: 317) that, 'the boundary between Amalgam English and International English is fuzzy'.

Amalgam English, as the terms suggests, is a mixture of native speaker varieties whose aim is described as the easy intelligibility of foreign-accented

English by native speakers. It is a hybrid between American and British varieties with some features transferred from the learner's L1 and with the focus on those contrasts which carry a high functional load. With respect to consonants, Amalgam English is almost identical with the LFC, but differs from it in the treatment of vowels and prosody. Thus, in initial position /p, t, k/ must be aspirated, as in the LFC, and /l, r, w, j/ following /p, t, k/ should be devoiced. Intervocalic flapping of alveolar plosives ought to be avoided, as in Jenkins' proposal. In the fricative series no distinction needs to be made between /θ/ and /ð/ nor between /ʃ/ and /ʒ/ since they are of a low functional load. /r/ can be pronounced whenever it is written, as in the LFC, which is also rhotic. The lateral can be dark or clear in all positions. The dropping of /h/, as highly stigmatized, should be eliminated. Much latitude is allowed in the realization of almost all consonants with respect to their place of articulation. Moreover, word-initial consonant clusters should be preserved, as proposed in the LFC. In Amalgam English five short and six long vowels and three diphthongs are postulated, selected because of their high functional load. The correct vowel-length distinctions must be made before fortis and lenis consonants, again in agreement with Jenkins' suggestion. Since Amalgam English is rhotic, it contains no centring diphthongs and the long schwa. In this proposal (Cruttenden, 2008: 328) 'the preservation of correct word accentual patterns remains paramount'. Unlike in the LFC, vowel reduction in unstressed syllables and weak forms should be employed. No native English processes of elision and assimilation belong to it; however it includes two suprasegmental features: proper nuclear stress placement and basic intonation patterns.

Amalgam English (Cruttenden, 2008: 329)

(1) *General aim*: easy intelligibility by native speakers.
(2) *Consonants*:
  (i) Insist on aspirated plosives but allow dental or retroflex /t, d/ and palatal /k, g/;
  (ii) Insist on /f, v, s, z/ but allow conflation of /ʃ, ʒ/ and /θ, ð/. /h/ required but allow velar/uvular replacements;
  (iii) Insist on /tʃ, dʒ/ distinct from /tr, dr/;
  (iv) Allow any variety of /l/. Allow pre-pausal and pre-consonantal /r/ = Allow insertion of /g/ following /ŋ/. Discourage /w/ = [ʊ];
  (v) Insist on consonantal clusters (apart from usual reductions allowable in RP).
(3) *Vowels*: a possible reduced inventory:
  (i) Short vowels /ɪ, e, æ, ʊ, ə/;
  (ii) Long vowels /i:, e:, a:, ɒ:, o:, u:/;
  (iii) Diphthongs /aɪ, aʊ, (ɔɪ)/.
(4) *Connected speech*:
  (i) Insist on nucleus movement and basic tunes.

Thus, Amalgam English bears a great resemblance to the LFC with respect to the majority of consonantal features, but also in its insistence on preserving context-dependent vowel length distinctions and nuclear stress placement. In Cruttenden's proposal, however, emphasis is placed on preserving some vowel contrasts, proper word stress, basic intonation patterns, vowel reduction and weak forms, which are excluded from the LFC. In brief, Amalgam English contains more phonetic features than the LFC, mostly concerning the vowel system and prosody.

International English is (Cruttenden, 2008: 330) 'set up as a target for those who use English as a *lingua franca* (...) as a means of international communication not necessarily involving native speakers at all'. Thus, International English corresponds to ELF with respect to its goals. It is based on Amalgam English, but tolerates more features of the L1 and allows the reduction of all contrasts of a low functional load. The same tolerances as in Amalgam English are postulated and even extended. With regard to consonants, International English retains the distinction between /p, t, k/ and /b, d, g/ without, however, insisting on aspiration. It tolerates substitutions of the interdental fricatives with corresponding (dental or alveolar) plosives. The same conflations of fricative pairs as in Amalgam English are allowed and extended to /f, v/ and /s, z/. /h/ is not necessary at all; it can be dropped or replaced with velar and uvular realizations. Different renditions of /l/ and /r/ are tolerated, but the contrast between them must be maintained. The distinction between /v/ and /w/ receives high priority. Further simplifications of consonant clusters are allowed, particularly of initial /s/ + C. International English is rhotic. The vowel system is largely reduced and follows the structure of many languages which have a five-vowel system, with length distinctions in each position, and no diphthongs (replaced with sequences of vowels followed by the glides /j/ and /w/). The vowel schwa and weak forms are considered unnecessary. Word stress is retained, but no native patterns of elision, assimilation and intonation are required.

International English (Cruttenden, 2008: 333)

(1) *General aim*: minimal intelligibility in the use of English in international lingua franca situations.

(2) *Consonants*:
   (i)   Allow voicing distinctions to be made using different features from those used by native speakers;
   (ii) All forms of /r/ and /l/ are allowed but distinction between the two should be given high priority;
   (iii) Distinction between /v/ and /w/ should be insisted on; use of /ʊ/ for either or both discouraged.

(3) *Vowels*:
   (i)   A reduction in the vowel inventory to five short and five long vowels is allowable.

(4) *Connected speech*:
  (i)   Some attempt should be made to place the accent on the usual syllable of polysyllabic words, that is, no reduction to /ə/ need be made;
  (ii) No effort need be made to learn the native intonation patterns of English.

The above proposal shares a number of features with the LFC: it includes no prosody (apart from word stress), no weak forms and vowel reduction, but is more radical than the latter with regard to its largely impoverished consonantal system. Moreover, International English comprises 10 vowels, but mentions no diphthongs.

A.2.2.3 Collins and Mees' Error Ranking

Below we present yet another proposal for pronunciation priorities in communication with native speakers, offered by Collins and Mees (2003: 186), who isolate three categories of phonetic errors in learner English.

Category 1: Errors leading to breakdown of intelligibility
  (1) Confusion of crucial phonemic contrasts in vowel system, e.g. /ɪ – iː/, /e – æ/, /ɜː – aː/, /ɒ – ʌ/;
  (2) Confusion of fortis/lenis;
  (3) Consonant clusters;
  (4) Crucial consonant contrasts, e.g. /b – v/, /f – h/, /l – n/, /l – r/, /ʃ – s/;
  (5) Deletion of /h/ or replacement by /x/;
  (6) Word stress, especially if not on initial syllable.

Category 2: Errors which invoke irritation or amusement
  (1) Inappropriate /r/ articulations, e.g. uvular, strong alveolar trills;
  (2) Dental fricative problems, e.g. replacement of /Θ/ by /t/ or /s/, of /ð/ by /d/ or /z/;
  (3) Less significant vowel contrasts, e.g. /u: – ʊ/, /o: – ɒ/;
  (4) Incorrect allophones of /l/, especially replacement by dark 'l' throughout;
  (5) Weak and contracted forms;
  (6) Inappropriate rhoticism/non-rhoticism for particular models of pronunciation;
  (7) Strong retroflex setting.

Category 3: Errors which provoke few such reactions and may even pass unnoticed
  (1) Intonation errors;
  (2) Lack of syllabic consonants;
  (3) Compound stress.

Table 2.3 Comparison of LFC, Amalgam English, International English and Error Ranking

	LFC	Amalgam English	International English	Error ranking
Consonants	Aspiration of word-initial voiceless plosives; all consonants preserved (approximations allowed) except interdental fricatives; dark 'l' unnecessary; untapped /t/; rhotic pronunciation; the glottal fricative preserved; word-initial consonant clusters preserved, word-medial and word-final clusters simplified according to native speaker norms.	Aspiration of voiceless plosives; /f, v, s, z/ preserved; approximations of /t, d, k, g, h, l/; conflation of /ʃ, ʒ/ and /θ, ð/ allowed; insertion of stops after the velar nasal allowed; rhotic pronunciation; consonant clusters preserved (simplifications as in native English allowed).	Voicing distinctions preserved, but using different features; /r/ – /l/ distinction must be preserved, but different realizations allowed; /v/ – /w/ distinction preserved.	Preservation of fortis – lenis distinction; preservation of crucial consonant contrasts: e.g. /b – v/, /f – h/, /l – n/, /l – r/, /ʃ – s/; no deletion of /h/ or replacement by /x/; appropriate /r/ articulations, e.g. no uvular or alveolar trills; preservation of dental fricatives; correct allophones of /l/; appropriate rhoticism; preservation of consonant clusters.
Vowels	Vowel length (inherent and contextual) of vital importance; vowel quality irrelevant (consistent substitutions allowed).	A reduced vowel inventory (5 short vowels and 5 long vowels, 3 diphthongs).	A reduced vowel inventory (5 short and 5 long vowels).	Preservation of vowel contrasts: /ɪ – iː/, /e – æ/, /ɜ – ɑː/, /ɒ – ʌ/.
Prosody	Nuclear stress preserved; other prosodic features (rhythm, intonation, connected speech changes) unimportant.	Word stress preserved; nuclear stress preserved; weak forms and vowel reduction preserved; basic tunes (intonation patterns) preserved.	Word stress preserved; no vowel reduction, no intonation.	Word stress preserved; weak and contracted forms; no strong retroflex setting.

Collins and Mees argue that the errors of the first category, which frequently result in unintelligibility, should be viewed as the top pronunciation priorities. Those in the second group should not be ignored either, as they may trigger listeners' irritation or amusement and this diminishes comfortable intelligibility. Consequently, they can be regarded as secondary pronunciation priorities. The third category of errors is unimportant and may be neglected. In this proposal much importance is attached to crucial phonemic consonantal and vocalic contrasts, preservation of consonant clusters and voicing distinctions. Less importance is attached to the majority of prosodic issues, except word stress.

Several comments are in order in connection with this proposal. First of all, it is not research based, but is theoretical in character, just like Cruttenden's. To be more exact, Error Ranking reflects the common pronunciation difficulties of various L1 learners observed by the authors without, however, empirical evidence as to their alleged communicative impact. Secondly, it fails to provide answers as to the significance of many aspects of English phonetics, such as, for example, aspiration, sentence stress, rhythm and connected speech changes or linking, which are not listed in any of the three categories. This leaves teachers and learners without any guidance as to the amount of attention that should be devoted to these features.

Let us compare all three sets of pronunciation priorities presented in this section (see Table 2.3). Recall that the LFC and International English are designed for international learners while Amalgam English and Error Ranking are intended for communication with native speakers. All four proposals take a similar stance with regard to the importance attached to the consonantal system of English as well as general negligence of most aspects of prosody and connected speech. The major difference concerns the advocated approach to vowels, with the LFC focusing on the strict preservation of vowel length and a general disregard for vowel quality while Amalgam English, International English and Error Ranking postulate a reduced inventory of vowels and vowel contrasts, based on their high functional load. In all these proposals segmentals occupy a more important position than suprasegmentals. With respect to prosody, the LFC insists on preserving nuclear stress, whereas Amalgam English insists on preserving word stress, nuclear stress, basic intonation patterns, weak forms and vowel reduction. In International English only word stress is regarded as significant and in Error Ranking weak and contracted forms as well as word stress are singled out as particularly relevant for safeguarding comfortable intelligibility.[13]

Let us sum up all these proposals and see whether they provide clear guidance as to pronunciation priorities for EFL learners. The following aspects of English phonetics emerge as having a particularly important communicative value according to the majority of the proposals discussed above:

- preservation of word-initial consonant clusters;
- preservation of the fortis-lenis distinction (phonetically expressed either through voicing, vowel length or, in the case of plosives, aspiration);

- rhotic pronunciation allowed;
- preservation of consonantal contrasts with a high functional load (e.g. /b – v/, /f – h/, /l – n/, /l – r/, /ʃ – s/;
- approximations of consonants allowed (of a slightly different place of articulation);
- preservation of vocalic contrasts with a high functional load (e.g. /ɪ – iː/, /e – æ/, /ɜː – aː/, /ɒ – ʌ/);
- preservation of the phonemic distinction between long and short vowels;
- word stress;
- nuclear stress.

While the above list contains phonetic aspects of English which should be prioritized according to the presented meta-analysis, there is no sufficient clarity in many areas of pronunciation. Substantial differences of opinion concern the role of allophonic distinctions (e.g. variants of /l/, aspiration), the role of various aspects of prosody and connected speech (intonation, weak forms, vowel reduction) and other significant elements (e.g. the interdentals). It can therefore be concluded that the above list provides only general guidelines with respect to pronunciation priorities with many important details remaining unclear. In brief, current research has so far failed to provide a fully-fledged, consistent and empirically supported set of phonetic features that could guarantee achieving comfortable intelligibility to EFL learners. This pessimistic conclusion stems, perhaps, from the impossibility of the task of establishing universally valid pronunciation priorities, an issue which we address in Section A.2.5.

A.2.3 Focus on the Pronunciation of Phonetically Difficult Words

In this section we will depart from our earlier discussion and put forward a proposal that it should be the pronunciation of phonetically difficult words rather than individual sounds, sound contrasts and prosodies that should be prioritized in the phonetic instruction for EFL learners, particularly at lower levels of language proficiency. This claim, developed below, is further supported empirically in Section B.2.1.

When we start learning another language, words and some clichéd phrases are what we acquire in the first place, long before we get acquainted with any rules of grammar. As a matter of fact, with the global popularity of English, many people who have never learnt it know at least several English words and phrases, such as *thank you, sorry, I love you, OK*. For most learners, particularly beginners, words constitute the basic units of language whose pronunciation, together with their meaning, is stored in their language memory, ready to be used when a need arises. Of course the phonological and phonetic shape in which lexical items are remembered often departs from the original version due to learners' L1-driven perception, storage and articulation. When words are retrieved from the lexicon, they are recalled in that frequently imperfect form, which explains why phonetic practice with the focus on individual sounds and sound contrasts often has little impact on the pronunciation of items that contain the same consonants or vowels, but in a different segmental and prosodic context.

This reasoning can be illustrated by some examples. The contrast between two English high front vowels /iː/ and /ɪ/ has a high functional load as it serves to distinguish numerous minimal pairs of the *'ship – sheep'* type. Polish learners typically mispronounce the first of them as /i/, i.e. as a vowel similar in quality to English /iː/, but shorter and less tense, due to interference from Polish spelling-to-sound rules according to which the letter <i> is pronounced as /i/. The difficulty is not articulatory in nature as Polish has a high front-centralized vowel /ɨ/ that resembles /ɪ/ and could be used as an approximation of the English vowel. It is striking that, in spite of intensive phonetic training of the /iː/ – /ɪ/ contrast, the incorrect pronunciation of the latter vowel remains one of the most persistent features of Polish English (e.g. Scheuer, 2003). Thus, Polish learners tend to use it in such frequent words as *his, sister, children, give* and *little*. We can account for this fact if we assume that such items have been stored in learners' memory with the Polish vowel and when employed in an utterance, they are recalled in their fixed incorrect phonological shape, not influenced by the phonetic practice which approaches this aspect of pronunciation in global rather than item-specific terms. To put it differently, learners usually fail to realize that they are using a wrong vowel in a given word, even if they know about the /iː/ – /ɪ/ distinction and can pronounce pairs like *ship – sheep* correctly. Simply, familiarity with this vowel contrast and awareness of its importance in English are not automatically carried over to the pronunciation of individual words, particularly when items such as *sister* or *children* do not form minimal pairs with other words containing /iː/. Learners can pronounce them correctly only when they restructure the phonological shapes of such words. Consequently, showing students that some contrasts must be preserved because they serve to differentiate phonemes is certainly useful but insufficient in those numerous cases where there are no such consequences.

Obviously, in the course of phonetic training sounds are not practised in isolation, but in words and phrases. The problem is, however, that once the focus of instruction is on sounds and sound contrasts, the items selected for practice are of secondary importance and serve only as carriers of particular segments. Put differently, for phonetic activities words are usually selected according to the specific sounds they contain and not on the basis of the degree of phonetic difficulty they pose for learners. Thus, in typical pronunciation practice materials (e.g. Ponsonby, 1982) a given sound is introduced and illustrated with some examples. Next, it is contrasted with other sounds, usually by means of minimal pairs. Finally, it is used in sentences, dialogues or poems constructed in such a way as to contain many occurrences of the segment in question. The problem is, however, that tasks with the focus on specific sounds do not prepare learners properly to deal with the pronunciation of whole words, which requires control over many different segments and their combinations, the placement of stress and, in the case of reading, mastering spelling-to-pronunciation rules.

Take a common and seemingly simple word, *brothers*. For Polish learners both vowels it contains are problematic since they are not found in their mother tongue. The consonants are not easy either, not only because of the notoriously difficult dental fricative, but also due to a differently articulated /r/ (in Polish it is an alveolar trill), the dilemma of what to do with the second <r> letter (to pronounce it or not – many learners tend to follow spelling, others drop it) and, finally, the plural suffix, which Poles devoice in word-final position (devoicing is additionally reinforced by spelling). If a frequently used item which consists of only six sounds poses so many pronunciation problems, it is easy to imagine the number of difficulties that arise in the case of longer or less common items (see also Section A.2.3.2).[14] This means that phonetic training which focuses only on specific sounds, but disregards frequent and systematic work on the pronunciation of whole words prone to be mispronounced cannot be effective.

While teaching the pronunciation of all words is necessary, there are certain types of lexical items that are particularly difficult for learners and which deserve special attention since their mispronunciation often leads to intelligibility problems. We discuss these below, focusing first on local errors, then on other problematic items which include phonetic 'false friends' as well as longer and frequently mis-stressed words.

A.2.3.1 Local versus global errors

In Szpyra-Kozłowska (2013) a claim is advanced that recent pronunciation research on intelligibility which focuses on the role of various segmental contrasts and different aspects of prosody, i.e. on the so-called *global errors* made by the learners, fails to take into account a particularly important aspect of foreign-accented English, namely that of numerous seriously deformed words, known as *local errors*, the use of which, it is argued, frequently hinders successful communication far more than other phonetic errors. Apparently EFL learners find many words of this language difficult to remember in their phonetic shape not because they contain problematic sounds or sound sequences, but due to a variety of interference factors (to be discussed later). To put it differently, such items are stored in the learners' memory with phonologically deviant representations.

For instance, many Polish learners of English mispronounce a seemingly phonetically simple word *foreign* as [fo'rejn] although it contains no particularly difficult segments and has penultimate stress which is typical of Polish. Clearly, the digraph <ei> that occurs in the spelling suggests to Poles a diphthongal pronunciation (found, for instance, in items with the same sequence of letters, such as *reign* and *feign*) or, to be more exact, a sequence of a vowel and the palatal glide. The penultimate stress placement, alien to Polish, is somewhat more mysterious. It can be attributed to the presence of what is assumed to be a heavy stress-attracting final syllable (as in *insane, polite*) or to analogy with the stress pattern of words with the prefix *for-*, such as *forget, forgive* and *forbid*. The same item, when pronounced without such distortions, is rendered in Polish English as ['forʲin]. In this version global errors are present, i.e. each English segment is replaced with a corresponding Polish consonant and vowel, with an additional palatalization of the rhotic by the following high front vowel.

Thus, the phonetically deviant words examined here are characterized by segmental errors in which English phonemes are substituted not with their closest counterparts in the learners' native language (e.g. the replacement of the English glottal fricative with the Polish velar fricative), but with segments which are often phonologically and phonetically remote from them (e.g. English /ɪ/ rendered as Polish [ej]). Such substitutions frequently involve more than one segment (as in *Disney* pronounced as [dʲisnej]) and may be accompanied by the incorrect placement of stress (e.g. *foreign* realized as [fo'rejn]).

Table 2.4 summarizes the distinction between global and local errors. While the exact number of local errors is evidently impossible to establish as it largely depends on the learners' level of language proficiency and their individual phonetic aptitude, it is certainly large enough to deserve a prominent place in pronunciation instruction. Sobkowiak (1996) presents about

Table 2.4 Characterizing global and local errors

Global errors	Local errors
Recurring mispronunciations of foreign sounds and prosodies which create a foreign accent and result mainly from L1 phonological and phonetic transfer, e.g.: E *jazz* > PE [džes] E *foreign* > PE ['for'in]	Idiosyncratic mispronunciations of individual words in which, apart from global errors, there are other phonological and phonetic deviations from the original, due to various interference factors. They are stored in the learner's memory with the incorrect segmental and/or prosodic structure, e.g.: E *foreign* > PE [fo'rejn], E *Disney* > PE ['dʲisnej]

700 of what he calls 'words commonly mispronounced' in Polish English, but this list can easily be extended, particularly if we include numerous proper names like *Disney*, *Turner* or *Presley*, which are also problematic for foreign learners. The importance of local errors lies not only in their large number, but in their high frequency in learner English and a considerable degree of fossilization and resistance to improvement.

It should be noted that the failure to make a distinction between global and local errors often has some serious consequences and leads to false conclusions. As noted in Chapter 3, many authors, in their advice to pronunciation instructors, maintain that Polish learners of English should be trained in the production of [v], as they often say *willage* or *walley* instead of *village* and *valley*. This is an obvious instance of confusing local errors with global ones, since Poles do not have to practise the labiodental fricative as it is found in hundreds of Polish words. What they do need to practise, however, is to pronounce the words *village* and *valley* with the initial fricatives and not labiovelar glides.

In Section B.2.1 we provide empirical evidence that local errors, extremely frequent in learners' English and generally disregarded both in teaching materials and in current pronunciation research, pose a considerable threat to various aspects of effective communication and intelligibility in particular. Consequently, they should be regarded as a top pedagogical priority. The question that arises in connection with this conclusion is why the serious issue of phonetically distorted words fails to be addressed in phonetic manuals. In order to answer it, it is necessary to examine the major sources of such local errors. Their classification presented below is largely based on Sobkowiak (1996) and illustrated with some examples taken from Polish English (PE).

Interference from L1

Below we provide some examples of common local errors in Polish English and examine the sources of such mispronunciations.

(A) Interference from sound
E *author* > PE [awtor] (P *autor*)
E *fauna* > PE [fawna] (P *fauna*)
E *alibi* > PE [aˈlibi] (P *alibi*)

(B) Interference from spelling
E *front* > PE [front] (E <o> > PE [o])
E *mountain* > PE [mowtajn] (E <ou> > PE [ow])
E *tomb* > PE [tomp] (E <b> > PE [b/p])

This group of errors is caused by interference from Polish pronunciation and spelling correspondences. The items in (A), which are discussed in more detail in the following section, are cognates, found not only in English, but also in Polish. Consequently, Polish learners, while speaking English, frequently pronounce them in the same way they do in their native language. The examples in (B) are cases of spelling pronunciation in which English letters are interpreted according to the Polish letter-to-sound rules. Since

Polish spelling is more phonemic than English, in the former almost all letters are pronounced. Thus, many items in this set comprise silent letters (e.g. *answer, half, tomb*).

Interference from English

Let us now turn to the errors which originate due to learners' familiarity with other English words and spelling-to-sound rules.

(C) Interference from sound
says > PE [sejs] (*say*)
southern > PE ['sawdern] (*south*)
variety > PE ['verˈjetˈi] (*various*)

(D) Interference from spelling
butcher > PE [bačer] (E <u> > PE [a], *cut*)
climate > PE [klajmejt] (E <ate> > PE [eit], *mate*)
blood > PE [blut] E(<oo> > PE [u], *food*)

The errors in (C) are triggered by the pronunciation of related, usually more frequently used English words. For example, the diphthong of *know* is transferred to the phonetic rendition of the less frequent *knowledge*. The items in (D) are often mispronounced due to incorrect overgeneralizations concerning English spelling-to-sound rules. For instance, the fact that <oo> in many words is pronounced as [u:], (*food, root, loose*), often leads to an erroneous assumption that this is true in other cases as well. Consequently, *blood* is frequently mispronounced in Polish English as [blut]. It should also be added that many errors have multiple sources. For example, the mispronunciation of *says* as [sejs] results both from the pronunciation of the infinitive with the diphthong as well as from the written form of this item in which the digraph <ay> suggests a diphthongal realization (as in *may*).

The above brief discussion of the major sources of local errors provides an explanation as to why such cases are generally not discussed in phonetic manuals published by big publishing houses. Since the majority of such books are addressed to international learners of English, their authors probably assume that local errors, resulting from the negative transfer between the L1 and L2, are L1-specific, and usually focus on more general pronunciation issues of interest to a larger audience. Another reason for this neglect might be the assumption that this is a small-scale local phenomenon, unworthy of more assiduous attention. Finally, local errors seem more typical of EFL students rather than of ESL learners, as in the former case, as argued earlier, the impact of written English is greater than in the latter. In Section A.3.6 of Chapter 3 we demonstrate that the majority of pronunciation instruction textbooks (e.g. Celce-Murcia *et al.*, 1996) primarily concern the ESL context.

In order to check how widespread local errors indeed are, we have examined the way learners from several countries pronounce 50 items problematic for Poles. Fifteen students of five different nationalities, all intermediate to advanced learners of English, attending an English language school in Dublin were recorded having been asked to read a list of words prepared by the author.[15] It turned out that all the items were mispronounced by the majority of the subjects, regardless of their mother tongue. Table 2.5 presents a selection of learner versions of 10 such words. Of course many other phonetically incorrect renditions of the test items can be encountered.

Even this small set of data is sufficient to show that we are dealing with a problem that concerns not only Poles, but other learners of English with different first language backgrounds as well. Interestingly, the same items turned out to be phonetically difficult for the participants, which suggests that a list of words prone to distortion by various international users of English can probably be compiled. This, however, remains a task for future research.

In Szpyra-Kozłowska (2013) an experiment, summarized in Section B.2.1, is presented in which two groups of English English and Irish English native speakers listened to two recordings by two Polish learners of English. The first version contained global errors but no local errors, i.e. it involved segmental and prosodic inaccuracies typical of Polish-accented English.

Table 2.5 Phonetic versions of 10 items produced by learners of five nationalities

Tested items	Brazilian Portuguese	Mauritian Creole	Mexican Spanish	Italian	Polish
meadow	['miːdow]	['miːdow]/ ['midow]	['miːdow]/ ["midow]	['miːdow]	['mʲidow]
climate	[kliˈmeit]/ ['klimat]	['klaimet]	['klimeit]/ ['klaimeit]	['klaimet]	['klajmejt]
guinea pig	[giˈnea pik]/ ['gwinja pik]	['gaini pik]/ [giˈnea pik]	[giˈnea pik]	[giˈnea pik]	[gvʲiˈnea pik]
preface	['priːfeis]/ ['prefaːs]/ [preˈfeis]	[ʲprifeis]	[preˈfeis]/ ['priːfeis]	['priːfeis]	[priˈfejs]
colonel	['kolonel]	['kolonel]	['kolonel]	['kolonel]	[koˈlonel]
captain	['kaptajn]	['kaptejn] ['kaptajn]	['kaptajn]	['keptajn]	['keptejn]
Leonard	['leonart]	['liːonaːrd] ['leonar]	['liːonart]	['leonart]	['lʲionart] ['leonart]
mountains	['mountains]	['mountinz] ['mauntin]	['mountains] ['mountejns]	['montejns] ['mauntejns]	['moutajns] ['montejns]
vegetables	[vedʒiˈtabls] [vedʒiˈtebls]	[vedʒiˈtejblz] [vegiˈtejbl]	['vedʒetebls]	['vejdʒetebels]	[vedžeˈtejbls]
Turkey	['turkaj]	['teːrkej]	['torki] ['turki]	['torki]	['tarkʲi]

The second version was native-like in terms of sounds and suprasegmentals, but comprised a number of local errors, common in Polish English. The listeners evaluated the experimental samples in terms of intelligibility, accentedness and acceptability. The results show that on all three counts the recording with global errors but no local errors received higher scores, i.e. was considered more intelligible, less foreign-accented and less irritating, than the other sample with global but no local errors. Thus, a common occurrence of local errors in learner English[16] and their negative impact on foreign accent evaluations suggests that such items should be pedagogically prioritized.

In a study by Stasiak and Szpyra-Kozłowska (2010), it is demonstrated how this proposal can be implemented in the language classroom. We present a report on the experiment in which 25 Polish secondary school pupils underwent special training in the pronunciation of 50 commonly mispronounced words with the use of specific, teacher-designed materials. We provide evidence for the effectiveness of the employed instructional procedures and show that within a short period of phonetic training all the learners managed to eliminate the majority of such errors. Moreover, in a questionnaire administered to them after the experiment, the pupils reported considerable improvement in their pronunciation and expressed a sense of achievement which they had not felt in the course of traditional instruction. The following fairly common opinion was provided: 'My pronunciation has improved a lot because now I can pronounce many words correctly which I mispronounced before. Because of that, my English is much better now.'

A.2.3.2 Other types of problematic words

The phonologically distorted words discussed in the preceding section are not the only items which are problematic for many foreign learners of English and which abound in their speech. Therefore, it is important to identify the major sources of the phonetic difficulty of words in order to devise effective pronunciation training for EFL students. Evidently, compiling a list of troublesome items is certainly useful, but insufficient as there can be nothing more boring and counterproductive than asking learners to memorize lists of any sort. If we could, however, formulate some meaningful and simple generalizations, they could easily be incorporated into pronunciation practice.

In Szpyra-Kozłowska (2011, 2012) an attempt is undertaken to isolate the major sources of phonetic word difficulty for intermediate and advanced Polish learners of English, with some of the results being presented in Section B.2.2. While some of the issues discussed there may reflect the problems of a specific group of learners, others seem to be more universal and can be applicable in the case of other L1 students as well. Below we present selected types of items problematic in terms of their pronunciation which have been identified empirically in our study and which appear to be difficult not only for Poles, but for many other foreign learners.

Phonetic 'false friends'

Many languages of the world contain numerous very similar sounding words, which can be viewed as phonetic 'false friends' since, in spite of their apparent similarity, they are pronounced differently in various L1s, in accordance with the phonological and phonetic rules of a given language. They may also be termed 'bilingual minimal pairs' (Rogerson-Revell, 2011). We discuss them briefly in this section, providing selected examples from English and Polish.

Such items stem from several different sources. The first group comprises cognates, i.e. older borrowings which in European languages come mainly from Latin and Greek, and more recent loanwords from a variety of other languages. A representative sample of such international cognates is provided below in their English version, e.g.[17]

> *atom, proton, neutron, psalm, hymn, Apollo, Venus, Saturn, Zeus, opera, karate, pizza, spaghetti, lasagne, goulash, salami, tequila, vodka, judo, sauna, corrida*

A particularly large group of phonetic 'false friends' originates in English from which they have been borrowed by many languages, e.g.[18]

> *weekend, lunch, disco, party, whisky, gin, tonic, business, cocktail, drink, spray, marketing, golf, football, rugby, tennis, match, bulldog, sweater, camera, hacker, quiz, talk show, cheeseburger, hot dog, dress, musical, monitoring, parking, out, knock-out, panel, patchwork, polo, pullover, mascara, push-up, recycling, record, reporter, baby-sitter, banjo, business, businessman, walk-over, trend, trick, shock, jeans, goal, bestseller, blues, jazz, rap, top, hit*

A large subgroup of internationally used items comprises proper nouns of various types. They include geographical names of planets, continents, countries, towns, mountains, seas, rivers, deserts, peninsulas, islands, bays, channels, e.g:

> *Africa, America, Australia, Venezuela, Colombia, Vietnam, Chicago, London, Korea, Egypt, Madagascar, Texas, California, Massachusetts, Himalayas, Mars, Mississippi, Missouri, Sahara, Ontario, Rio de Janeiro, Caracas, Thailand*

Names of famous people, such as historical figures, past and present political leaders, poets, writers, composers, painters and scientists as well as current celebrities, film stars, film directors, singers, musicians, sportsmen and sportswomen of different nationalities also belong here, e.g.:

> *Mozart, Chopin, Beethoven, Bach, Shakespeare, Milton, Strauss, Einstein, Rembrandt, Van Gogh, Picasso, Leonardo da Vinci, Lincoln, Washington, Michael Jackson, Murphy, Turner, Rourke, Beyonce, Beckham, Spielberg*

Names of numerous popular fictional literary and film characters are also used in L1 versions, e.g.:

> *Lear, Hamlet, Macbeth, Othello, Sherlock Holmes, Robin Hood, Don Quixote, Carmen, Don Giovanni, D'Artagnan, Dr Jekyll, Mr Hyde, Dorian Grey, Frankenstein, Darth Vader, Batman, Spiderman, Superman, Rambo, James Bond, Lara Croft, Tomb Raider, Indiana Jones, Dracula, Harry Potter*

We might also add a list of first names, both old and new, used in English but also in other languages, e.g.:

> *Abraham, Isaac, Daniel, David, Adam, Robert, Adrian, Philip, Matilda, Anna, Amanda, Patrick, Patricia, Theresa, Leonard, Stephen, Edward, Maria, Isabella, Emma, Nina, Nora, Alexander, Henry, Anastasia, Thomas, Anthony*

In addition to cognates, two languages may contain pairs of similar sounding, but completely unrelated words, as shown in the translations of the Polish forms below, e.g.:

E *ten* – P *ten* 'this, masc.'	E *pan* – P *pan* 'mister'
E *brat* – P *brat* 'brother'	E *gnat* – P *gnat* 'bone, augmentative'
E *sock* – P *sok* 'juice'	E *ham* – P *cham* 'boor'

Lexical items such as those presented in this section, the numbers of which run into hundreds if not thousands, are frequently used by speakers of English and other languages, who pronounce them, however, differently, and not only because their sound inventories are not the same. Borrowings are subject to loanword adaptation with regard to their phonetics and phonology as well, which proceeds in many ways, depending on a given sound system. In many cases this leads to the rise of very different phonetic shapes of the same words in various languages. Take, for instance, the name of the Dutch painter Van Gogh, pronounced in the original as [vanⁱxɔx]. According to Wells' (1990: 758) dictionary, in English it can be realized in several ways, i.e. as [væn/væŋ gɒx/gɒf/gəʊ]. The Polish spelling-based version coupled with word-final obstruent devoicing is [van gok], i.e. it differs both from the Dutch and English forms. Below I include some cognates/borrowings with their Polish pronunciation to show how much they often depart from their English counterparts:

alibi [aˈlʲibʲi]   *psalm* [psalm]   *autor* [ˈawtor]
Shakespeare [ˈšekspʲir]   *Lindsay* [ˈlʲiintsej]   *Rourke* [ˈrurke]

Many learners, however, are unaware of these differences and assume that look-alike and semantically identical items are pronounced in English in the same way as in their mother tongue, which view, in the languages employing the Latin alphabet, is often additionally reinforced by similar or the same spelling. The problem is expressed precisely and succinctly by one the participants of our study on phonetically difficult words, summarized in Section B.2.2, in the following comment: 'They look like Polish words so when I see them, I pronounce them in the Polish way though I know it's wrong.'

We would like to suggest that bilingual minimal pairs should be practised together, as proposed by Szpyra-Kozłowska and Sobkowiak (2011), i.e. a given item in its L1 version should be juxtaposed with its English counterpart for practice to make learners realize that they are not pronounced identically. Appropriate lists of minimal pairs can be prepared for learners of different levels of proficiency. For instance, beginners can be given simple monosyllabic words, e.g.:

E *back* – P *bak* 'tank'   E *book* – P *buk* 'beech'   E *peak* – P *pik* 'spade'

More advanced learners can use bisyllabic examples, e.g.:

E *radio* – P *radio*   E *doctor* – P *doktor*   E *actor* – P *aktor*

or even longer items, e.g.:

E *parliament* – P *parlament*   E *gentleman* – P *dżentelmen*   E *Washington* – P *Waszyngton*

Apart from improving learners' pronunciation of such words, practising them appears to have yet another advantage, namely that of raising their awareness of differences in the sound systems of their L1 and L2.

Mis-stressed words

Many foreign learners, particularly those in whose mother tongues word stress is fixed, find it difficult to remember the correct stress pattern of many English lexical items. Gilbert's (2008) example, discussed in Section A.2.1.1, of the item *committee* with the stress shifted to the initial syllable which makes it sound like *comedy* serves well to illustrate this issue.

While stress errors made by foreign learners are noted by all pronuncia-tion specialists, the importance attached to them varies from author to author. Jenkins (2000), as pointed out in Section A.2.2.1, on the one hand appreciates the importance of word stress but, on the other hand, considers rules of stress placement unteachable and excludes this issue from the LFC. Other specialists disagree and prioritize word stress. Thus, Cruttenden (2008) includes it both in International English and Amalgam English. Collins and Mees (2003) place stress errors into their Category 1, i.e. among those inaccuracies that may cause communication breakdown, and regard eliminating them as a pronunciation priority.

It appears that the major problem with mis-stressed words is that, as noted by several specialists, they considerably increase the processing diffi-culty of accented speech. Brown (1992: 51) maintains that: 'The stress pat-tern of a polysyllabic word is a very important identifying feature of the word (...). We store words under stress patterns (...) and we find it difficult to interpret an utterance in which a word is pronounced with the wrong stress pattern.' Gilbert (2008: 5) adds that, 'the combination of stress errors with other types of errors can seriously disrupt communication' and con-cludes that wrong stress is an added burden for listeners. This conclusion is supported by the empirical findings of van den Doel (2006) who, on the basis on native English speakers' judgements, places word stress among the top pronunciation priorities for Dutch learners of English. A similar result has been obtained in Szpyra-Kozłowska's (2004) study of the perception of Polish-accented English, reported in Part B.

While the importance of stress errors in communication with native speakers of English appears to be well documented, it is not clear how to approach this issue in the EFL classroom; teaching English stress rules, with their complex morphological, phonological and lexical conditioning as well as a considerable number of irregularities is very difficult and discouraging for learners. It seems, however, that, in view of its undeniable importance, this aspect of word pronunciation deserves proper attention in phonetic instruc-tion in spite of the problems it poses. We propose to regard word stress not as a truly prosodic issue, such as sentence stress, rhythm or intonation, which concern phrase and sentence phonetics, but as an important property of lexical items that should be learnt together with their segmental make up. To put it differently, we should help learners realize that stress constitutes an important aspect of word identity and, as argued by Cruttenden (2008: 235), 'the accentual shape of a word (...) is a reality for both the speaker and the listener'. This can be done by the teacher in a simple way; it is enough to mis-stress some words in the learners' L1 (if lexical stress is part of the L1, of course) and then ask them to comment on such pronunciation. They usually regard it as strange and annoying, sometimes amusing.

Thus, in teaching word pronunciation more attention should be given to their stress pattern, particularly those cases which tend to be frequently mis-stressed. As shown in Section B.2.2, learners with the same L1 background usually have similar problems with the correct placement of stress. This means that a list of items prone to be mis-stressed should be made for each L1 learner group, to be later employed in pronunciation training.

Apart from practice in commonly mis-stressed words, more advanced learners may benefit from explicit training concerning selected English word stress rules, which are discussed in detail in other sources (e.g. Cruttenden, 2008; Rogerson-Revell, 2011) and need not be repeated here. For example, it is very useful to introduce students to a distinction between stress-neutral, self-stressed and stress-determining suffixes, particularly the first two categories which are not only fairly regular and thus phonodidactically useful, but which constitute a very frequent source of stress errors. A more detailed analysis of common stress errors in learner English is found in Section B.2.2.

Longer words

The pronunciation of longer words fails to be addressed by the majority of phonetic manuals, which usually do not recognize it as a phonodidactic issue at all. Yet, such a category is often isolated by learners (see Section B.2.2), as shown by their comments like *'this word is difficult because it's long'*. Apparently, longer items are problematic because of a variety of factors they have to control: spelling-to-pronunciation rules, the placement of stress, the articulation of many different new sounds and complex sound sequences. This means that many single words become almost tongue twisters for many students, especially beginners.

Long words are difficult to pronounce (frequently for native speakers as well), not only by virtue of their length, but also due to the accumulation of many troublesome phonetic features. Take the word *pronunciation* [prə,nʌnsi'eɪʃ(ə)n], which contains five syllables. The placement of the main stress should not cause much difficulty since it falls on the suffix -ation, which is always stressed in nouns, extremely frequent in English. Secondary stress, however, may constitute a problem. So may the quality of the vowel in the initial syllable, which is schwa, absent in many languages, and the vowel between two nasal consonants because of the alternation in *pronounce – pronunciation*, where the verbal stem comprises the diphthong [aʊ] and the noun the mononphthong [ʌ]. As shown in Section B.2.2, morphological alternations contribute to the phonetic difficulty of words. The next problematic aspect of this item is a cluster of a nasal and a fricative, which in many languages tends to be eliminated. Poles, for instance, in such cases employ nasal gliding, which turns the nasal stop into a nasal glide. The vowel following this cluster is somewhat unusual; in terms of quality it is like /iː/, but with regard to length it is like /ɪ/. Moreover, it is followed by another vowel with which it forms a vowel hiatus not tolerated in many languages. In such instances, Poles change high vowels into the corresponding glides, in this case pronouncing /j/ instead of /i/, shortening the word to four syllables.

Finally, the last syllable is difficult because of the presence of the palatoalveolar fricative, the schwa vowel or a syllabic nasal, segments which might be absent in the learners' L1. Thus, a common Polish English version of this word is [pronaw̃sjejšɨn].

A question that arises concerns the length of words regarded as difficult. This largely depends on the phonetic and morphological complexity of a given item and the students' level of proficiency. Intermediate learners who participated in our study listed some trisyllables (e.g. *Australia, picturesque*), quadrisyllables (e.g. *relaxation, surprisingly*) and quintisyllables (e.g. *encyclopaedia, exaggeration*). Advanced learners, however, admitted problems with the pronunciation of lexical items which consist of more than three syllables.[19]

The above discussion does not exhaust the issue of phonetically difficult words which include many other types, for example, homophones, homographs and words with an idiosyncratic relation between the spelling and pronunciation. As they are well known and discussed in various other sources, we have omitted them here, focusing on important, but less frequently noted cases. It must be added that the focus on phonetically difficult words advocated here does not mean neglecting general phonetic practice, since it would be absurd if learners mastered the pronunciation of difficult items, but mispronounced those which seem phonetically easy.

It should be pointed out that current English pronunciation teaching materials generally fail to address the problem of word pronunciation. They focus almost entirely on sounds, sound combinations and suprasegmental issues. This is true of older classics (e.g. Baker, 1981; Ponsonby, 1982) as well as of more recent sources (e.g. Kelly, 2000). Thus, typically, we can find sections devoted to vowels, consonants, sometimes difficult consonant clusters, word and sentence stress, intonation, rhythm and changes occurring in connected speech. Occasionally some spelling-to-pronunciation rules are discussed. The question of phonetically problematic words is generally ignored, although some authors propose exercises concerning certain types of vocabulary they consider difficult for learners. Hewings (2004) should be singled out because he offers many tasks which involve the pronunciation of whole words, such as first names, place names, products, planets and nationality words. Sobkowiak's (1996) book deserves a special mention, with its list of about 700 'words commonly mispronounced'. Interestingly, although the list is placed in the appendix and thus is marginalized in the book, it belongs to the most frequently used parts of it. This proves many teachers' intuition concerning the importance of mispronounced words. The conclusion is evident; in order to reduce/eliminate such errors, pronunciation instructors cannot rely on the existing publications but should produce their own phonetic materials suited to the specific needs of their learners. The reduction of mispronunciations under discussion is not an easy task since they are often fossilized and reinforced by the fact of their high frequency in learner English.

Let us sum up this section. We have suggested that phonetic instruction should, first and foremost, focus not on segments and suprasegments, but on the pronunciation of whole words, particularly those where distortion might lead to intelligibility problems. This shift of emphasis appears to have the following advantages:

- Learning to pronounce whole words without major phonological deviations is easier than achieving mastery of individual segments and prosodic features, as was proved by the experiment we carried out (Stasiak & Szpyra-Kozłowska, 2010) in the course of which very little segmental and prosodic progress could be observed, with, however, striking improvement in the elimination of word pronunciation errors.
- Mastering individual sounds and sound contrasts does not necessarily lead to improvement in the production of problematic words since mispronounced forms are not the result of articulatory difficulty, but stem from the incorrect storage of these items in learners' phonetic memory.
- The suggested procedure is more rewarding for the learner as it results in immediate communicative gains and a feeling of accomplishment which is difficult to achieve in the training of segments and suprasegmentals.

The claim about the necessity of prioritizing phonetically difficult words which can all be regarded as instances of local errors made in this section (so-called item learning) does not mean, of course, that other, more global aspects of pronunciation should be neglected (so-called system learning). Numerous other segmental and prosodic issues must find their way into the EFL pronunciation classroom. For example, connected speech phenomena (e.g. Shockey, 2003) deserve special attention as without some familiarity with them understanding spoken English is next to impossible.[20] Nevertheless, eliminating severely distorted words from learners' vocabulary, largely neglected in current phonodidactic instruction, should remain in focus, particularly at lower levels of phonetic proficiency. At the more advanced levels where such mispronunciations are less frequent, various other elements of phonetics should be given close attention.

A.2.4 Pronunciation and Spelling

In the preceding sections we have demonstrated that the major source of many phonetic problems can be found in spelling (both of English and the L1) and the influence it exerts on learners' pronunciation. Thus, Poles can be heard to say, for example, [tomp rajders] (*Tomb Raiders*), ['egzemajn] (*examine*), [pe'lejs] (*palace*). During my recent visit to France I heard (on the radio) in the titles of songs *promise* pronounced as ['promais] and *about* as [a'but]. Moreover, in Section B.2.3 some empirical evidence is provided to show that native speakers of English consider cases of foreign speakers' spelling pronunciation a major hindrance to the intelligibility of accented speech. We would therefore like to suggest that teaching the major spelling-to-sound correspondences should constitute the next phonodidactic priority for foreign learners.

It should be noted that, as pointed out in Chapter 1, EFL learners differ from ESL students in that while in the latter case the exposure to spoken English is unlimited, in the former it is often restricted to the language classroom.[21] This means that in EFL contexts learners are exposed to written English far more frequently than to spoken English. Basetti (2008: 1) also argues that 'for many instructed second language learners much second language input is not spoken, but written input'. She adds that although L2 learners are often familiarized with the written form of the L2 from the early stages of the learning process, 'SLA researchers have mostly shown little interest in the differences between spoken and written input'. The impact of the orthographic form of L2, however, cannot be ignored, as it interacts with the acoustic input 'thus affecting L2 learners' mental representation of L2 phonology'. Such non-targetlike phonological representations in turn result in the incorrect pronunciation of segments and words.

There are some positive effects of L2 orthographic input. When the spelling of words is phonemic, the written forms are the teacher's and students' friend. For example, in items such as *street*, *Spain*, *play*, *cry*, *tree*, *proud*, the initial letters correspond to consonant clusters which appear in pronunciation. In this case spelling reminds learners of the need to articulate all of them without any elisions or insertions, as is often done by learners in whose L1 such initial clusters are disallowed. Thus, a simple rule can be formulated against epenthesis: 'Do not add any segment (a vowel or a consonant) if it is not written.' Other advantages of access to orthographic input can also be noted. As shown by Bassetti (2008), Japanese learners of English who find it difficult to perceive the difference between English /l/ and /r/ can be helped to articulate these consonants when they see the written words. The same is true of Korean learners of English. Erdener and Burnham (2005) demonstrated that monolingual adult speakers of English and Turkish could repeat Irish and Spanish words more accurately when they had seen them written compared with words they had only heard. Bassetti (2008: 2) concludes that 'for literate L2 learners, the orthographic input provides a visual and permanent analysis of the acoustic input, which may complement a defective perception and thus enable learners to produce phonemes they have difficulty perceiving'.

In the majority of cases, however, spelling is not a friend, but an enemy. According to Bassetti (2008: 2), 'while orthographic input can help L2 learners produce target L2 pronunciations, it can also lead to some non-targetlike pronunciations which would probably never occur if learners were only exposed to acoustic input'. Such negative effects can involve phone additions (adding a segment for which there is no evidence in spelling), phone omissions (omitting a segment which is present in speech, but absent in writing), phone substitutions (replacing one phone with another because of its spelling) and producing contrasts which do not exist in the L2 acoustic input. Such mispronunciations occur mainly due to the application of L1 spelling-to-sound rules to the L2, overgeneralization of L2 spelling and sound correspondences, or a mixture of these factors coupled with phonetic input.

In order to show the extent to which the written forms can affect EFL learners'[22] pronunciation, below we present the most common types of spelling-induced mispronunciations, common in Polish English, but also in other L1 versions of English, which cannot be explained by native English auditory input. In (1) and (2) we provide typical examples of spelling pronunciations which arise when learners apply L1 spelling-to-sound rules to English, e.g. *key* pronounced as [kej]. (3) contains very frequent cases of mispronunciations which result from the incorrect overgeneralizations of L2 letter and sound correspondences, e.g. <ate> pronounced as [ejt]. In (4) we place particularly interesting cases which cannot be accounted for by one of the factors above, but which constitute a mixture of both, e.g. *law* pronounced as [low]. Finally, in (5) we include some cognates in which Polish learners' versions can be attributed to the pronunciation of a similar Polish word, additionally reinforced by the influence of English spelling, e.g. *honour* pronounced as [xonor].

(1) Pronunciation of silent letters and letter combinations, in agreement with L1 spelling-to-sound rules:
   (a) consonants (e.g. *half, calf, walk, doubt, handsome, castle, answer, iron, honest*);
   (b) vowels (e.g. *bottom, cotton, prison, political, historical, fruit*);
   (c) letter sequences (e.g. *aren't, weren't*).
(2) Pronunciation of letters and letter combinations according to L1 spelling-to-sound correspondences, e.g.:
   <o> as P[o], e.g. *don't, only, old, cold, worry, onion, roll, oven word, world, work*[23];
   <i> as P[i], e.g. *sit, did, sister, city, live, if, give, picture, possible*;
   <ch> as P[x], e.g. *technology, technical, chrome, loch, Bach*;
   <ei> as P[ej], e.g. *foreign, their, geyser, Seymour*;
   <ou> as P[ow], e.g. *curious, dangerous, enormous, south*;
   <au> as P[aw], e.g. *aunt, sausage, haunt, audience*;
   <ou> as P[ow], e.g. *soup, group, mountain, cough, enough, through, thorough*;
   <ey> as P[ej], e.g. *key, donkey, monkey, hockey, jockey*.
(3) Pronunciation of letters and letter combinations based on false generalizations concerning L2 spelling-to-sound rules, e.g.:
   <u> as P[a], e.g. in *butcher, difficult, Turkey, nurse, urgent, Turner, purple, cushion* (as in *shut, but, cut*);

<ea> as P[i], e.g. *instead, deaf, dead, sweat, steady, meadow, steak* (as in *meat, teach, read*);

<ate> as P [ejt], e.g. *delicate, chocolate, separate (adj.), private, accurate, certificate* (as in *debate, irritate, relate*);

<able> as P[ejbl], e.g. *capable, available, suitable, vegetable* (as in *able*);

<ace> as P[ejs], e.g. *surface, palace, necklace* (as in *face, race, lace*);

<i> in <ial, ion, ious> as [j], e.g. *special, potential, region, national, precious, delicious*.

(4) Pronunciation of letters and letter combinations which follows neither L1 nor L2 spelling-to-sound patterns, but is a mixture of both, e.g.:

<aw, au> as P[ow] (according to Polish rules it should be pronounced as [aw]), e.g. *saw, draw, Warsaw, hawk, law, lawn, claw, because*;

<oa> as P[ow] (according to Polish rules, it should be pronounced as [oa]), e.g. *broad, abroad*;

<ai, ay> as P [ej] (according to Polish rules, it should be pronounced as [aj]), e.g. *says, said, captain, certain, mountain*;

<ou, ow> as P[aw] (according to Polish rules, it should be pronounced as [ow]), e.g. *country, own, known*.

(5) Mispronunciations due to the existence of cognates, additionally reinforced by English spelling, e.g.:

E *honour* – P *honor* [xonor] > PE [xonor]/[xono]

E *author* – P *autor* [awtor] > PE [awtor]/[awto]

E *alibi* – P *alibi* [aˈlʲibʲi] > PE [aˈlʲibʲi]

E *cowboy* – P *kowboj* [kovboj] > PE [kovboj]

E *hobby* – P [xobbʲi]/[xobbɨ] > PE [xobbʲi]/[xobbɨ]

As shown above, spelling-induced errors are extremely numerous in learner English and cannot be ignored in EFL instruction. Bassetti (2008: 9) reaches the same conclusion and states that: 'it appears that the spoken language is not primary in second language acquisition (at least in instructed contexts) as it is in first language acquisition. Researchers and language teachers should therefore take the role of written language into account more than it has hitherto been the case.' In other words, in the course of language instruction more attention should be given to reducing the negative effects of orthography on pronunciation. We suggest that in order to counteract the phenomenon in question phonetic training should maximize auditory input, employ phonemic transcription (both discussed in Chapter 3) and include teaching the major English spelling-to-sound rules (see below).

The discussion in this section focuses on the spelling-induced pronunciation problems of Polish learners whose native language makes use of an alphabetic writing system which, unlike English, has a high degree of phonological transparency, i.e. a fairly regular correspondence between letters and sounds. In such instances, according to Bassetti (2008), the impact of orthographic input is particularly strong. Other writing systems (e.g.

consonantal, syllabic and morphemic) pose other types of difficulties which will not be considered here (see, for example, Bassetti, 2006; Sipra, 2013).

Our proposal is to approach the issue of English spelling–pronunciation relations first of all in those instances when it is an ally and then deal with its less friendly aspects. As observed by Kelly (2000: 123), English spelling is not as irregular as it seems. 'Surveys of the system have shown that over 80% of English words are spelled according to regular patterns, and that there are fewer than 500 words (out of an estimated total of over half a million words) whose spelling can be considered completely irregular.' He adds that the fact that some of these exceptions belong to the most common lexical items 'gives a distorted impression of irregularity'. He concludes that teachers should focus on the regular features of English spelling and tie them in with pronunciation work.

The necessity of teaching the basic spelling-to-pronunciation rules has been noted by other pronunciation specialists as well. Gilbert (2008), for instance, argues that learners need help in guessing how to pronounce English spelling and offers some suggestions as to how it can be done. Hewings (2004: 9) points out that, 'although pronunciation is a feature of speech and spelling a feature of writing, spelling will often have an influence on the learning of pronunciation as the majority of learners use written texts in their studies'. He adds that the relationship between spelling and pronunciation is often thought to be complex and chaotic, which is not true. He considers it important to help students develop their awareness of the sound and letter correspondences and, with this purpose in mind, proposes a set of very useful exercises. Celce-Murcia *et al.* (1996: 419) also maintain that 'it is important for ESL and EFL teachers to understand the correspondences between English phonology and English orthography so that they can teach their learners (1) how to predict the pronunciation of a word given its spelling and (2) how to come up with a plausible spelling for a word given its pronunciation'. We might add here that while points (1) and (2) are undoubtedly important, the major reason for studying the issue in question is to minimize the impact of spelling on pronunciation and to eliminate cases of spelling pronunciation which, as shown in Section B.2.1, are frequently detrimental to intelligibility.

Thus, pronunciation specialists appear to agree about the importance of teaching foreign learners selected sound and letter correspondences and formulate basic rules which account for them. It seems, however, that providing such rules and illustrating them with appropriate examples is rather boring and should sometimes be replaced with simple tasks in which students themselves are supposed to uncover a given regularity (a problem-solving approach). For example, they can be given the following minimal pairs and can be asked to point to the differences in their pronunciation and relate it to the spelling:

(a) *rid – ride, kit – kite, fin – fine, pill – pile, strip – stripe*
(b) *hop – hope, mop – mope, not – note, rob – robe, pop – pope*

(c)   *mat – mate, fat – fate, hat – hate, lack – lake, tap – tape*

Learners usually come quickly to the conclusion that the items in (a) contain two vowels: /ɪ/ and /aɪ/, in (b) /ɒ/ and /əʊ/, and in (c) /æ/ and /eɪ/. In all instances the short vowels are followed by a single word-final consonant whereas the diphthongs are followed by a consonant and the <e> vowel letter. Next they can provide their own examples which follow this pattern.

   Another task which requires finding out some regularities in letter-to-sound relations concerns the pronunciation of vowels in the provided sequences of segments, i.e. students are asked to answer the following questions: what sound do the words in each row have in common? How are these sounds spelt?

(a)   *park, Charlie, bark, Mars, marble, shark, carve, scarf*
(b)   *pork, storm, York, morning, torn, born, port, horse*
(c)   *turn, purple, curb, curly, Murphy, purse, nurse, Turner*
(d)   *firm, Shirley, flirt, shirt, girl, Irwing, Birmingham, bird*

More advanced students should also be encouraged to add their own examples, as well as to find counter-examples to the generalizations they have formed.

   A simple type of activity consists in deciding whether the vowels in the provided pairs of words are the same or different, e.g.:

   monkey – donkey, lane – lain, ton – on, pair – bear, pin – pine, litter – litre

   The cases presented above are relatively simple and should be followed by tasks devoted to more complex instances, particularly those involving less regular correspondences between English spelling and pronunciation. For example, students can be given sets of words to find the odd man out, i.e. an item in which some letter or letter sequences are pronounced differently from in the remaining words, e.g.:

(a)   *man, bat, many, lamb, happy, sad, lamp* (*many* pronounced with [e], not [æ])
(b)   *thousand, think, birthday, Thomas, bath* (*Thomas* pronounced with [t], not [Θ])
(c)   *read, seat, meat, steak, heating, least, meaning,* (*steak* pronounced with [eɪ], not [iː])
(d)   *bitter, tip, list, police, sister, children, official* (*police* pronounced with [iː], not [ɪ])

   A useful task which can be used with advanced learners consists of providing them with a list of non-words which they can attempt to pronounce in accordance with the spelling-to-sound rules of English. They can be asked to justify their decisions by providing real items which realize a given convention, e.g.:

>*sab* (pronounced with [æ], as *lab, cab, crab*)
>*sade* (pronounced with [eɪ], as *shade, blade, grade*)
>*nath* (pronounced with [Θ], as *bath, path, maths*)
>*pham* (pronounced with [f], as *photo, physics, phone*)

It should also be added that to counteract spelling-induced mispronunciations many specialists suggest introducing new vocabulary items to learners only in their auditory form, without access to any visual input. As sooner or later some contact with the latter is inevitable, e.g. while using course books or the internet, it seems that a different procedure may turn out to be more fruitful, i.e. presenting and then learning new words simultaneously in their written and spoken form (and preferably also in the phonemically transcribed shape – see Chapter 3) to enhance and integrate audiovisual learning which should remain inseparable.

To sum up, minimizing the powerful impact of spelling on EFL learners' pronunciation should not be just one of the many elements of phonetic instruction, but must be placed among its top priorities. In order for this requirement not to remain purely programmatic, however, pronunciation instructors need appropriate exercises, adjusted to the specific learner groups. Since such sources are probably unavailable, teachers are encouraged to devise some activities like the ones proposed above.

A.2.5 Segmentals Versus Suprasegmentals

An important part of the search for pronunciation priorities is what has been dubbed a 'segmentals versus suprasegmentals' debate concerning the communicative role of these two aspects of English phonetics. Some pronunciation specialists argue that segmental features are crucial for maintaining intelligibility while others claim that it is prosody that is of primary importance. While in earlier approaches to pronunciation instruction segmentals occupied a central position, the majority of more recent publications appear to subscribe to the latter view. It should be stressed that this is indeed a significant issue as it determines not only the shape of phonetic syllabuses and the order in which specific problems are introduced (the so-called 'top down' approach when instruction starts with training in suprasegmentals and proceeds to segmentals versus the 'bottom up' view, in which this order is reversed), but also the amount of time and effort that is devoted to practicing segmentals and suprasegmentals at every stage of language instruction.

A shift of emphasis from segments to prosody has been a result of a series of experiments, the authors of which (e.g. Anderson-Hsieh *et al.*, 1992; Derwing & Rossiter, 2003; Field, 2005; Munro & Derwing, 1999) presented cases of communication breakdown when suprasegmentals were not sufficiently mastered by learners. Consequently, they argue that it is prosody that should be prioritized. Jenner (1989: 3), for example, maintains that 'we should be spending a lot less time on contrasts in vowel shape and a good deal more on suprasegmental aspects of pronunciation'. Roach (1991: 204) also claims that 'rhythm and timing are important in successful communication', which is supported by 'evidence of problems arising from inappropriate rhythm in language learners'. Various authors (e.g. Gilbert, 2008: 8) provide examples of conversational interchanges in which the use of inappropriate intonation patterns has led to misunderstandings or even communication breakdowns. She claims that: 'without a sufficient, threshold-level mastery of the English prosodic system, learners' intelligibility and listening comprehension will not advance, no matter how much effort is made drilling individual sounds. That is why the highest priority must be given to rhythm and melody in whatever time is available for teaching pronunciation.'[24]

The results of the 'segmentals versus suprasegmentals debate' are reflected in the construction of phonetic syllabuses; an analysis of several English course books published up to the 1990s shows that segmentals were introduced first at lower stages of language proficiency and prosody later, for advanced learners. In more recent EFL materials, prosodic issues appear to dominate over segmental ones. In Table 2.6 we present a list of the phonetic issues most frequently covered by 20 popular course books[25] in British English (the majority of which were published after the year 2000).[26] Table 2.6 demonstrates that 14 of the 20 phonetic issues most frequently dealt with by the analyzed course books concern various aspects of prosody and only five segmental problems, which proves that current teaching materials tend to prioritize suprasegmentals.

In recent years, mostly under the influence of Jenkins (2000) and her claims concerning the vital role of segments and the negligible contribution of prosody to intelligibility in international contexts, another shift in phonodidactic practices can be noted towards prioritizing segments over suprasegmentals (e.g. Walker, 2011). According to Jenkins, there is a striking difference in the manner in which speech is processed by native speakers of English and foreign learners; in the former case 'top down' processing is employed, i.e. from larger to smaller units, while in the latter it proceeds in a 'bottom up' fashion, i.e. from segments to prosodic patterns. Rogerson-Revell (2011: 242) attempts to reconcile these two conflicting viewpoints by stating that 'it might be more important for EFL learners, who will be communicating with native English speakers, to give more attention to suprasegmental aspects of pronunciation than ELF learners who might be better improving segmental accuracy primarily'. If she is right, NELF students who

Table 2.6 Phonetic issues most frequently covered by 20 English course books

No.	Phonetic issues	Number of course books dealing with a given issue
1	Word stress	20
2	Stressed versus unstressed syllables	20
3	Stressed and unstressed words	19
4	Sentence stress	19
5	Strong and weak forms	19
6	Contractions	19
7	Intonation of statements expressing emotions	16
8	Vowel contrasts	16
9	Interdental fricatives	16
10	Pronunciation of inflectional endings	16
11	Word linking	15
12	Linking 'r'	13
13	Linking glides	13
14	Intonation of questions expressing emotions	13
15	Intonation of general and wh questions	12
16	Intonation of question tags	12
17	Intonation of neutral statements	12
18	Palatoalveolars	12
19	Elision of /t, d/	12
20	Spelling-to-sound correspondences	12

wish to communicate both with native and non-native speakers of English are placed in the particularly difficult position of having to learn segmentals as well as suprasegmentals, but prioritizing one or the other aspect depending on their interlocutors.[27]

Below, we should like to argue that the approaches under discussion are misguided and that the issue of intelligibility does not reside in the segmentals versus suprasegmentals dichotomy, but follows from the degree of phonetic and phonological distance/similarity between the L1 and L2 in terms of these two aspects of pronunciation.

In order to clarify this viewpoint, let us consider the hypothetical examples of two languages, A and B, which are similar in terms of their segmental inventories and phonotactics, but which differ markedly in their prosodic properties, such as stress and intonation. It is evident that mutual learners of these languages will acquire segments easily, but will face considerable difficulties with the prosodic system of the other language and that gross departures from it will lead to intelligibility problems. Take another example of languages C and D, sharing many prosodic features, but differing radically in their segmental make-up. In such instances we can predict that segmental issues will play a major role in the intelligibility of learner speech. In other words, in the first case prosody has to be prioritized while in the other one segments are crucial.

Thus, we should like to advance a claim that the debate on the communicative relevance of segments and prosodies is misdirected since it ignores the major issue of the relation between the L1 and L2 phonetic/phonological systems. Put differently, these are properties of the learners' L1, juxtaposed with those of their L2 which, to a large extent, determine what is crucial for ensuring intelligibility. It is impossible to generalize as to which of the two phonetic aspects of English, segmental or suprasegmental, is more important since this largely depends on the degree of similarity/difference between the learners' mother tongue and English. If segments are similar, but suprasegmentals are very different, then the latter will be the major source of learning difficulty and intelligibility problems. The opposite is true as well.

Let us provide some empirical evidence for this claim. In a series of articles (e.g. Szpyra-Kozłowska & Radomski, 2012, Radomski & Szpyra-Kozłowska, 2014) we have examined Poles' perception of foreign-accented Polish. In these studies we have elicited listeners' judgements concerning, among other things, the most striking and the most intelligibility-hindering phonetic features in speech samples provided by learners from different, but mostly European, countries. Care has been taken to select samples of a comparable (medium) degree of foreign accentedness. The results show that in all instances listeners pointed to foreign pronunciation of some consonants and vowels, but made no mention of prosodic issues with one exception. In their assessment of a Polish sample provided by a Chinese learner, the participants emphasized the speaker's flat intonation and lack of marked word stress. This means that in Poles' perception of foreign-accented Polish used by speakers of intonation languages, segmental issues come to the fore, but in their evaluation of samples by speakers of a tone language, prosody (intonation and stress, to be more exact) occupies the central position. The conclusion is simple; in the former case segments should be prioritized and in the latter suprasegmentals.

It should be added that real languages differ from our hypothetical examples in that very few of them display the neat pattern of A and B having similar segmentals and different suprasegmentals, or C and D with similar suprasegmentals and different segmentals. In the majority of cases, natural languages display various types of similarities and differences, both segmental and prosodic. For example, the six-vowel inventory of Polish and fixed penultimate word stress makes it fully predictable that Polish learners of English will have problems with the rich English vowel system (a segmental issue) and its extremely complex word stress (a prosodic issue). Furthermore, the interdental fricatives are absent from Polish and thus are very problematic for Poles (a segmental issue). As Polish is a syllable-timed language and English is stress-timed, Polish learners have problems with English rhythm, vowel reduction and the use of weak forms (prosodic issues). Thus, the question is not always whether these are all segmentals or all suprasegmentals that should be prioritized, but which particular segmental and prosodic aspects should be targeted in phonetic instruction.

For example, in the already quoted studies of Poles' perception of foreign-accented Polish an interesting case concerns East Slavic (Russian, Ukrainian and Belarus) learners of Polish. What many listeners noticed was a frequent lengthening of stressed vowels and a specific 'singsong' intonation, which depart from the prosodic patterns of Polish, as well as various segmental inaccuracies concerning both consonants and vowels. In such instances both segmental and prosodic issues should be given similar attention in phonetic instruction.

While comparative analysis and differences between languages indicate the major areas of learning difficulty and potential threats to intelligibility in foreigners' speech,[28] these are empirical studies that must determine which of them are particularly important for successful communication and which are not. In other words, in our view, pronunciation priorities cannot be established theoretically, in an a priori fashion, for all learners of English, but must be decided on the basis of research concerning their impact on spoken interactions between its users. To put it yet differently, the confusion as to the role of segmentals and suprasegmentals in safeguarding intelligibility follows from the fact that no generalizations which concern all learners with different L1 backgrounds can be formulated as they depend on language-specific rather than universal factors. If this conclusion is true, intelligibility should be studied empirically with reference to specific L1 and L2 language pairs.

Consider now the usefulness of some proposals of pronunciation priorities meant to be universal, i.e. directed at all foreign learners. Gilbert (1999), for example, formulates a list of six pronunciation priorities for the beginning student whose native language is not specified. They include the following: decoding print, i.e. teaching basic spelling-to-pronunciation rules, grammar sounds, i.e. those sounds which make a grammatical difference, e.g. tense markers *he's/he'd, I'll/I'd*, number markers *book/books,* linking (to help students to identify beginnings and endings of words, necessary in listening comprehension), preservation of the number of syllables in a word (no vowel deletion and insertion), rhythm, understood as lengthening stressed syllables and shortening unstressed ones, and emphasis, i.e. proper placement of nuclear stress in phrases.[29]

Let us now try to apply these suggestions to specific learners, for instance, Poles. Of the six priorities proposed by Gilbert, only two, i.e. spelling-to-pronunciation rules and rhythm are relevant to Polish learners who do not have problems with the remaining features. It might be concluded that Poles should simply focus on the two problematic issues and skip the other ones. Empirical research (discussed later in this section) shows, however, that while eliminating spelling-related errors should indeed be prioritized, there are several other properties of Polish English pronunciation that are crucial to its intelligibility and which do not include rhythm. This means that Gilbert's proposal fails to indicate some genuinely problematic aspects of Polish English that should be dealt with in the course of pronunciation training.

Examine now the major phonetic problems of Brazilian Portuguese learners of English discussed by da Silva (2011), who defines several pronunciation priority areas for them which, according to him, are crucial for intelligibility. They comprise four issues: confusion between /r/ and /h/ in initial position (Brazilian learners tend to say *hetired* instead of *retired*), strong reduction (deletion) of vowels in final unstressed syllables (they say *happ* instead of *happy*), nuclear stress placed on the wrong word (e.g. *I like IT* instead of *I LIKE it*) and 'Brazilianized' pronunciation of loanwords (e.g. *cowntrie* instead of *country*). Clearly, only two items, i.e. nuclear stress placement and preservation of the number of syllables in a word, appear in Gilbert's and da Silva's lists. The remaining issues, essential for the intelligibility of Brazilian English, are absent in Gilbert's approach since they can only be established on a language-specific and not a universal basis.

It should also be noted that other proposals for universal pronunciation priorities presented in Section A.2.2 fail to predict all of the unintelligibility-causing phonetic features of Polish English or Brazilian English since no such general lists can be applicable to all learners with different L1 backgrounds. On the one hand, they provide too much by including phonetic features irrelevant for many learner groups. On the other hand, they offer too little and are not detailed enough for specific L1 students. This conclusion finds full support when we examine a staggering array of pronunciation difficulties encountered by EFL learners of different L1s, discussed, for instance, in Swan and Smith (2001), which concern segments, phonotactic restrictions and various aspects of prosody, and which cannot be generalized to other languages.

The need to establish an empirically based set of priorities for L1 learners requires making a decision concerning the 'intelligibility to whom' issue. As in the approach to pronunciation teaching/learning advocated here native speaker models are adopted, it follows that it is their perception and evaluation of foreign-accented speech that should be taken into consideration in the first place. Thus, what we are suggesting here is establishing pronunciation priorities for L1 learners on the basis of native speakers' reactions to foreign-accented English. Note that this is a far more realistic enterprise than intelligibility research involving countless pairings of various L1 versions of English, which differ also depending on the learners' level of language proficiency.

This is not to say, however, that empirical studies on the intelligibility of foreign accents are devoid of problems since their results often vary due to differences in the employed research methodology and experimental designs.

For example, analyzed samples of accented speech differ in terms of their number, length and degree of accentedness, the method of their collection (read versus extemporaneous speech) and the speakers' level of foreign language proficiency. Raters show much diversity with respect to their number, linguistic experience (trained versus naïve judges), mother tongue (native versus non-native listeners) and various sociolinguistic factors (e.g. age, sex, education, place of living). What also matters in the case of English native speaker judges is the type of accent they use. As shown by van den Doel (2006) for Dutch English and by Bryła-Cruz (2013) for Polish English, native Scottish, Irish, American and English listeners do not perceive foreign accents in exactly the same way and differ in their evaluations of accented speech. Finally, numerous differences characterize the adopted rating procedure pertaining to the number and types of tasks expected of the assessors, the employed rating scales and other details of assessment.

While this variety of methodological approaches allows the researcher to examine accent issues from many different perspectives, the obtained results often vary. In such a situation it seems advisable to resort to meta-analysis, i.e. a critical comparison and evaluation of the results obtained in several studies (if they are available). If the majority of them support a given conclusion, then we can assume that it is correct. The opposite is also true; if the importance of a given phonetic feature is argued for by a single source, then we might approach this result with due caution.

In order to demonstrate how such meta-analysis works, let us consider the top pronunciation priorities which emerge from four studies on the perception of Polish-accented English by native speakers.[30]

Table 2.7 demonstrates that, in spite of various methodologies adopted by different authors, there is a considerable degree of convergence in the obtained results. Thus, all the studies point to the salience of maintaining proper vowel quality and quantity, and single out the need to preserve the /iː/ – /ɪ/ distinction in particular. They are also unanimous in attaching special importance to the pronunciation of the interdental fricatives and the velar nasal without the following plosive, for instance at the end of words such as *sing, long, going*. Moreover, all four lists comprise a typical feature of phonetic transfer from Polish to English, i.e. word-final devoicing of obstruents.[31] It should also be pointed out that two studies, i.e. Szpyra-Kozłowska's and Bryła-Cruz's, which included the category of spelling-induced word mispronunciations and word stress errors (not examined in the remaining papers), argue that these issues should be considered a top priority.[32] Moreover, it is striking that no prosodic features, except word stress and fluency in Bryła-Cruz's column, are found in Table 2.7.[33]

Finally, yet another important issue concerning teaching segmentals and suprasegmentals should be addressed here, namely that of sequencing them in the course of phonetic training. As mentioned earlier, traditionally segments were taught at earlier stages of instruction and prosodic

Table 2.7 Comparison of pronunciation priorities for Polish learners according to four studies

Scheuer (2003)	Gonet and Pietroń (2004)	Szpyra-Kozłowska (2004)	Bryła-Cruz (2013)
		Spelling pronunciation	Spelling pronunciation
Vowel quality and quantity (especially /iː/ – /ɪ/ distinction)	Vowel quality and quantity	Vowel quality and quantity (especially /iː/ – /ɪ/ distinction)	Vowel quality and quantity (especially /iː/ – /ɪ/ distinction)
	Interdental fricatives	Interdental fricatives	Interdental fricatives
Word-final obstruent devoicing	Word-final obstruent devoicing	Word-final obstruent devoicing	Word-final obstruent devoicing
	The velar nasal (without the following plosive, e.g. in *sing*)	The velar nasal	The velar nasal
		Word stress	Word stress
	Palatoalveolars		Fluency
	Aspiration		Vowel reduction

features to more advanced learners, which is known as the 'bottom-up' approach. The studies which argued for the salience of prosody in successful communication suggested the reversal of this order (the 'top-down' approach). From the arguments presented in this section it should be clear that none of these options can be universally adopted since we believe that the sequencing of phonetic issues should be dictated by pronunciation priorities specified for L1 learners. For example, the quoted studies on the intelligibility of Polish-accented English provide compelling evidence that Polish learners require more training in segments than in suprasegments. Whether the same holds true for other L1 speakers remains to be tested and empirically verified.

Part B

In Part B some empirical evidence supporting several claims made in Part A concerning pronunciation priorities is provided. First, in B.2.1. it is demonstrated that local errors should be prioritized in phonetic instruction since they hinder intelligibility and are irritating for native listeners more than global errors. Next the focus is on different types of phonetically problematic words, isolated by intermediate Polish learners, and on examining the major sources of their pronunciation difficulty. Finally, we present a study meant to evaluate the impact of 24 phonetic features typical of Polish English pronunciation on intelligibility and accentedness judgements made by native raters in order to establish segmental and suprasegmental pronunciation priorities for Poles.

B.2.1 Intelligibility and Global Versus Local Errors

In order to investigate the impact of local and global errors on communication via English, we conducted a two-part experiment, the design and results of which are presented in Szpyra-Kozłowska (2013). Below the major observations made in this study are summarized.

The major goal of the experiment was to examine English native speakers' judgements concerning two types of mispronunciations commonly made by Polish learners: one which involves typical segmental and suprasegmental inaccuracies, i.e. global errors, but which is devoid of local errors, and another version which is segmentally and prosodically correct, i.e. in which there are no global errors, but where local errors can occur. The aim was to find out how these two types of inaccuracies are evaluated by native speakers of English in terms of comprehensibility, intelligibility, foreign accentedness and the degree of irritation/annoyance they trigger in native listeners.

For the purposes of the experiment a brief text containing 20 words commonly mispronounced by Polish learners of English was compiled by the author. The test items are transcribed below in their Polish English versions. Needless to say, in all cases several other pronunciation variants are possible in learner English. The transcription symbols refer to Polish sounds.

Disney [ˈdⁱisnej]	*area* [eˈrⁱija]
worked [workt/workit]	*lettuce* [letⁱjus]
butcher [ˈbačer]	*fruit* [fruit]
climate [ˈklajmejt]	*meadow* [ˈmⁱidow]
steak [stⁱik]	*captain* [ˈkeptejn/ˈkeptajn]
foreign [foˈrejn]	*radar* [ˈradar]
walk [wolk]	*mountains* [ˈmowtajns/ˈmawtejns]
colonel [koˈlonel]	*soup* [sowp]
Turkey [ˈtarkⁱi/ˈtarkej]	*cabin* [ˈkejbⁱin]
nurse [nars]	*Japan* [ˈdžapan]/[ˈdžepen]

The local errors which occur in these forms stem from different sources. Most of them result from the interference of English spelling and involve: pronouncing silent letters (*walk, fruit*); incorrect overgeneralization of English spelling-to-sound rules (e.g. <u> interpreted as P [a] in *butcher, nurse, Turkey*; <ea> pronounced as [i] in *steak, meadow*; <ate> as [eit] in *climate*; <ai> and

<ei> as [ei] in *captain, foreign, mountains*); and interference from Polish pronunciation (*radar, Japan*).

The diagnostic passage was recorded in two versions produced by two adult Polish men.

(a) Version A: here the speaker, an intermediate learner of English, read the passage using consonants, vowels and prosodies typical of Polish English, but without any major distortions of words provided above (global errors, but no local errors).
(b) Version B: in this case the speaker, an experienced English phonetics teacher, employed English sounds and prosodies, but mispronounced the test items in the manner indicated above (local errors, but no global errors).

It should be added that both samples were characterized by a comparable speaking rate, volume and clarity of articulation, which factors, according to Munro and Derwing (1999), affect the comprehension of accented speech.

In the first part of the experiment the participants were a group of 20 adult native speakers of Irish English, of mixed sex, aged between 25 and 55, all inhabitants of Dublin and having college education. The majority of them are teachers of English, employed in a language school and teaching English to foreigners from various countries. Thus, all the subjects are familiar with different versions of foreign-accented English. They all admit to having conversed in English with many Poles.

The Irish listeners were divided into two groups of 10 persons each. The first group listened to Version A while the second group listened to Version B. Then they were all asked to complete a questionnaire which contained four questions. The first of these was intended to measure the comprehensibility of the recorded samples and asked how easy/difficult it was to understand the speaker. The next question concerned the evaluation of the speakers' accentedness and asked how foreign the speaker's accent sounded to the subjects. Question 3 dealt with the degree of irritation caused by the speaker's pronunciation in the listener. Finally, the participants were requested to list those pronunciation inaccuracies which they considered particularly detrimental to successful communication. The subjects selected one of the four answers to Questions 1, 2 and 3,[34] which were then given numerical values from 1 to 4 (the higher the score, the harsher the judgement). Subsequently mean scores for every question were calculated. The experimental results are summarised in Table 2.8.

The data show that the participants' evaluation of the samples' degree of comprehensibility, foreign accent and annoyance on all three counts are more severe in the case of Speaker B. Thus, Speaker A scored 1.5 points for comprehensibility with the assessment varying from 'very easy' to 'rather easy to understand', while Speaker B's speech, with 2.72 points, was most

Table 2.8 Experimental results: Part I

Question	Speaker A (global errors, no local errors)	Speaker B (local errors, no global errors)
Comprehensibility	1.5 (very easy/rather easy to understand)	2.72 (rather difficult to understand)
Foreign accent	2.5 (slight foreign accent/ rather strong foreign accent)	2.9 (rather strong foreign accent)
Annoyance	1.3 (not irritating at all/ somewhat irritating)	1.9 (all options – from not irritating to very irritating)
Most important pronunciation errors	Flat intonation, no pauses in listing foods, every syllable pronounced too carefully	Mispronounced words: soup, Turkey, nurse, worked, fruit, steak, captain, meadow, etc.

frequently regarded as 'rather difficult to understand'. The differences in the evaluation of foreign-accentedness were somewhat less marked; Speaker A, with 2.5 points, sounded slightly foreign to half of the subjects and strongly foreign to the other half, whereas Speaker B was described by the majority as having a rather strong foreign accent. Speaker A's accent was generally viewed as 'not irritating at all' (1.3 points), whereas in the evaluation of Speaker B's pronunciation, with the general score of 1.9 points, there was no agreement between the subjects who employed all the options presented in the questionnaire, from 'not irritating at all' to 'very irritating'. Apparently, native listeners differed considerably in their degree of tolerance of local errors made by Speaker B, but were not annoyed by Speaker A's global errors.

It is interesting to note that in the case of Speaker A there was a strong correlation between answers to Questions 1 and 3. This means that the fact that Speaker A was judged as being easy to understand was correlated with the opinion that his pronunciation was not annoying for the listeners, regardless of the assessment of his accentedness. As for Speaker B, here a correlation was noted between answers to Questions 1 and 2. In other words, the ease or difficulty of understanding this speaker was correlated with the assessed degree of his foreign accent.

Finally, the last question was open and asked the participants to list those pronunciation errors in the two samples which they considered particularly detrimental to successful communication. The majority of comments on Speaker A's version concerned prosodic issues. He was claimed to have flat intonation, to make no pauses were they were required and to use too careful pronunciation (e.g. 'each and every syllable pronounced too carefully and in a precise manner, there is no flexibility that a more fluent and confident *speaker would have'*). Interestingly, no segmental inaccuracies of this speaker were pointed out (e.g. *'I didn't really find too many errors in his pronunciation'*). In the case of Speaker B, the participants presented lists of mispronounced words with frequent comments, such as *'I would normally have no problem understanding a Polish accent, but this one was difficult'*.

Twenty subjects took part in the second part of the experiment.[35] They were all university-educated adults (aged 28–57), native speakers of English English, of both sexes, living in London and working at an exhibition centre. They admitted having minimal contact with Poles and Polish-accented English. The participants formed two groups of 10 persons each of whose task was to transcribe orthographically the diagnostic passage read by Speaker A (Group 1) and by Speaker B (Group 2) in order to examine how intelligible the two samples were to the listeners.

The dictation of Speaker A's version resulted in completely accurate transcriptions written by all the participants. This means that in this case the intelligibility score was 100%. The transcription task of Speaker B's version turned out to be considerably more difficult with a mean intelligibility score of 76%. The words and phrases where understanding was particularly problematic are presented in Table 2.9 in order of decreasing difficulty.

Table 2.9 Experimental results: Part II

Test item	Subjects' versions
the Disney family (100% incorrect)	Dista, Distay, Distin, Destain, Distone
they worked on a radar (90%)	they walked on a rudder, they walked on a ladder, they walked on water
sister was a nurse (80%)	was an arse, was an ass, was an aunt
a meal of soup, steak (70%)	soap stick, steep, a reel of soap stick
Turkey (60%)	Talky, Takhi, Taki
colonel (50%)	a colonial, Appolonia
captain (50%)	Katung
butcher (50%)	bachelor
fruit [fruit] (50%)	Freud
walk in the meadow (40%)	walk in the middle
Japan (40%)	Chatham, Chapan
for its climate (30%)	for their environment, for its time it, for its timing
lettuce (30%)	the juice, let choose
cabin (30%)	cave
in the area they liked (20%)	is there a rear, the rear the light
foreign (10%)	(?)
mountain (0%)	(?)

These results demonstrate that the two experimental samples differ strikingly in terms of their intelligibility. While Speaker A's version turned out to be fully intelligible, Speaker B's version in many cases was partly or completely unintelligible to native English listeners.

It is interesting to compare the intelligibility scores of the test items. The least intelligible word was *Disney*, mis-transcribed by all the participants, which can be accounted for by the phonetic unpredictability of surnames and other proper names in general, additionally reinforced by the rarity of morpheme internal occurrences of clusters of voiceless fricatives and nasals present in the Polish English version [dᵻisnej] and perceived by all the listeners as the [st] sequence, far more frequent in this position in English.

The phrase *they worked on a radar*, with 90% of incorrect transcriptions, came second in terms of difficulty to understand, due to the mispronunciation of both the verb and the noun, followed by *sister was a nurse* (80% of misperceptions) and *a meal of soup, steak* (70% of misperceptions). The easiest words to decipher turned out to be *foreign, mountain* and *area* (0–20% of incorrect responses). This result means that not all types of local errors represent the same level of processing difficulty for the listeners, which is strictly connected with their phonological make-up (e.g. the word *mountain*, even when grossly distorted, cannot easily be confused with any other item) and contextual transparency. Thus, the expression *foreign countries*, for instance, created a lexical, syntactic and semantic context which made the adjective comprehensible to the listeners in spite of its deviant phonetic realization. Clearly, further tests with these and other expressions used in different contexts are needed to establish their intelligibility values.

In the preceding pages we have argued that the major obstacle to successful communication between foreign learners and native speakers of English is posed not so much by global segmental and prosodic inaccuracies as by idiosyncratically deviant words, i.e. local errors, which abound in foreign-accented English. Such items, generally disregarded in intelligibility research and in pronunciation training materials, have been shown to negatively affect native judges' ratings of Polish-accented English in terms of its comprehensibility, intelligibility, foreign-accentedness and the degree of irritation triggered in the listeners far more than corresponding ratings of global errors.

The phonodidactic implications of this research are clear; it is not the articulation of individual sounds and prosodic patterns of English that should be the focus of communicatively oriented pronunciation instruction, but rather whole words prone to be commonly mispronounced by EFL learners. This does not mean, of course, that other elements of English phonetics should be disregarded altogether, but simply that pronunciation work on segments and suprasegmentals is insufficient if it does not eliminate the mispronunciations discussed above.

B.2.2 Other Phonetically Difficult Words

In Section B.2.1 we have argued that local errors, which are highly detrimental to successful communication, should be prioritized in English phonodidactics. In the following pages we examine the issue of other phonetically difficult words in the speech of intermediate and advanced Polish learners of English, based on two studies (Szpyra-Kozłowska, 2011, 2012). We attempt to analyse the major sources of word pronunciation errors, both well-known and lesser known, in the case of these two groups of students. It is hoped that, in spite of the Polish context of our investigations, many observations made here will be relevant for other varieties of foreign-accented English.

In the first study we asked 100 secondary school pupils, aged between 14 and 18, of both sexes, all intermediate learners of English,[36] to list those words whose pronunciation they found particularly difficult and which they tended to mispronounce in spite of their teachers' corrections. They were also requested to point to the problematic aspects of these items. The applied procedure yielded about 400 different words. In order to ensure that a given item was difficult not only for individual learners, it was further analyzed when it was found in several pupils' responses. Over 200 such cases are discussed in this section.

The participants adopted different strategies when dealing with the second task, i.e. pointing out the pronunciation difficulties posed by the provided items. In the majority of cases they did not write anything or made a comment such as '*I don't know why I mispronounce this word, I just do*' or '*somehow my tongue refuses to pronounce these letters*', which was to be expected as judgements of this sort require some linguistic and analytic skills, largely unavailable to teenage learners. Thus, a more common method consisted of underlining the problematic parts of words, which the subjects were encouraged to do. In several cases, however, some specific remarks on the encountered phonetic difficulty were offered, some of which are presented in what follows.

A comment on the choice of intermediate learners for this study is in order. While, in terms of pronunciation, for beginners almost everything is difficult (L1 dominates) and for advanced students there is relatively little that remains problematic (L2 dominates), those who have achieved an intermediate level of proficiency seem to be the most interesting group to study not only because they are probably more numerous than other learners but also because they are at an interesting stage in their linguistic development at which there is a strong tug-of-war between L1 and L2 influences. In other words, at this level the learners' interlanguage is bound to display some interesting phonetic and phonological properties.

Below we present and discuss briefly the obtained data, grouping the collected items into some categories. We start with the most numerous types and proceed to the less frequently mentioned instances of phonetically difficult words.

Words with difficult spelling-sound correspondences

One of the major culprits responsible for Polish learners' phonetic difficulties is English spelling or, to be more exact, the irregularities found among spelling-to-pronunciation rules as well as differences between such correspondences in Polish and English. In what follows we shall focus on those cases which were particularly frequent in the participants' responses. Interestingly, most of them did not concern vowels, notorious for being spelt in a variety of ways, but consonants. Silent letters were only rarely mentioned, probably due to the sufficient practice the pupils received in this regard.

The following difficult words were provided by the participants, all of which share multiple phonetic realizations of a given consonant letter or a sequence of letters. The subjects' typical comment was as follows: '*I never know whether to pronounce [s] or [z] in this word.*'

<s>
(a)   *base, basic, basis, isolate, isolation, crisis, fantasy*
(b)   *comparison, curiosity, generosity, consist, insist, increasing, exclusive*
(c)   *close* (verb)/*close* (adj,), *loose/lose, use* (verb)/*use* (noun)

What the items in (a) and (b) have in common is that here the letter <s> tends to be pronounced by learners as a voiced fricative, although for different reasons: in (a) because of the presence of [z] in similar Polish words (e.g. *ba[z]a, i[z]olować, kry[z]ys, fanta[z]ja*) and in (b) because of some kind of s-voicing rule (operating mostly intervocalically and next to sonorants) that students tend to develop. Interestingly, this is not a case of interference from Polish, which allows for both [s] and [z] in the two contexts (e.g. *o[s]a* 'wasp', *kon[s]ekwencja* 'consequence'). The items in (c) represent yet another problem: here pairs of English words differ in the voicing of the final fricative depending on their grammatical category, which is bound to lead to learning difficulties. In such instances a general tendency in Polish English is to use the voiceless fricative due to word-final obstruent devoicing operating in Polish.

<g>
The following items containing the letter <g> were claimed by the subjects to be difficult because of confusion as to whether it should be pronounced as the voiced velar plosive or the palatoalveolar affricate:

stingy, urgent, agent, gorgeous, gigantic

This group is not very numerous but is included here since *gigantic* appeared in several papers.

<c> and <cc>

The pronunciation of the letter <c> or a sequence of two such letters was problematic for the participants in the following words:

<c>   *civil, scene, cement, cycling*
<cc>   *success, accent, accelerate, accident*

The source of difficulty here lies in the presence of the voiceless dental affricate [ts] in the corresponding Polish words in the first set, e.g. *[ts]ywil, s[ts]ena, [ts]ement,* and the cluster [kts] in the second set, e.g. *su[kts]es, a[kts] ent, a[kts]elerator,* and this type of pronunciation is carried over to the English words under discussion. What helps in such cases is reminding students that English has no dental affricate /ts/ at all.

<ch>

This digraph was often underlined by the subjects as difficult to pronounce in the following words:

technique, technology, techno (music), chaos, choir, orchid

in which cases it tends to be pronounced as the voiceless velar fricative spelt as <ch> in Polish, additionally reinforced by the presence of the fricative in Polish equivalents of these items.

<ous>, <able>, <ate>, <ace>, <ough>, <augh>

Some suffixes and sequences of letters are known to cause pronunciation difficulties. The pupils who took part in our study underlined these formatives in the words listed below:

<ous> *dangerous, famous, jealous, nervous, marvellous, continuous*

This suffix is frequently rendered as [ows] or [us] in Polish English as a case of spelling pronunciation.

A common problem concerns the pronunciation of <a> in <able>, <ate>, and <ace>, often interpreted as [ej], due to an incorrect overgeneralization, based on the phonetic shape of such sequences in, for example, *able, tolerate* and *race.*

<able>   *capable, available, valuable, comfortable, vegetable*
<ate>   *delicate, certificate, ultimate, separate* (adj.)
<ace>   *surface, preface, necklace, palace*

In many of these items an additional side effect is the incorrect stress placement on these suffixes.

Two more sequences of letters were mentioned as problematic by the pupils:

| <ough> | *tough, enough, although, through, cough* |
| <augh> | *taught, caught, laugh, draught* |

The source of pronunciation difficulty lies in the different phonetic realizations of such letter sequences, which is confusing to learners.

Phonetic 'false friends'

The second largest group of problematic words contains lexical items which we have dubbed phonetic 'false friends' and which are usually cognates. The following items in the collected data have been found to belong to this category:

> *taxi, karate, alibi, album, chaos, panel, atom, tandem, safari, mania, horror, boa, baobab, jaguar, contact, robot, echo, stereo, video*

Some of the participants commented on such cases in the following way: *'They look like Polish words so when I see them, I pronounce them in the Polish way though I know it's wrong.'*

Words with a difficult stress pattern

As argued in Section A.2.3.2, English word stress belongs to the most difficult areas of English phonetics for Poles (e.g. Sobkowiak, 1996; Waniek-Klimczak, 2002) who, with their fixed-stress mother tongue, find the intricacies and irregularities of the former very hard to master. Since this issue is discussed in more detail in other studies, here we will list the items which some subjects provided with comments such as: *'I keep forgetting how to stress this word correctly.'*

The following bisyllabic items appear in the collected dàta (typical Polish English stress placement is indicated):

(a) 'guitar, 'hotel, 'event, 'technique, 'alarm, 'success, 'Japan, 'exam, 'support, 'suspense
(b) e'ffort, fe'male, fo'reign, da'maged, ca'pable (when pronounced as [e'fo:rt], [fˈi'mejl], [fo'rejn], [de'mejčt], [ke'pejbl])

The examples in (a), with ultimate stress in English, tend to receive penultimate stress in Polish English, partly due to the pronunciation of corresponding Polish words (when they exist) and partly due to the transfer of Polish penultimate stress. The forms in (b) are particularly interesting since here an opposite tendency can be observed, i.e. stressing the ultimate syllable. It might be the case that learners develop some sensitivity to syllable weight and emphasize the final syllable as they regard it, correctly or incorrectly, as heavy and therefore stress-attracting.

Problems with the correct stress placement in longer words was signalled by the participants in the following cases:

(a)   *valu'able, avai'lable, Janu'ary, e'nergy, edu'cated, orga'nizer, in'teresting, fasci'nating*
(b)   *unfor'tunately, 'successful, 'September, 'October, 'interpret, e'conomic, ar'tificial*
(c)   *'computer, 'museum, 'professor*

In the items in (a), with initial stress in English, learners frequently shift it onto the penultimate syllable, in accordance with the Polish rule. The examples in (b) and (c) depart from this pattern in a curious way; here the antipenultimate syllable tends to be stressed in Polish English, which is particularly surprising in the case of the words in (c) with cognates in Polish stressed on the penult like in English. i.e. *kom'puter, mu'zeum, pro'fesor*. This phenomenon is often viewed as a tendency to avoid too Polish-sounding pronunciation since words with the Polish stress pattern are approached with some suspicion by students. It seems, however, that the items in (a) and (b) contradict this assumption and an alternative explanation can be offered. It might be assumed that in these instances learners develop the English antepenultimate stress rule which operates in numerous items, such as *A'merica, uni'versity, 'marvelous,* and apply it to the examples in (b) and (c).

To sum up, it appears that a tug-of-war takes place between Polish and English stress rules in the students' interlanguage, with winners on both sides. This indicates that in the course of phonetic training more attention should be devoted to word stress and those items which tend to be mis-stressed.

Words with difficult consonant clusters

Polish learners, whose mother tongue abounds in a rich variety of consonant sequences, generally have no major problems with the pronunciation of English clusters, with some exceptions, however. Many participants of our study regard as phonetically difficult those words which contain an interdental fricative in combination with another consonant.

(a)   <th+C> *three, throw, threw, through, throat, thriller, threaten, birthday, maths*
(b)   <C+th> *sixth, seventh, eighth, length, strength, month, depth, width, warmth, although*

Thus, the interdental fricatives, difficult for Poles in any context, are particularly troublesome when they appear next to another consonant. As shown above, the order of consonants is irrelevant since in (a) the spirant appears as the first segment while in (b) as the second one. The quality of the other consonant does not seem relevant either; the provided examples comprise combinations of 'th' with rhotics, nasals, plosives, laterals and fricatives. It should be pointed out, however, that in our data the most frequently repeated examples involve 'th' followed by /r/.

The issues discussed so far, that is, the occurrence of cognates, interference from spelling, word stress and consonant clusters which make English words difficult to learn, cause well-recognized problems not only for Poles, but for learners of other L1 backgrounds as well. In what follows we focus on the lesser known sources of phonetic errors uncovered by our study.

Long words

Several students placed the following comment next to some items: *'this word is difficult because it's long.'* As mentioned earlier, longer items are problematic for many learners as they require from them the skill of controlling several different factors: spelling-to-pronunciation rules, the placement of stress (primary and secondary), the articulation of many different new sounds and complex sound sequences.

A important issue concerns the length of words regarded by learners as difficult. Let us consider the data below:

(a)   trisyllables: *excitement, adventure, jewellery, Australia, picturesque, quotation*
(b)   quadrisyllables: *relaxation, astonishing, surprisingly, competition, desperately*
(c)   quintisyllables: *encyclopaedia, occasionally, exaggeration, association, opportunity*

The provided items contain three, four and five syllables. Evidently, for intermediate learners even words which are three syllables long may be difficult, which does not mean, of course, that every word of this length will be regarded as such. It is not obvious, however, which particular phonetic aspects of the forms listed above make them troublesome for learners as this requires a detailed examination of their learner versions.

Words with several liquids

One of the most surprising results of our study has been a discovery that the presence of several liquids, i.e. both rhotics and laterals, in one word contributes to its pronunciation difficulty for intermediate learners. One source of such problems is the failure to master the restrictions on the occurrence of /r/ in RP and a frequent case of articulating it word-finally and preconsonantally. Such realizations of /r/ result in the presence of several rhotics in one item and learners' complaints that it is difficult since *'there are too many r's in this word'*. The following examples have been supplied by the subjects:

murderer, appropriate, library, portray, cartridge

Nevertheless, these were forms which contain both laterals and rhotics (found in pronunciation and/or in spelling) that were frequently provided with angry comments such as *'I can't get my tongue around it'* or *'I get my tongue in a twist when I say it.'*

regularly, particularly, rarely, barely, burglary, world, rural, literally, cellular

In such cases learners frequently attempt to pronounce all the r's present in spelling, which with the lateral and other consonants create phonetically difficult clusters. The problem with liquids is expressed clearly by one pupil: *'red lorry, yellow lorry – this is a true tongue twister.'*

Words with several high front vowels

For intermediate Polish learners phonetically difficult English words are also those which contain two different high front vowels, i.e. [iː] and [ɪ], e.g.:

reading, sleeping, feeling, dreaming, cheating, ceiling, greeting, leaving

In such instances they tend to employ two [iː] vowels (or rather its shorter and less tense Polish counterpart [i]). Interestingly, the reverse order of these vowels causes no such problems, e.g.:

believe, receive, deceive, precede, repeat, release

However, when the progressive -ing suffix is attached to the verbs above, a very difficult sequence of [ɪ] – [iː] – [ɪ] is created, e.g.:

believing, receiving, deceiving, preceding, repeating, releasing

Here the vowels in all syllables tend to be pronounced as [i].

Words with morphological alternations

The collected data also contain words regarded as phonetically difficult by the respondents due to the fact that some of the segments found in them are subject to morphological alternations. Since in English such changes are often highly irregular and idiosyncratic in character, this fact contributes to the perceived pronunciation difficulty of items in which they take place. Some examples are given below:

(a) *so**c**iety* (so**c**ial) – /s~ʃ/, *nor**th**ern* (nor**th**) – /ð~Θ/, *sou**th**ern* (sou**th**) – /ð~Θ/, *lon**g**itude, lon**g**evity* (lon**g**er) – /ʤ~g/, *an**x**iety* (an**x**ious) – /z~kʃ/

(b) *can't* (c<u>a</u>n) – /a:~æ/, *var<u>ie</u>ty* (var<u>i</u>ous) – /aɪ~ɪ/, *br<u>ea</u>the* (br<u>ea</u>th) – /i:~e/, *n<u>u</u>merous* (n<u>u</u>mber) – /ju:~ʌ/, *w<u>i</u>dth* (w<u>i</u>de) – /ɪ~aɪ/, *d<u>e</u>pth* (d<u>ee</u>p) – /e~i:/, *sinc<u>e</u>rity* (sinc<u>e</u>re) – /e~ɪə/, *b<u>a</u>the* (b<u>a</u>th) – /eɪ~a:/, *n<u>a</u>tural* (n<u>a</u>ture) – /æ~eɪ/

In (a) we find items which involve consonant alternations while those in (b) involve vowel alternations. In some examples (*south – southern, breathe – breath*) both types of changes take place. It is likely that pupils first learn the more frequent words provided in parentheses and when faced with less common related items, they transfer the pronunciation of the underlined segments from the former to the latter. The degree of difficulty increases due to the fact that in most cases the alternating sounds are spelt in the same way.

The lexical items presented and analyzed in this section provide a rich and valuable source of information on the issue of phonetically difficult words for Polish intermediate learners of English[38]. It should be stressed that since we have dealt here with the pupils' subjective judgements, the emerging picture is far from complete and needs to be supplemented by a direct observation of the learners' performance.

B.2.3 Pronunciation Priorities for Polish Learners

In this section we examine the most important phonetic features of Polish-accented English which impair its intelligibility and contribute most to the impression of a Polish accent. The study, based on the judgements of phonetic error gravity made by native teachers of English employed in Polish schools, colleges and universities, was carried out in order to establish phonetic priorities for Polish learners (Szpyra-Kozłowska, 2004).

An anonymous questionnaire was distributed among 30 native speakers (13 British, 13 Americans, two Canadians and two Australians), who have been teaching English in Poland from several months to 12 years. They were given a list of 25 aspects of Polish English pronunciation and asked to evaluate their impact on the intelligibility of Polish-accented English and their contribution to the Polish accent. The following features were subject to assessment[37]:

(1)   Spelling pronunciation, e.g. *[ps]alm, mu[sk]le, bo[mp]*.
(2)   Mispronunciation of individual words (local errors) (*recipe* [ri'saip], *delicate* ['delikeit]).
(3)   Incorrect placement of word stress (*deve'lopment, 'success*).
(4)   Incorrect pronunciation of the interdental fricatives (substituted by /t, d/, /f, v/ or /s, z/).
(5)   Devoicing of word-final obstruents (*bad, dogs,* pronounced as *bat, docs*).
(6)   Stop insertion after the velar nasal (*'ing'* in *bring, sitting* pronounced as [ɪŋk]).

(7)   Lack of aspiration (in *pen, team, come*).
(8)   Replacing the glottal fricative (in *house*) with the velar fricative /x/.
(9)   Trilled pronunciation of /r/ whenever it is written (in *dark, door*).
(10) Voice assimilation in obstruent clusters (*a[ps]olutely, foo[db]all*).
(11) Replacing palatoalveolars, e.g. /ʃ/ in (*shoe*), /tʃ/ in *chin* with Polish alveolars.
(12) No syllabic sonorants (in *bottle, cotton*).
(13) Palatalization of consonants before /i:/ and /j/ (in *meet, tea, new*).
(14) No length distinction between long and short vowels.
(15) No distinction between /i:/ (*read*) and /ɪ/ (*rid*), both pronounced as /i/.
(16) No distinction between the vowels /æ/ (*cat*), /e/ (*get*) and schwa (*girl, ago*), all pronounced as P/e/.
(17) No distinction between /a:/ (*cart*) and /ʌ/ (*cut*), both pronounced as P/a/.
(18) No distinction between /ɒ/ (*cot*), and /o:/ (*caught*), both pronounced as P/o/.
(19) No distinction between /ʊ/ (*foot*) and /u:/ (*food*), both pronounced as P[u].
(20) Dipththongs /oɪ/ (*joy*), /aɪ/ (*buy*), /eɪ/ (*take*), /aʊ/ (*now*) and /əʊ/ (*go*) pronounced as /oj/, /aj/, /ej/, /aw/ and /ow/.
(21) The final vowels in *radio,* pronounced as [o] and schwa in *sister* as /e/.
(22) Diphthongs /ɪə/ (*here*), /ʊə/ (*fewer*), /ɛə/ (*chair*), pronounced as /ije/, /uwe/ and /ea/.
(23) Word-final vowel in *America, banana* pronounced as /a/.
(24) No vowel reduction and weak forms.
(25) Rising intonation of 'wh' questions.

As the participants were not professional linguists and either had no or very little training in phonetics, an attempt was made to formulate all the questions in a non-technical fashion, comprehensible to non-specialists. They were illustrated with typical examples of mispronunciations, presented in a simplified phonetic transcription as well as transliteration (whenever possible). The respondents were asked to make judgements concerning the role of individual phonetic features with respect to intelligibility and the Polish accent by circling one of the following answers: *very important, rather important, unimportant* and *no opinion*. Next they were requested to select three features of Polish English pronunciation which they found particularly salient for the issues of intelligibility and accentedness, and to justify their choice. Finally, the participants supplied answers to questions concerning their nationality, their period of teaching English in Poland, types of schools where they work and their ELT qualifications.

The provided answers were subsequently converted into points (*very important* = 2, *rather important* = 1, *unimportant* = 0). The higher the score, the more important a given feature, in the respondents' view, for the issue of intelligibility and accentedness.

Intelligibility

The phonetic features which, according to the participants, most hinder the intelligibility of Polish-accented English and which have been given over 50% (over 30) in points include the following issues which can be regarded as pronunciation priorities for Polish learners:

- spelling pronunciation and mispronunciation of individual words – 89
- no distinction between /iː/ and /i/ – 46
- incorrect placement of word stress – 46
- incorrect pronunciation of the interdental fricatives – 42
- devoicing of word-final obstruents – 38
- no distinction between long and short vowels – 36
- no distinction between the vowels ash, /e/ and schwa – 33

Thus, the absolute winner in this category is spelling pronunciation and mispronunciation of individual words which received almost twice as many points as the remaining issues. Two of the listed features refer to consonants and two to vowel length and quality, with the lack of distinction between /iː/ and /ɪ/ being regarded as a particularly grave error. The incorrect placement of word stress also occupies a high position in this ranking.

The importance of the above phonetic features for the intelligibility of Polish English finds further support in the comments made by many respondents, a representative selection of which is provided below:

- *the difference between the vowels in 'slipping' and 'sleeping' can change meaning significantly;*
- *making no distinctions between different vowels can create confusion between listener and speaker;*
- *when 3 sounds like 'tree' it takes 10 minutes to figure out what the students are saying;*
- *'th' when mispronounced drives me nuts since I have to work hard to try and figure out what is being said;*
- *word-final devoicing results in confusing homophones;*
- *spelling pronunciation sometimes leads to completely anomalous gibberish;*
- *incorrect stress in words throws the listener off and makes him concentrate much more on figuring out what is being said;*
- *these features affect comprehension and hinder communication;*
- *they cause breakdown in interaction.*

Observe that many comments refer not so much to the impossibility of understanding mispronounced items (many of which can be disambiguated by the context in which they are used), but to the resulting confusion and delay in processing a given piece of information. As stated by several teachers, some types of phonetic errors require much concentration on the part of the listener and considerable effort to understand a Polish speaker of English.

The aspects of Polish English which received between 20 and 30 points, and can therefore be regarded as less important for intelligibility, are provided below:

- no distinctions between the vowels /a:/ and /ʌ/, /o/ and /o:/, /ʊ/ and /u:/ – 27–29
- stop insertion after the velar nasal – 25
- lack of aspiration – 24
- rising intonation of 'wh' questions – 23
- mispronunciation of closing diphthongs – 22

The remaining features were regarded as irrelevant for intelligibility and were either not indicated by the respondents or only by a few of them. This means that of 25 properties of Polish English less than half were mentioned in this category.

Accentedness

An important goal for more advanced learners of another language is to suppress those elements of their pronunciation which create the effect of a heavy foreign accent and which, in consequence, might hinder successful communication. As argued by Kenworthy (1987: 3–4): 'if the person pronounces in such a way that we have to constantly ask for repetitions, then at some stage we reach our threshold of tolerance. We become irritated, and maybe resentful of the effort that is being required of us. (...) We expect conversations with non-native speakers to be "comfortable".' In other words, heavily accented speech might be intelligible, but it may cause listeners irritation.

According to the respondents the features which contribute most to the Polish accent in English, with the scores above 50% (above 30 points), are listed below:

- spelling pronunciation and mispronunciation of individual words – 72
- mispronunciation of the interdental fricatives – 61
- word-final devoicing of obstruents – 39
- incorrect placement of word stress – 37
- no distinction between between /ɪ/ and /iː/ – 36
- trilled pronunciation of /r/ whenever it is written – 36
- stop insertion after angma – 34

As in the previous error ranking, spelling pronunciation and mispronunciation of individual words occupies the top position. The remaining features refer mostly to the realization of consonants (four out of seven), one to vowels and one to prosody.

The accent-revealing features which scored between 30 and 20 points are the following:

- voice assimilation in obstruent clusters – 28
- no distinction between long and short vowels – 27
- no distinction between /ɒ/ and /oː/ – 26
- no distinction between /ʌ/ and /aː/ – 24
- no distinction between /ʊ/ and /uː/ – 23
- mispronunciation of closing diphthongs – 23
- mispronunciation of palatoalveolars – 23
- mispronunciation of final vowels – 22
- pronouncing /h/ as a velar fricative – 21

The above list includes mostly features which pertain to vowels (six out of eight) and only two which concern consonants. These results suggest that, in assessing the degree of accentedness of Polish English, native speakers pay attention to the quality of some consonants in the first place and only then to the pronunciation of vowels. The remaining features are considered less significant in their contribution to the Polish accent. It should also be pointed out that more properties of Polish English were provided by the respondents as indicators of a Polish accent than as hindering the intelligibility of accented speech.

Intelligibility versus accentedness

Although distinguishing between the features responsible for intelligibility and foreign accent is not always easy, it is fairly obvious that these are two interrelated but distinct issues. This means that while incomprehensibility results mainly from a foreign accent, the opposite is not always true. As observed by Kenworthy (1987: 123):

> there are features, which, although they may contribute to a very noticeable foreign accent, will usually not lead to intelligibility problems because:
>
> (1) native listeners are generally used to these features of foreign accents, or
> (2) there are regional accents or varieties of English that use the particular feature so it is familiar to English ears, or
> (3) the feature is 'close enough' to the native feature, or
> (4) relatively few words are kept apart by the feature or sound.

Let us examine the relationship between the two aspects of Polish-accented English in terms of the phonetic features that are most salient for

Table 2.10 Comparison of phonetic features of Polish English relevant for intelligibility and accentedness

	Intelligibility	*Accentedness*
1	**Spelling pronunciation and mispronunciation of individual words – 89**	**Spelling pronunciation and mispronunciation of individual words – 72**
2	**No distinction between /iː/ and /ɪ/ – 46**	**Mispronunciation of 'th' – 61**
3	**Incorrect word stress – 46**	**Word-final devoicing of obstruents – 39**
4	**Mispronunciation of 'th' – 42**	**Incorrect word stress – 37**
5	**Word-final devoicing of obstruents – 38**	**No distinction between /iː/ and /i/ – 36**
6	**No distinction between long and short vowels – 36**	Trilled pronunciation of /r/ – 36
7	No distinction between /æ/, /e/, /ǝ/, /ɜː/ – 33	**Stop insertion after angma – 34**
8	**No distinction between /ʌ/ & /aː/, /o/ & /oː/, /u/ & /uː/ – 28**	Voice assimilation of obstruent clusters – 28
9	**Stop insertion after angma – 25**	**No distinction between long and short vowels – 27**
10	Lack of aspiration – 24	**No distinction between /ʌ/ & /aː/, /ʊ/ & /uː/ /ɒ/ and /oː/, 23–26**

them. Table 2.10 juxtaposes the ranking of 10 phonetic features with the highest scores in both categories. The number of points indicates how strongly the respondents feel about the importance of a particular factor.

It is striking that among the 10 features which received the highest scores in both categories, as many as eight can be found in the two columns, which means that they are viewed by the respondents as important for accentedness and intelligibility. Consequently, they should be regarded as pronunciation priorities for Polish learners of English. Spelling pronunciation and local errors appear at the top of both lists, which provides further support for the experimental results presented in Section B.2.1 and for the need to focus on word pronunciation as well as spelling and sound correspondences as advocated in this chapter. According to the presented rankings, stress errors occupy a prominent position as contributing significantly to the issues under consideration, which confirms our reasoning concerning the importance of misstressed words voiced earlier. Three consonantal properties found in both rankings involve the mispronunciation of the dental fricatives, stop insertion after the velar nasal and word-final devoicing of obstruents. It should be pointed out that the first two features can be found in many native varieties of English, yet in spite of this fact they are serious irritants for native listeners. The respondents are also bothered by the lack of qualitative and qualitative distinctions between the vowel pairs in Polish English.

There are, however, some differences between the two rankings as well, mainly concerning the importance given to various features. Mispronunciation of the interdental fricatives is considered indicative of the Polish accent (61 points), but as less relevant for intelligibility (42 points). The participants also agree that although a trilled articulation and spelling-based distribution of /r/ identifies Poles (36 points), it is not essential for understanding them (18 points). On the other hand, the lack of aspiration is considered more relevant for comprehension (24 points) than for accent detection (13 points). The same holds true of qualitative and quantitative distinctions among vowels, voice assimilation in obstruent clusters and stop insertion after the velar nasal.

Several issues have been considered equally (ir)relevant for comprehension and accentedness, i.e. devoicing of word-final obstruents (38 and 39 points, respectively), no qualitative distinctions between vowels (33 and 31), mispronunciation of English diphthongs (22 and 23) and no syllabic consonants (17 and 18).

Let us now present the joint scores of several top-ranked features in both categories.

- spelling pronunciation and mispronunciation of individual words – 161
- mispronunciation of the interdental fricatives – 103
- no distinction between [ɪ] and [i:] – 84
- incorrect placement of word stress – 83
- devoicing of word-final obstruents – 77
- no distinction between long and short vowels – 64
- stop insertion after angma – 61

If the goal of phonetic instruction is comfortable intelligibility, then the above aspects of English phonetics must be given priority in teaching pronunciation to Polish learners. Observe that the top position of spelling pronunciation and mispronunciation of individual words fully supports our claims in Part A that phonetically difficult words as well as spelling-induced errors deserve particular attention in EFL phonodidactics. Interestingly, two features, i.e. mispronunciations of the interdental fricatives and stop insertion after angma, frequently found in native English varieties, have been harshly evaluated by the native judges. Apparently, what is acceptable in native speech might be annoying in foreigners' mouths.

Notes

(1) According to Derwing and Munro (2005: 389), 'relying on experiences and intuitions sometimes serves teachers well. (...) However, expecting teachers to rely solely on intuition is unrealistic and unfair.'

(2)   This is known as the Interlanguage Speech Intelligibility Benefit, which refers to the intelligibility advantage of L2 learners over native listeners in comprehending speakers of their own L1.

(3)   This is not to say, of course, that teachers should not decide about pronunciation priorities for specific learners and in concrete situations.

(4)   One of the problems with reported stories, as argued by Hahn and Watts (2011), is the lack of recordings which would allow for an exact description of a mispronunciation.

(5)   A frequently quoted example of communication breakdown provided by Jenkins (2000) concerns the /r/ – /l/ distinction. A speaker pronounced the phrase *red cars* as *let cars*, which the listener took to mean 'cars to hire'. Clearly, apart from the mispronunciation of /r/ as /l/, a decisive factor was the existence of the minimal pair *red – let* as well as the meaning of the verb *let*.

(6)   Native speakers' adjustment of speech in terms of pitch, intensity and rhythm to noisy conditions is known as the Lombard Effect.

(7)   Munro (2011: 12) claims that: 'In general older listeners have greater difficulty than younger listeners at understanding an accent other than their own. While the effect may be partly due to hearing loss, central processes in speech perception deteriorate with age. As a result, geriatric listeners have a harder time processing speech in general, and a novel accent may become particularly challenging.'

(8)   Frequently a distinction is made between intelligibility (understanding of individual words) and comprehensibility (understanding the meaning of the whole utterance). According to Field (2005: 400), 'intelligibility is measured by the ability of judges to transcribe the actual words of an utterance, comprehensibility by an overall rating of how easy it is to understand a given speaker'.

(9)   Preserving native articulatory setting is not a priority, but is considered to be of some importance in the LFC. The question that arises is which setting it should be as it is not the same for all English accents.

(10)   In the phonemic transcription of Polish words the symbols /š, ž, č, dž/ represent postalveolar obstruents and depart from the IPA notation with the symbols /ʃ, ʒ.tʃ,ʤ/, which wrongly suggests that the two sets of consonants are identical. Raised ⁱ marks the palatalization of the preceding consonant.

(11)   As a matter of fact, the Polish front mid-vowel is half-open and should be transcribed as [ɛ]. We use here the symbol /e/ as it corresponds to the vowel letter found in spelling.

(12)   In more recent versions of the LFC, for example the one found in Walker (2011), there is no mention of the need to preserve the glottal fricative or the long schwa.

(13)   Moreover, a distinction is usually made between phonetic features which need to be learnt receptively, but not productively. Generally, all authors who postulate a limited set of phonetic features for foreign learners' pronunciation also maintain that it must be complemented with auditory training, necessary for understanding native speakers. Other researchers, however, point to the mutual relationship between these two skills. Trudgill (2005) claims that learners who cannot make certain phonemic distinctions will have greater difficulty in perceiving them.

(14)   An interesting attempt at measuring the phonetic difficulty of English words for Polish learners has been made by Sobkowiak (2004), who proposes a Phonetic Difficulty Index, which is a numerical measure of the pronunciation difficulty of lexical items.

(15)   I am grateful to Darek Bukowski for preparing the recording.

(16)   The problems discussed here concern those EFL students who use the Latin alphabet in their L1. Learners who employ other writing systems face different difficulties. For instance, in the case of analphabetic writing (e.g. Chinese, Japanese) the major issue is the division of speech into phonemes.

(17)   In many cases it is difficult to establish which language a given word was directly borrowed from.

(18) For example, Mańczak-Wohlfeld's (2010) dictionary of recent loanwords from English into Polish contains 2000 items.

(19) It appears that word length alone is not always a predictor of pronunciation difficulty, as frequently items of the same length are problematic to a different degree. Their other phonetic properties are of relevance here as well as their morphological transparency.

(20) An important difference between changes in connected speech and prosodic phenomena should be noted. While both operate when words are combined into phrases and sentences, connected speech processes, such as linking, assimilations and elisions, concern changes in the segmental aspects of utterances and differ strikingly from suprasegmental issues such as stress, rhythm and intonation which refer to the prosodic, i.e. non-segmental properties of speech. For this reason it might be advisable to regard the former as part of segmental phonetics and the latter as genuine prosodic phenomena.

(21) The amount of spoken input in an EFL classroom is usually very limited as teachers often use their own and their learners' native language rather than English.

(22) The number of spelling-induced mispronunciations discussed here depends on various learner-related factors (e.g. learners' level of proficiency, their phonetic coding ability, length of study), the learning context (according to Bassetti (2008) instructed learners may be more affected than uninstructed learners) and the teaching methods (e.g. the use of written materials versus spoken input, the amount of phonetic instruction and attention attached by the teacher to pronunciation accuracy).

(23) Sometimes the opposite is also true, i.e. <o> is pronounced as P[ow], e.g. in *glove, above, shone.*

(24) Apart from these two radical and opposing views, attempts have been made at a compromise as various pronunciation specialists came to the conclusion that a balanced treatment of segmentals and suprasegmentals should be advocated.

(25) The following course books have been examined: *New Headway, Matters, Lifelines, Reward, Wavelength, Inside Out, Go/Go for Poland, Blueprint, Choice, Prospects, Opportunities, English File, New Streetwise, Snapshot, Distinction, Cutting Edge, Open Doors, The New Cambridge English Course, Enterprise, Landmark.* It should be added that all these titles comprise several parts, all of which were included in the analysis.

(26) The list has been prepared by the author and her collaborators as part of a paper presented at the Phonetics Teaching and Learning Conference in Wąsosze in 2006.

(27) This might be particularly problematic in communicative situations involving both native and non-native speakers.

(28) Lists of phonetic problems encountered by EFL learners, such as those provided by Swan and Smith (2001), are insufficient as they fail to indicate those properties of accented speech which affect intelligibility most and should be prioritized in phonodicatic instruction.

(29) Gilbert does not provide any empirical support for her proposal so it is not clear how the list of her priorities has been compiled.

(30) Scheuer's study included four features, Gonet and Pietroń (2004) included 10, Szpyra-Kozłowska (2004) included 24 and Bryła-Cruz (2013) included 20. The first two sources were concerned with defining the major perceptual properties of Polish-accented English. Only the latter two authors dealt with selected prosodic features (stress, rhythm, intonation, fluency) and examined their impact on perceived intelligibility, accentedness and annoyance.

(31) In Polish vowel length is not significantly affected by the following consonants (Rojczyk, 2010), so word-final obstruents devoicing has the serious consequences of making pairs of words such as *kot* 'cat' and *kod* 'code' homophonous.

(32) Majer (2002) in his study on phonetic error gravity also points to the importance of proper word stress.

(33) It should be pointed out, however, that in the studies under consideration segmental issues were given more attention than prosodic aspects, mainly because of the difficulty of examining the impact of suprasegmental inaccuracies.

(34) The following options to choose from were provided: Question 1 – very easy to understand (1 point), rather easy to understand (2), rather difficult to understand (3), very difficult to understand (4); Question 2 – slight foreign accent (1), medium foreign accent (2), rather strong foreign accent (3), very strong foreign accent (4); Question 3 – not irritating at all (1), somewhat irritating (2), rather irritating (3), very irritating (4).

(35) I am very grateful to Graz Kalenik for her help in carrying out this part of the experiment.

(36) They attend a private secondary school in Lublin. The school in which the study took place attaches much importance to teaching foreign languages, including their pronunciation. The pupils have six English lessons a week in groups of 10–15.

(37) The readers will probably notice that the features of Polish English subject to evaluation concern mostly segmental issues. Prosodic aspects, represented by word stress and the intonation of questions, are less numerous, mainly due to the difficulty of providing brief non-technical explanations to teachers with little knowledge of phonetics.

(38) Interestingly, in an experimental study carried out with Finnish students of English by Lintunen (2013) and modeled after Szpyra-Kozłowska (2011) similar sources of phonetic word difficulty have been identified. They include the presence of two liquids in one word, word length and stress.

3 Pronunciation Inside and Outside the Classroom: A Holistic Multimodal Approach

So far we have been concerned with the issue of what should be taught to EFL learners in terms of selecting an appropriate phonetic model (Chapter 1) and establishing pronunciation priorities (Chapter 2). Such considerations would not be complete, however, without a discussion about how these goals could be accomplished. Therefore, this chapter is devoted to the major aspects of effective instructional procedures that should be adopted in the language classroom as well as outside it. In other words, we shall focus on the question of how to teach English pronunciation in a way that is both effective and at the same time attractive, which is both learner friendly and teacher friendly. While the major principles and techniques of phonetic instruction are similar for all L2 learners, in EFL contexts, because of their specificity, some of them take priority over the others. Thus, as elsewhere in this book, we shall deal with the needs of EFL students and the selection of the procedures most appropriate for them.

We employ here what can be dubbed a multimodal approach, according to which pronunciation teaching and learning should involve the development of appropriate motor habits needed in sound perception and production, work on the formation of the L2's sound system in the learner's mind and appeal to multisensory speech perception and processing. In what follows we are going to argue that effective pronunciation instruction should be holistic and should develop in learners, to use Dalton and Seidlhofer's (1994) terms, 'sounds in the body' and 'sounds in the mind'. While individual elements present in this approach are well known and have been postulated separately in various publications on English phonodidactics, it is an attempt to develop and integrate them into a coherent method to be applied in EFL phonetic training that is novel.

Before the relevant details of pronunciation instruction are considered, first addressed are some preliminary but important issues, such as developing learners' concern for good pronunciation, and suggest various ways in which it can be done. Next, in Section A.3.2 the major assumptions and principles which underlie the holistic motor-cognitive multimodal approach advocated here are presented and its four main components are introduced. First, the focus is on articulatory training, necessary for motor habit formation. Then we proceed to discuss auditory training which must accompany pronunciation practice. Section A.3.2.3 deals with the role of explicit phonetic and phonological instruction as an important part of learners' cognitive training, aimed to foster their understanding of how L1 and L2 sound systems work and how interference between them affects students' phonetic performance in their L2. Section A.3.2.4 is devoted to the use of multisensory reinforcements in the acquisition of L2 phonetics. It is followed by the presentation and discussion of selected types of pronunciation teaching techniques that are particularly useful for EFL learners. In Section A.3.4 we point to the necessity of pronunciation learning outside the classroom and developing students' autonomy. Section A.3.5 is concerned with providing feedback on learners' phonetic performance, with the focus on the correction of pronunciation errors. Finally, Section A.3.6 takes up some problematic aspects of pronunciation teaching materials addressed to international learners of English.

As usual, also in this chapter much importance is attached to the empirical verification of various theoretical claims. Thus, in Part B we summarize several experimental studies devoted to examining the effectiveness and attractiveness of selected pronunciation teaching techniques presented in Part A, such as, for example, using phonetic drills, articulatory descriptions, phonemic transcription, comparison of L1 and L2 phonetic systems, songs, poems and elements of drama as well as employing error correction.

Part A

A.3.1 Developing Concern for Good Pronunciation

In order to teach English pronunciation effectively, teachers must convince their students that this is an important aspect of language without which successful communication is not possible. To put it another way, they must develop in their learners care and concern for good pronunciation. If teachers do not attach sufficient importance to the phonetic training of their students and the quality of their pronunciation, it should come as no surprise that students will also adopt this attitude.

Recall that written tests and language examinations, frequent in EFL settings, contribute significantly to downplaying the role of pronunciation. Moreover, a view common among EFL learners, additionally fostered by the communicative approach to language teaching/learning as well as the concept of ELF discussed in Chapter 1, is that what matters is being able to communicate in English, regardless of the quality of this communication. Such an attitude, however, is fraught with genuine dangers; as argued by Porzuczek *et al.* (2013), if pronunciation training is ignored, after some years of learning English it might turn out that the learner is understood mainly by other students of the same L1 background and hardly anyone else.

There are many different ways in which due care for good pronunciation can be developed in students. First of all, instructors must explain to them why this aspect of language is just as important and worth mastering as grammar and vocabulary. They should also point out various negative consequences of having poor pronunciation (see Section A.1.1). Learners can be invited to take part in the discussion on their perception and evaluation of accented speech. An excellent opportunity is provided by TV appearances of some foreign celebrities who speak the students' L1, usually with a strong accent. Such cases can be discussed in the classroom.

Secondly, as theory should go hand in hand with practice, nothing will convince learners more about the importance of good pronunciation than regular and consistent phonetic training, carried out according to the earlier prepared syllabus. Kelly (2000) observes that pronunciation instruction tends to be done in response to errors which students make in the classroom. While such reactive teaching is necessary (see Section A.3.7 on the importance of error correction), he emphasizes the fact that pronunciation work cannot be restricted to it, but should be planned carefully. If possible, it should be coordinated with the phonetic sections in the chosen course book. We consider it a serious error to omit the pronunciation activities included there as it gives students a clear message that such tasks are unimportant and can be skipped without any significant loss. Ideally, some time (about 10 minutes) should be found for pronunciation practice, if not during every lesson than at least every other or every third lesson.

Contrary to many other specialists, we think that, if students are to attach due importance to pronunciation, from time to time a whole lesson should devoted to it. We do not mean here 45 or 60 minutes of tedious drills. After some drilling, other phonetic activities can also be employed. For example, you could make part of the lesson a 'question and answer' session in which learners are encouraged to ask questions concerning various problematic aspects of English pronunciation and the rest of the group should try to provide, with the teacher's help, answers to them. For example, they can collect words and phrases, the pronunciation of which they are not sure of or which they find particularly difficult and feel they need help with. Students who listen to English songs are usually surprised by some phonetic forms that appear in them and want to have them explained. Such lessons also provide a perfect opportunity to practise the use of pronouncing dictionaries or computer software that deals with pronunciation as well as to introduce English accents other than the variety they are learning. The teacher should also have some games at hand to bring some fun into the class (see Section A.3.4.3 for suggestions).

A good idea is to organize on a regular basis, perhaps once a month, an English Pronunciation Day, in which special attention is paid to pronunciation issues through additional activities, e.g. reciting poems, acting out scenes from plays or films, playing games, singing songs, making posters devoted to some phonetic problems (e.g. commonly mispronounced words), all with the intention of promoting the idea that ENGLISH PRONUNCIATION IS IMPORTANT AND FUN!

The next rule to follow is to pay attention to pronunciation every time an opportunity arises to do so, not only during proper phonetic practice. Take introducing new vocabulary, for instance. As argued in Chapter 2, it is important to learn the proper pronunciation of new items from the very beginning to avoid their incorrect storage in the students' phonetic memory. An excellent way of teaching phonetically difficult words employed by a colleague of mine is to pin up several such items, both in the orthographic and phonemically transcribed form, on a cork board placed in the classroom and called 'the phonetic corner'. Students are encouraged to add their own examples of troublesome words. Teaching various elements of morphology and syntax can also be combined with pronunciation practice. Many books (e.g. Celce-Murcia, 1996; Kelly, 2000; Rogerson-Revell, 2011) show how pronunciation can be integrated with instruction on other aspects of English.

With advanced students I practise what I call 'phonetic alert', that is, paying attention to the pronunciation of English words which appear in various radio and TV commercials and which are often grossly mispronounced. For example, in Poland *Dove* soap was advertised as [douf] and in a KFC commercial there appeared *Colonel* [ko'lonel] *Sanders*. KFC sells *coleslaw* salad which got polonized as [ko'leswaf]. In other commercials some car oil called *Ultimate* is pronounced as ['altimejt] and *surface* in *Surface Protector* is realized as ['serfejs]. A student of mine has recently bought a *Citizen* watch advertised as [ki'tajzen]. And popular Polish chocolate-coated wafers *Prince Polo* are commonly called ['priintse 'polo]. We collect such examples, analyse them and point to the sources of pronunciation errors.

In the English Department where I work, in order to enhance students' care for good pronunciation and their greater involvement in its improvement, we organize yearly English pronunciation competitions. At first, students compete against their colleagues within the same year of study and next the winners compete against each other for the title of the Master of English Pronunciation. English pronouncing dictionaries are given to the best of them as awards. It seems that similar competitions can be organized with any group of learners or between various groups of a similar level of language proficiency. They should be announced well in advance in order to give students plenty of time for preparation.

Other events which promote English pronunciation learning can also be organized. For instance, every year I am invited to be a jury member in a foreign language (i.e. English, German and Russian) poetry reciting competition for the secondary school pupils of the whole region which, in addition to developing young people's interest in poetry, enhances the participants' pronunciation practice as an important element of assessing their performance is pronunciation proficiency. The English language 'Scenes from Shakespeare' festival for secondary schools, which has been held several times in my town, plays a similar role.

Finally, in the school context, the importance attached by students to a given skill substantially depends on the role it plays in the teacher's system of assessment or, simply speaking, in the marks given for it. If pronunciation is not tested and evaluated, just like other aspects of language learners are required to know, it will tend to be ignored by the majority of them. Consequently, if we want our students to put some effort into pronunciation practice, both in the classroom and at home, we should assess it regularly. The issue of providing feedback is addressed in more detail in Section A.3.6.

Apart from developing learners' concern for good pronunciation, phonetic instruction should follow the same didactic rules as the effective teaching of other elements of language; it must be principled (with the major principles specified in this chapter), well planned, i.e. not incidental and only remedial, and long term, that is carried out at various educational stages. Moreover, a recursive approach, in which the training of the same phonetic issues is repeated, should be adopted.

A.3.2 A Holistic Multimodal Approach to Phonetic Training

It is the present author's conviction that, in order to be effective, EFL phonetic training must fulfil several requirements. First, it must be learner centred in that it should cater for the needs and abilities of different students and be suited to their individual learning styles and preferences. Secondly, it should be holistic in the sense of involving not only traditional and commonly employed 'listen and repeat' activities, based mostly on auditory and articulatory skills, but should make use of various channels of perception and information processing. In other words, in holistic pronunciation teaching and learning L2 sounds must not only be heard and imitated as faithfully as possible but, metaphorically speaking, they should also be seen, touched, tasted, smelled, felt, understood and appropriated, emotionally as well as intellectually, by EFL learners. Thus, since 'one size does not fit all', and the effectiveness of pronunciation instruction depends on the type of learner and the type of procedures employed, phonetic training should include various kinds of activities that appeal to as many different modalities as possible.

In this section the above general ideas are developed in greater detail. Four types of phonetic training are discussed: articulatory, auditory, cognitive (phonetic and phonological) and multisensory, all of which should find their way into the pronunciation class. Articulatory and auditory activities should be regarded as basic and indispensable in all cases, whereas cognitive and multisensory training is subsidiary in character. Moreover, we offer numerous suggestions for tasks which can be employed in the course of holistic pronunciation instruction, the majority of which are easy to prepare and carry out in the EFL classroom.

A.3.2.1 Articulatory training

There is no doubt that learning new sounds and sound combinations requires from students the acquisition of new motor skills, i.e. the formation of new articulatory habits. Put simply, the muscles found in our vocal tract, accustomed to producing the sounds of our L1 for years, must be retrained to meet the challenge of articulating different, alien segments.

These assumptions underlie the Audiolingual Method, according to which phonetic drills, involving numerous repetitions of sounds, words and phrases, constitute the most efficient type of exercise for the development of automaticity in pronouncing the L2. In the Communicative Method the use of such mechanical drills has been criticized not only as tedious and boring (often called 'drill and kill'), but also as failing to bring the desired results since correct pronunciation obtained in the course of drilling is not always carried over into communicative situations. Consequently, phonetic drills stopped occupying the prominent position they held during the audiolingual era and have largely been replaced by communicatively oriented pronunciation activities.

It seems, however, that giving up phonetic drills altogether means throwing the baby out with the bathwater as they are necessary in any approach to language teaching and learning. Basically, some amount of drilling is needed for the formation of new motor skills and automaticity without which fluent speech is not possible.

Nevertheless, the use of phonetic drills, in order to be effective, should follow some simple rules. First of all, it cannot be the only type of phonetic activity employed in the classroom as drills to tend to be boring when over-used.[1] Secondly, the teacher should limit the amount of drilling to a few minutes in a single session. In other words, it is less tiring for learners to have frequent, but short drilling sessions. It is also a good idea to explain to them why such exercises are necessary so that they feel motivated to do them. Thirdly, various types of drills should be employed, e.g. using minimal pairs (word-level and sentence-level drills, both paradigmatic and syntagmatic), contextualized minimal pairs, tongue twisters and developmental approximation drills (Celce-Murcia *et al.*, 1996), in order to make drilling less mechanical and more meaningful. As a matter of fact, any newly introduced word or phrase can and should be drilled. Finally, it is essential for drilling to be followed by communicatively oriented activities in which the drilled units are employed in a variety of meaningful contexts. To put this differently, in addition to activities which focus on phonetic form, learners need communicative tasks which focus on content. All the major textbooks on pronunciation instruction (e.g. Celce-Murcia *et al.*, 1996; Rogerson-Revell, 2011) include sections devoted to a communicative approach to pronunciation teaching and suggest many ways in which it can be done.

The latter issue is particularly important since, as noted by Firth (1992: 215):

> One of the most serious problems facing all ESL/EFL instructors who deal with pronunciation is that of 'carry over'. Too frequently, students achieve near-standard versions of segmental articulation, stress patterns, or intonation contours during class time, only to revert to their former non-standard patterns as soon as they leave the classroom.

Communicative pronunciation activities, which focus on meaningful practice and learners' needs in real-life situations, are therefore necessary to foster phonetic 'carry over' (Morley, 1991).

Nevertheless, we consider it harmful to replace phonetic drills and other more traditional forms of phonetic instruction with communicative activities completely, since both are needed as they have different and mutually complementary functions; the former aim at achieving accuracy, the latter, fluency. It seems that good, easily intelligible pronunciation in L2 combines some degree of accuracy with fluency, and fluency is not possible without a considerable automaticity of sound production.

It should also be pointed out that phonetic drills, if not limited to minimal pairs, but extended to other units of language, have yet another advantage apart from motor habit formation. Faithful frequent repetition, which lies at the bottom of drilling, is pivotal for memorizing lexical items and their retention in long-term memory.

Let us take an example. A common spelling-induced error among Polish EFL learners is to pronounce the negative forms *aren't* and *weren't* as bisyllabic words [arent] and [werent]. In order to eliminate such mispronunciations, we can first do a series of drills involving several repetitions of each of the sentences below:

*We **aren't** hungry. You **aren't** hungry. They **aren't** hungry.*
*We **weren't** lazy. You **weren't** lazy. They **weren't** lazy.*

Then the teacher can ask students some questions which should be answered in the negative, e.g.:

Teacher: *Are they hungry?*   **Student:** *No, they* **aren't.**
Teacher: *Were they lazy?*   **Student:** *No, they* **weren't**.

Next students can do the same asking similar questions of each other and providing negative answers. Finally, you can suggest a guessing game of the 'what/who are they?' type, in which negative statements are used, e.g.:

They are African animals. They **aren't** *lions, they* **aren't** *elephants, they* **aren't** *crocodiles. What are they?*
They live in the north of Europe. They **aren't** *Swedes, they* **aren't** *Finns. They* **aren't** *Norwegians. Who are they?*
These are geometrical figures. These **aren't** *squares. These* **aren't** *circles. These* **aren't** *triangles. What are they?*

The teacher can start this game to show how it works and then students can take over and continue with it.

It should be added that various researchers (e.g. Archibald, 1992; Celce-Murcia *et al.*, 1996; Wrembel, 2005b) maintain that pronunciation practice should be preceded by some articulatory warm-up exercises, the function of which is to prepare speech organs for the production of L2 sounds and to teach learners to control them to some extent, similar to those employed by drama coaches. They include, for instance, voice modulation and changing the pitch, volume and rate of speech. Students can also practise repeating some sequences of sounds. Such exercises should relax learners, as relaxation is considered to be an important prerequisite of successful pronunciation practice.

Many pronunciation specialists (e.g. Honikman, 1964; Jenner, 1997; Mompean-Gonzales, 2003) claim that an important part of articulatory training is developing in learners native voice quality or articulatory setting. It refers to the habitual positions of speech organs typical for a given language, and involves 'pitch level, vowel space, neutral tongue position and degree of muscular activity that contribute to the overall sound quality or "accent" associated with the language' (Celce-Murcia *et al.*, 1996: 11). Jenner (1997: 38) defines articulatory setting as 'general features of pronunciation which underlie all the separate sounds of a language and which enable us to recognize speakers as "native" or "non-native", irrespective of the clarity of their pronunciation'. Honikman (1964: 73) argues that, 'where two languages are disparate in articulatory setting, it is not possible completely to master the pronunciation of one whilst maintaining the articulatory setting of another'. In other words, without training in L2 articulatory setting learners will speak this language with a noticeable foreign accent.

Mompean-Gonzales (2003) claims that the issue goes beyond using accented speech and proves empirically that training in L2 articulatory settings brings numerous benefits; it facilitates the correct production of foreign sounds, enhances EFL speakers' intelligibility and helps students to improve the image they project when they speak their L2.

According to Laver (1980), there are three types of articulatory settings: supralaryngeal settings, which involve habitual tongue and jaw position, lip shape (spreading or rounding, degree of protrusion) and nasality (the habitual position of the soft palate), laryngeal settings, which determine types of phonation, i.e. whether the voice is whispery, creaky, neutral or falsetto, and overall muscular tension and range settings (which concern the extent of articulatory movements). All these settings may differ not only from language to language, but also from one language variety to another. For example, the so-called 'nasal twang' characterizes some accents of American English, but is generally absent in British English.

In order to make phonodidactic use of articulatory settings, it is necessary to compare those of the L1 and L2. As an example, Table 3.1 provides such a comparison of Polish and English, presented in Święciński (2006). This table demonstrates that the two languages differ with regard to phonation, laryngeal (longitudinal, mandibular and velopharyngeal) settings, the position of the tongue tip and tongue root as well as supralaryngeal and laryngeal tension, but also in the mandibular and lingual ranges. In view of these differences, it should come as no surprise that acquiring a genuine English accent for Poles and native-like Polish pronunciation for native speakers of English is an extremely difficult task.

According to Święciński (2004: 148), Poles wishing to adopt the English articulatory setting should practise, among other things, the following:

- to lower the larynx;
- to limit the movements of the jaw;
- to switch from articulating English alveolars with the blade of the tongue in the post-dental region to apical articulations in the alveolar region;
- to keep the tongue root in the neutral (non-advanced) position;
- to decrease laryngeal and supralaryngeal muscular tension;
- to decrease the range of lingual movements.

An important question concerns the teachability/learnability of the articulatory setting of another language, that is, whether it is possible to switch to a different setting when we speak another language, the way it is done by bilingual speakers. Various authors maintain that it is, in fact, not as difficult as it seems. Mompean-Gonzales (2003), for instance, carried out such training with a group of Spanish learners and demonstrated that after it they had better English pronunciation, a more native-like accent and a less strong foreign accent.

Table 3.1 Comparison of Polish and English articulatory settings

Setting	Polish	English
1	Phonatory	Modal	Breathy
2	Laryngeal – longitudinal	Raised	Neutral or lowered
3	Labial – longitudinal	Slight protrusion	Slight protrusion
4	Labial – cross-sectional	Slight spreading and rounding	Slight spreading and rounding
5	Mandibular	Slightly open	Loosely closed
6	Lingual tip/blade	Advanced setting	Retracted setting – tip as the main articulator
7	Lingual body	Advanced and heightened	Advanced and heightened
8	Lingual root	Advanced	Neutral
9	Velopharyngeal	Slight nasalization	Moderate nasalization
10	Supralaryngeal tension	Slightly tense	Lax
11	Laryngeal tension	Slightly tense	Lax – causing whisperiness
12	Labial range	Narrow	Narrow
13	Mandibular range	Wide	Narrow
14	Lingual range	Wide	Narrow

Source: After Święciński (2006: 205).

As far as Poles' learning of the English articulatory setting is concerned, an interesting experiment was carried out by Święciński (2006), who made an attempt to teach a group of 15 students to use breathy phonation (as shown in Table 3.1, Polish is characterized by modal phonation). For two months the participants were trained in various elements of the English articulatory setting, with particular emphasis on breathy phonation and reduced supralaryngeal and laryngeal tension. Next an acoustic analysis of pre-test and post-test recordings was done which showed that in the former case all students except for one used typically Polish modal and tense phonation, but after the training period as many as 13 out of 15 subjects changed 'the adopted phonation type towards a more relaxed and breathier voicing. In the control group, however, no such change has taken place' (Święciński, 2006: 212). Thus, the study under discussion has demonstrated that it is possible to teach the English breathy phonation to Polish learners within a brief period of two months.[2]

It is interesting to examine what types of activities were employed by Święciński (2006: 207) in his experiment. They included:

> quiet, relaxed, preferably initially whispered pronunciation of phrases, using a 'yawning' voice when counting in English and later in the pronunciation of longer phrases, pronouncing long vowels in sentences in a relaxed gliding manner with the exaggeration of their length, or pronouncing some phrases in a 'sexy' voice which is associated with breathiness.

Many useful suggestions as to the teaching of various elements of English articulatory settings to speakers of other languages can be found in Collins and Mees (1995), Jenner (1997), Jones and Evans (1995) and Mompean-Gonzales (2003). These authors also argue that training in articulatory settings should occupy an important and even privileged place in pronunciation teaching.

A.3.2.2 Auditory training

As argued in Chapter 1, one of the major differences between EFL and ESL language learning lies in the fact that in the latter case after leaving the classroom the learner continues to hear the L2 in the street, shops and buses while in an EFL context this is not possible and the classroom frequently constitutes the only place in which the student is exposed to English. What is more, it is exposure to the non-native English of the language teacher and other learners rather than authentic English speech. While this might be sufficient at the early stages of learning an L2, it is clearly not at more advanced levels.

An important principle of EFL students' pronunciation training should therefore be the **maximization of phonetic input**, by which we mean surrounding or even bombarding them with sounds of English both in the classroom and outside it in an attempt to imitate at least partially the conditions of ESL learning.[3] To put it differently, effective phonetic training requires learners' immersion in the world of English sounds.

Thus, starting as early as possible, students should be exposed to English recordings, first of single words and word pairs, then of phrases, sentences and, finally, of longer utterances or conversations. The teacher should also introduce an obligatory type of homework in which learners listen to the recordings that accompany the material studied in the class. When they are not available, instructors can prepare their own recordings for students to listen to with, for instance, new vocabulary items. With learners of a higher level of proficiency, more complex auditory input should be employed, first based on the variety selected as the pronunciation model and next including different English accents.

Auditory training serves several purposes. First of all, it is needed to foster sound discrimination as, according to a frequently voiced claim, learners are unable to produce a sound contrast they cannot hear. This point is generally well understood, as evidenced in numerous phonetic materials which contain various tasks involving sound discrimination.

Secondly, and this issue should be pointed out emphatically, auditory training should involve noticing tasks, i.e. listening to some spoken texts not with the purpose of listening comprehension, but in order for learners to notice particular pronunciation features of spoken English (analytic listening). In such activities the focus is on form rather than content, which means that they belong, in fact, to cognitive training as discussed in the next section. For example, a short recording of two or three sentences can be played and analyzed in the classroom with respect to the pronunciation of fortis plosives. Learners with an L1 like Polish which lacks aspiration will notice that English /p, t, k/ are pronounced with what is heard as more emphasis and this observation can constitute an excellent starting point for productive exercises on English plosives. The same can be done with regard to other phonetic features, particularly changes in connected speech which are a frequent source of miscomprehension (Nowacka, 2008).

Nevertheless, noticing tasks, in spite of their evident usefulness, are infrequently employed as they require language instructors to possess some theoretical knowledge not only of the English sound system, but also of learners' L1 which, in the case of multilingual classes, is impossible. It is less problematic, however, in an EFL context, in which teachers should be prepared to carry out such exercises.

A very useful type of activity is to get students to listen to a recording of a native English speaker using their language and then analyse their pronunciation in terms of foreign-sounding features. For instance, I did it with my students who listened to a recording by an Englishman speaking Polish and were asked to observe how he pronounced various Polish sounds. We selected one sentence and the students tried to imitate its English-accented version. A discussion on English-accented Polish followed. Next, they were encouraged to pronounce English sounds just like the recorded speaker did, which resulted in their considerably improved pronunciation.

Finally, the third major purpose of auditory training is developing learners' receptive skills concerning various English accents, both native and non-native, standard and non-standard. As is commonly acknowledged, students who follow one pronunciation model are disadvantaged in communication with speakers of other varieties of English whom they often fail to understand. To alleviate this problem, at a certain point, on achieving an upper intermediate or advanced level of proficiency, learners should be exposed to various speech samples. Clearly, a selection of different social and regional accents should be made by the instructor, who ought to choose those varieties which their students are most likely to encounter in their lives.

While listening to samples of different English accents is undoubtedly very useful, it has been pointed out that an ideal type of activity is listening to the same sentence or several sentences pronounced by various speakers using different accents. In such cases the content of the message is well known and the learner can concentrate on form, i.e. different phonetic shapes of the same utterance. This task can be followed by an analytic activity in which students are asked to notice a given speaker's specific pronunciation features, that is, those which depart from the model adopted in the classroom. Once such properties are identified, they should be discussed in reference to accentual varieties of English. Alternatively, this can be done in pairs or groups who get different speech samples to analyze and compare with the model. Advanced students can be encouraged to find information about a selected English accent as their homework to be later presented in the classroom.

If possible, a good idea is to invite some students from various countries to the class and ask them to deliver short speeches in English about their countries of origin, cultural differences, etc. and then encourage a general discussion. In this way, students can experience natural exposure to non-native English accents, practise communication in English with non-native speakers and can notice their particular pronunciation features which can later be discussed in the classroom.

A comment is in order on the relationship between perception and production. While there is no doubt that the former affects the latter since, as argued by Leather and James (1991), well-formed perceptual targets are necessary for productive success, it is also claimed (e.g. Ur, 1984) that production aids perception in that if learners can produce sounds accurately, they can hear them correctly. If this is indeed the case, articulatory and auditory training complement each other and should both be employed.

A.3.2.3 Cognitive phonetic and phonological training

While motor and auditory training constitutes the core of adequate pronunciation instruction and is often the only approach employed by many teachers, in this section we shall argue that it should be complemented with selected elements of cognitive training so that foreign sounds remain not only in the body, but also in the mind. It involves explicit instruction, the purpose of which is for learners to get some basic understanding of the working of the phonetics and phonology of both their L1 and L2 in order for them to better internalize this knowledge and to enhance their pronunciation learning. For instance, with regard to phonetics, students can be told in a simplified and easily accessible fashion how some sounds are articulated, how foreign sounds differ from those of the L1 and how these differences affect their pronunciation of the L2. With respect to phonology, they can, for example, get acquainted with the major phonotactic constraints of the L2, compare them with those of the L1 and study the impact of the observed differences on their phonetic performance in the L2. In other words, we promote conscious pronunciation learning and agree with Fraser (2006: 4), who argues that 'pronunciation is a cognitive skill ... [which] involves both "knowing" things about language and being able to do things physically with the body'. Also Moyer (2013: 3) maintains that 'phonology is unique compared to other language realms because it relies on both motor-based and cognitive skills for perception and production'. Meaningful learning which occurs when learners actively interpret their experience using cognitive operations has been proved to be superior, particularly in the case of adults, to rote learning which is based on memorization without full understanding of the material to be mastered.

In what follows we isolate and discuss two types of cognitively based procedures which are claimed to foster the acquisition of an L2 sound system: understanding the basics of the articulatory phonetics of the L2 and L1, and understanding the basics of the phonology of the L1 and L2,[4] which can also be referred to as developing learners' phonetic metacompetence and raising their phonological awareness.[5] According to Wrembel (2005b: 2), who discusses these issues under the heading of phonological metacompetence, explicit theoretical training plays a major role in enhancing L2 pronunciation learning in adults:

> Phonological metacompetence is postulated as a major facilitating device capable of enhancing the process of acquisition in a threefold manner as:
> (1) facilitator of intake – operating at the level of perception and helping input to become conscious intake through formal explicit instruction and guided ear training;
> (2) acquisition facilitator – forming adequate representations and preventing the mapping into the L1 system owing to the conscious analysis of the underlying process;

(3)   monitoring device – providing reflective feedback on the production by equipping L2 learners with necessary tools for self-monitoring and self-correction as well as promoting conscious awareness of the influencing potential of socio- and psychological factors.

A.3.2.3.1 Understanding the basics of L1 and L2 articulatory phonetics

Developing learners' basic understanding of the articulatory phonetics of the L1 and L2 consists of providing them with selected explicit information on the articulation of sounds in the L1 and L2, comparing sounds and prosodies in both languages (contrastive analysis), and discussing the major aspects of phonetic interference from the L1 on the L2. It includes presenting and explaining to students, for example, simplified articulatory descriptions of sounds and sound production, preferably with different kinds of speech visualization (e.g. head cross-sections, animations of speech organ movements, video close-ups of the mouth) as well as supplying them with theoretical knowledge about various prosodic aspects of the L1 and L2, for instance, drawing intonation contours of sentences and explaining the stress patterns of English words and phrases. Contrastive information is particularly important in helping learners to understand phonetic similarities and differences between two languages, which provides the necessary background for discussing various aspects of phonetic interference. In brief, this kind of training is meant to equip students with elementary theoretical knowledge of L1 and L2 phonetics, to be employed not to replace, but to supplement the intuitive-imitative techniques discussed in the preceding sections.

Evidently, this approach is fairly demanding of teachers as it requires some solid theoretical phonetic knowledge on their part, both of the L1 and L2. In this respect non-native instructors who share an L1 with learners have a clear advantage over native teachers due to two factors. First of all, as pointed out in Chapter 1, in EFL contexts language teachers are generally obliged to receive a college or university education which usually includes mandatory courses in English descriptive articulatory phonetics and phonetic interference. This means that they are (or at least should be) equipped with some knowledge of L1 and L2 sound systems, and can apply it to providing some necessary explanations to students. Secondly, as speakers of the same L1 and former learners of the L2, they know very well which aspects of English pronunciation are particularly problematic and how to overcome these difficulties. Native teachers who do not possess such knowledge and learning experience are thus disadvantaged in this regard.

It is important to add that mere familiarity with the rudiments of English articulatory phonetics without some knowledge of the learners' L1 sound system is insufficient, since the former allows instructors to describe what the target sounds should be like without, however, enabling them to understand properly the source of the students' pronunciation difficulties (no contrastive information). In other words, an illness can be successfully cured only when it is diagnosed accurately. For instance, Polish learners of English commonly mispronounce the English palatoalveolars (/ʃ, ʒ tʃ, ʤ/) by replacing them with Polish postalveolars and thus making them too hard, which is somewhat paradoxical as Polish abounds in soft consonants which Poles have no problem articulating. Thus, apart from the hard alveolar obstruent series, Polish contains soft prepalatal consonants. English palataoalveolars share with the former the position of the tip and the blade of the tongue, and with the latter the position of the front of the tongue which is raised towards the hard palate. To pronounce palatoalveolars correctly, Poles need to be told to make them softer than postalveolars, but a bit harder than prepalatals. Good results are yielded when they hear all three series of consonants, i.e. Polish postalveolars, English palatoalveolars and Polish prepalatals, and are asked to repeat all of them, as it makes students realize that that the quality of English consonants is intermediate between the two series of Polish segments. Evidently, explanations of this kind can only be provided by an instructor who is familiar with both sound systems and not only with the target language and who can pronounce all the sounds in question. Moreover, even basic information concerning the articulation of sounds, difficult to understand by anyone without training in theoretical phonetics, is much easier to absorb when it is provided in the learners' native language since only advanced students have sufficient command of English to be able to comprehend simple articulatory descriptions in this language (for more on this, see Section A.3.7).

For the reasons stated above it seems that the head cross-sections provided in many books on English pronunciation as well as in computer programs designed to visualize the articulation of English sound pronunciation are of a very limited usefulness to the majority of learners since they are too abstract, make frequent reference to movements of speech organs over which they have little or no control, and contain no contrastive information relating L2 sounds to those of the students' L1. Consequently, without proper and meaningful explanation such phonodidactic aids might discourage rather than encourage many learners.

It is evident that the approach which includes the development of phonetic metacompetence is not suitable for all learners as it depends on two factors: their age and learning style. It seems that children should only be given practice in listening and repeating as theoretical explanations are too difficult for them and are not likely to be of much use to them, except for the simplest ones, presented in a play-like fashion. Adults, however, whose cognitive skills are fully developed, are claimed to benefit much from explicit theoretical instruction and usually feel more confident when they understand what they are doing and are not only required to parrot what they hear. The same appears to hold true in the case of teenagers, who can follow rudimentary explanations without any problems and who, as frequently learners of more than one foreign language, generally show much curiosity about the working of other language systems. According to Gut (2009), more advanced learners profit more from theoretical training than beginners and show more improvement in production.

Moreover, what matters in the case of developing phonetic metacompetence is an individual's learning style, with some students preferring inductive and others deductive learning. Thus, some people learn through absorbing a set of data and formulating unconscious generalizations based on them while others, faced with raw data, feel lost and regain language confidence when they are provided with some rules and principles which allow them to control the material to be acquired. Take, for example, the pronunciation of the (regular) English inflectional endings, i.e. the plural ending, the third person singular present tense suffix, the Saxon genitive suffix and the past tense ending. For some learners, the rules concerning the distribution of the appropriate allomorphs are not necessary as sufficient exposure to a variety of inflected forms allows them to draw the correct conclusions and attach proper endings to nouns and verbs. Others will not be able to do that on their own and will require explicitly formulated rules of allomorph distribution to apply them in their speech.

As in a given group there are probably learners of both types, the question that arises concerns the approach to be adopted. On the one hand, learning specialists assure us that uncovering regularities within a set of data is an important aspect of human creativity and that knowledge based on it is more profound than ready-made rules supplied by the teacher or a book. On the other hand, many learners feel more comfortable when provided with some useful generalizations. It seems that an effective, though time-consuming, method is to adopt a problem-solving approach whenever possible. Consider the above example involving inflectional endings. Instead of presenting students with the principles governing their phonetic realization, we can ask them to formulate such rules themselves. First they should provide as many examples of, say, plural forms as possible, then group them according to the pronunciation of the ending to finally formulate the required generalization. In this way analytic learners will have a chance to analyse the data and uncover the regularities behind them, while those who work better with rules will get them in the end. It should be added that, of course, not all pronunciation problems can be handled in this way.

Needless to say, theoretical information must be carefully selected (we should not teach all we know) and presented to learners in an accessible way as too much of it or too complex a presentation is counterproductive. This, however, is not an easy task, as is shown in Section A.3.7 in which several phonetic instructions as to how to pronounce English sounds found in books on pronunciation teaching are critically evaluated. It is demonstrated that some of them are very difficult to understand, while others are simple but too imprecise and therefore are impossible to follow.

Finally, it should also be pointed out that knowing how to do something and doing it are two different things. This means that even expert theoretical knowledge of English articulatory phonetics does not guarantee having good pronunciation. As pointed out by Fraser (2006), learners can consciously know the rules of English pronunciation, but still break them when they speak since such rules remain at the conscious level. Is it only when they are filtered down to the unconscious level that they can influence learners' performance, in agreement with the following schema:

perception > conceptualization > articulation

Thus, theoretical knowledge must first be internalized before it can be applied in spontaneous speech.

Moreover, it must be remembered that developing learners' phonetic metacompetence is not the goal of instruction but only a means to achieve the real objective, which is improving their English pronunciation. That it indeed does that has been amply evidenced by various researchers (e.g. Blanco *et al.*, 2001; Dziubalska-Kołaczyk, 2002; Wrembel, 2005a).

A.3.2.3.2 Understanding the basics of L1 and L2 phonology

An important part of cognitive training is raising learners' phonological awareness of English and their native language, particularly of those students who have achieved higher levels of language proficiency. What is meant here is introducing various elements that have traditionally been assigned to the area of phonology and which rarely, if ever, find their way into pronunciation teaching materials. For this reason this issue will be discussed in more detail. As languages often differ considerably in terms of their phonological structure, such differences, due to transfer from L1 to L2, are often responsible for learners' pronunciation errors. Thus, we agree with those scholars who claim that making students aware of various phonological aspects of their L1 and L2 can help them to eliminate many pronunciation problems (see, for example, Dickerson, 1983; Dziubalska-Kołaczyk *et al.*, 2013).

Let us start with phonotactic constraints, which constitute a significant element of the phonological system of every language. Generally speaking, they concern restrictions on the occurrence of individual sounds (segmental constraints) and sound sequences (sequential constraints). They may refer to vowels, consonants and combinations of these segments. As is well known, languages often differ strikingly with respect to their phonotactic constraints, particularly as to allowed and disallowed consonant clusters, which frequently result in pronunciation difficulties.

Below we present selected examples of phonetic errors made by Polish learners of English which are caused by their lack of familiarity with English phonotactic constraints and interference from Polish and which can be largely reduced if the students' attention is drawn to them. Evidently, other learners of English are often faced with the same or similar types of problems as well.

We will start with some restrictions concerning English consonants which have no equivalents in Polish. If RP is taught, a common error consists of pronouncing /r/ whenever it is written since Polish has no such constraint and the rhotic can occur in various contexts. Thus, learners often articulate this consonant not only before vowels, as in (c), but also word-finally, as in (a), and before consonants, as in (b). Pronouncing /r/ in cases such as (a) and (b) also has an impact on the quality of the preceding vowels which become r-coloured.

(a) *car, door, bar, more, floor, fair, hear, sure*
(b) *card, storm, park, flirt, scarf, girl, torn, purple*
(c) *ride, read, very, sorry, roaring, carry, boring*

It is our experience that the problem can be dealt with successfully when students are explicitly provided with a simple phonotactic constraint of RP, namely that /r/ is pronounced only when followed by a vowel, as in (c). Such statements must, of course, be supported by many examples and appropriate pronunciation practice. This approach has the additional advantage of helping to introduce the issue of linking /r/. Advanced learners might also benefit from information concerning rhotic and non-rhotic English accents, with GA and RP being representative and well-known examples.

A similar procedure can be extended to several other English consonants. The glottal fricative is a case in point, sharing with /r/ a restriction on the occurrence in prevocalic contexts, as in (c) below (with the exception of the following palatal glide, e.g. in *huge, humour, Hugh*). As in Polish no such constraint is in operation, learners frequently pronounce <h.> and the <ch> digraph as a (velar) fricative word-finally as in (a), and preconsonantally as in (b), in accordance with Polish spelling-to-pronunciation rules.

(a) *Bach, Czech, Zurich, Munich, stomach*
(b) *technology, technical, chrome, chronic*
(c) *house, hotel, behind, rehearse, prohibit*

Here again, a presentation of the phonotactic constraint concerning the glottal fricative, coupled with the information as to how the letters in question are pronounced and a set of phonetic exercises, can bring the desired results.

The same simple rule is also responsible for the occurrence of English glides which are pronounced only when followed by vowels, as in (c). This restriction is useful for Polish learners who usually articulate closing diphthongs with a very prominent second glide-like element in cases such as those in (a) and (b).

(a) *buy, joy, may, go, now, show, try, toy*
(b) *take, bite, oil, goal, out, oak, write, boil*
(c) *yellow, yoke, yesterday, wish, wonder, water*

Students can also be told that the voiced palatoalveolar fricative [ʒ] in English generally appears word-medially (e.g. in *pleasure, measure, decision*) and in other positions only in borrowings, i.e. finally (e.g. in *massage, mirage, espionage*) and initially (e.g. in *Zhivago, Zhukov, genre*). This information can help them to avoid the erroneous pronunciation of words such as *gel, giraffe, Gerard*, in which Polish learners tend to use a fricative, under the influence of French.

Let us now pass on to the distribution of English vowels and the lack of short vowels different from /ɪ/ and /ə/ in word-final position. In Polish as well as many other languages with a small inventory of vowels and lack of reduction of unstressed vowels, no such restriction can be found. This means that many word-final English vowels are pronounced as Polish vowels, in accordance with the phonetic value given in Polish to the letters <a, o, e, u >, e.g.:

(a)   P /a/ – *Afric**a**, Americ**a**, Coca-Col**a**, pand**a**, Cinderell**a***
(b)   P /u/ – *val**ue**, virt**ue**, Hind**u**, contin**ue**, men**u**, Per**u**, fl**u***
(c)   P /o/ – *radi**o**, pian**o**, stere**o**, vide**o**, jumb**o**, volcan**o**, studi**o***
(d)   P /e/ – (i) *sist**er**, moth**er**, fath**er**, doct**or**, act**or**, direct**or***
             (ii) *clich**e**, attach**e**, blas**e**, caf**e**, pat**e**, fianc**e***

Thus, in Polish English the following vowels are used in the final position: open central in (a), high back rounded in (b), back half-open in (c) and front half open in (d). Learners must be made aware that such vowel segments do not appear in English word-finally and that English deals with them in several different ways; in (a) and (d(i)) the vowel is reduced to schwa and in (b) it is lengthened, while in (c) and (d(ii)) diphthongization takes place.

In all the cases presented above, instead of providing the rules responsible for the (non)occurrence of a segment in specific contexts, a problem-solving approach can be applied. The teacher can present sets of examples in which a given constraint operates and ask students to formulate an appropriate generalization. It should be remembered, however, that this method is effective, but time-consuming.

Also, to familiarize with vowel reduction those learners whose L1 contains no such phenomenon, we might place on the blackboard several transcribed words which contain schwa and ask them to figure out in what types of syllables this vowel can be found , e.g.:

ago [əˈgəʊ]   teacher [ˈtiːtʃə]   monotonous [məˈnɒtənəs]   today [təˈdeɪ]

Once the principle of the occurrence of schwa only in unstressed syllables is established, learners can provide their own examples of words with this vowel. This procedure can also serve as an introduction to the issues of stress/unstress and rhythm in English.

Sequential constraints refer to the restrictions on sound combinations, particularly those pertaining to possible and impossible consonant clusters. Languages differ considerably in this respect. On the one end of the spectrum there are those which either do not allow any consonant clusters and contain only open syllables as well as those with a limited number and type of consonant sequences. Korean, Hawaiian and Japanese are representative examples of such languages. On the other end of the scale there are languages such as Polish, Czech or Georgian, in which many different combinations of consonants are found. English can be claimed to be located between these two extremes. This means that many English consonant clusters will pose great difficulty to students whose L1 does not allow them. A frequently quoted example is the noun *product*, realized by many Japanese learners roughly as [perodakuto] and by Koreans as [podak]. Two different strategies for dealing with the difficult consonant clusters are employed here; in the first case vowels are inserted to separate neighbouring consonants, while in the second one some consonants are removed to eliminate such undesirable sequences. Needless to say, none of these two methods can be used in English.

Interestingly, speakers of languages with heavy consonant clusters, for whom words like *product* are not difficult to pronounce, often have a reverse problem caused by the fact that many consonant letters which are found in English orthography remain silent in this language, but not in the students' L1. Thus, Polish learners have a tendency to pronounce initial sequences of consonant letters in the items in (a) (most of which are cognates), as well as what they take to be medial clusters in (b) and final clusters in (c):

(a) *psychology, psalm, pneumatic, xerox, pterodactyl*
(b) *castle, muscle, fasten, nestle, soften*
(c) *column, hymn, bomb, strong, song*

To eliminate such incorrect forms, a whole series of constraints can be formulated, e.g.:

> *No English word can begin with /ps, ks, pn, pt/. In such cases only the second consonant is pronounced.*
> *No English word ends with /stl, skl, stn/. In such cases the plosive is not pronounced.*
> *No English word ends with /mn, mb, ŋg/. In such cases the last consonant is not pronounced.*

We can encourage learners to expand the above lists and add to them clusters impossible in English in word-initial and final positions. This can be contrasted with examples taken from their L1. It is possible, of course, to focus only on consonant clusters which can be found in English and make two lists: one of licit and another of illicit sequences of segments.

The best-known sequential constraint of English disallows word-initial three-consonant clusters different from those which consist of /s/, followed by a voiceless plosive /p, t, k/ and an approximant /r, l, w, j/, e.g.:

street, student, stew, spray, splash, square, scuba, scratch, sclerotic

If the teacher is willing to devote some time to this issue, instead of presenting the above constraint, they can ask students to try to formulate the appropriate generalization themselves. It is useful to introduce it to more advanced learners who might have problems with the pronunciation of some clusters appearing initially in mostly German names, e.g. *Strauss, Springer,* and pronounce the initial palatoalveolar fricative instead of the alveolar spirant. They can also be warned that whenever clusters which are impossible in English appear in borrowings into this language, they are usually subject to simplification, modification or schwa insertion, for example, *Brno,* pronounced as [ˈbɜːnəʊ] or [brəˈnəʊ] (Wells, 1990: 93).

As a matter of fact, with particularly enthusiastic students, it might be worthwhile devoting some time to the phonetic and phonological adaptation of loanwords into English by examining, for instance, the way in which words borrowed from the learners' L1 are pronounced in English. Thus, Spanish students may study the English versions of, for instance, *tequila, tortilla, corrida* and *guacamole,* Italians such items as *pizza, spaghetti, cello* and *concerto,* and Japanese learners loanwords into English like *ikebana, origami, sake* and *samurai.* Comparing the pronunciation of such items in two languages provides a valuable insight into the working of different phonological and phonetic systems.

Returning to the issue of phonotactic constraints, another consonantal restriction operating in English should be mentioned, i.e. a ban on geminates inside single morphemes. In languages such as Polish geminates are commonplace and the following minimal pairs can be found:

ga[m]a 'scale' – ga[mm]a 'gamma'	bu[l]a 'boule' – bu[ll]a 'bull'
o[t]o 'here'– O[tt]o 'male name'	bu[d]a 'doghouse' – Bu[dd]a 'Buddha'

Thus, when Polish learners speak English, they tend to employ geminates in many cognates in which they are pronounced in Polish as well as in various English items spelt with double consonant letters , e.g.:

ho[bb]y, mo[tt]o, pi[tsts]a, A[nn]a, Ste[ll]a, i[rr]egular, i[ll]egal[6]

Advanced learners can benefit greatly from a brief comparison of English and Polish with respect to the occurrence of geminates, supported by bilingual minimal pairs, such as E *ho[b]y* – P *ho[bb]y.* This issue also provides the teacher with an excellent opportunity to discuss spelling-to-sound correspondences related to the use of double consonant letters in English and differences in the pronunciation of root vowels in pairs such as *writing – written, riding – ridden, later – latter.*

In order to consolidate learners' knowledge of English phonotactic constraints, we can present them with a list of non-words, some of which are accidental gaps, i.e. forms in agreement with these restrictions, that is, potential words, and some of which are systematic gaps, i.e. strings of phonemes violating phonotactic constraints that cannot become English words. The students' task is to tell the two types of items apart, together with a justification for their decision. For instance:

/knæs/ – a systematic gap since an English word cannot begin with the cluster /kn/.
/krɪt/ – an accidental gap since English words can begin with /kr/, e.g. *crib, crane, cry,* and end with /ɪt/, e.g. *sit, quit, Brit.*

The following list of non-words can be subject to analysis:

/plɪm/	/sniːl/	/pseɪm/	/dlɒp/	/kɜː br/
/glebl/	/prʌk/	/tʃælsa/	/pəŋk/	/piː me/

To make studying English phonotactic constraints more attractive and appealing to learners, a more creative type of activity can be employed. In one of my phonology classes devoted to this issue students were supposed to be screenwriters of a science fiction film whose task was to suggest names of various characters: some of them, meant for Earthlings, were to be pronounceable in English (accidental gaps), while others, meant for aliens, were in a language in which words were very difficult for English speakers to produce (systematic gaps). This activity turned out to be very successful not only in terms of the fun it provided, but also in helping students to convert theoretical information into something real and practical.

A problem-solving approach can be adopted in teaching some aspects of allophonic variation. For instance, an explanation of the differences in the pronunciation of dark and clear 'l' in RP can be accompanied by a list of forms, such as those given below:

mi[ɫ]k, [l]ook, si[l]y, ba[ɫ], c[l]ear, he[ɫ]p, gir[ɫ], va[l]ey

After placing these items on the blackboard, we can ask students to formulate the principle beyond the distribution of the two variants and once it is done, they should make three lists of examples, to be practised later, of course, with the clear lateral before a vowel, as in (a), the dark allophone before a consonant, as in (b), and in the word-final position, as in (c):

(a) *like, lovely, look, belly, lily, sailor, colour*
(b) *belt, shelf, Malta, cold, pulse, help, milk*
(c) *call, feel, tell, roll, tail, pill, oil, owl, pull*

A similar approach can be adopted to deal with other allophonic phenomena, such as aspiration, sonorant syllabicity or pre-fortis clipping.

A wealth of phonological material to study is provided by the changes which occur in English connected speech, i.e. different kinds of assimilations, linking, elisions and insertions. Sets of examples in which such modifications occur (or fail to occur) can be presented to learners, as it is done in Szpyra-Kozłowska and Sobkowiak's (2011) *Workbook in English Phonetics*, where the problem-solving approach is adopted to connected speech phenomena and where the students' task is to uncover regularities that operate within the supplied data and formulate appropriate rules.

It is also advisable to discuss in the classroom selected phonological processes of the L1 and L2 that have a direct bearing on students' phonetic performance. What matter in particular are those phonological changes which are commonplace in their L1 and are automatically carried over to the L2 where they do not operate. A case in point is word-final obstruent devoicing occurring in German, Dutch, Russian, Polish and many other languages, but not in English. The phenomenon in question can be explicitly discussed and illustrated with pairs of cognates from the L1 and English in which final obstruents are devoiced in the former, but not the latter case, as in the examples taken from English and Polish below:

E *snob* [snɒb] versus P *snob* [snop]   E *band* [bænd] versus P *band* [bent]
E *dog* [dɒg] versus P *dog* [dok]   E *strip-tease* [strɪptiːz] versus P *strip-tease* [strʲiptʲis]

A similar procedure can be adopted in presenting other interference-causing phonological processes of the L1. For instance, in Polish, due to voice assimilation, clusters of obstruents become uniform in voicing, which rule is carried over to Polish English, e.g.:

football: E *foo[tb]all* versus P *foo[db]all*   *baseball:* E *ba[sb]all* versus P *ba[zb]all*

Another example concerns the palatalization of consonants in Polish triggered by the following high front vowel /i/ and the palatal glide /j/ (indicated by an apostrophe after the consonant):

E *team* [tiːm] versus P *team* [tʲim]   E *clip* [klɪp] versus P *clip* [klʲip]

Such processes, because of their automatic character, are extremely difficult to suppress in the L2. Learners' awareness of them might foster the reduction of undesirable phonological interference and help them to self-monitor their phonetic performance.

In this section we have provided selected examples of some phonological phenomena in English, the awareness of which can help learners to eliminate numerous common phonetic errors. They can be introduced by teachers when they realize that students are unable to form auditory input-based generalizations on their own and when their mistakes concerning some phonological issue are persistent. Our experience is that once learners are made aware of various phonological regularities, they make considerably fewer pronunciation errors. Moreover, problem-solving tasks provide intellectual stimulation for students and encourage their active participation in the learning process.

In the holistic approach advocated here, motor, auditory and cognitive training should complement each other since, as pointed out by Moyer (2013: 4), the mastery of L2 pronunciation 'relies on articulatory precision, auditory-perceptual processing and higher-order analysis'. In Section B.3.1 we juxtapose two approaches to phonodidactics: intuitive-imitative and analytic-linguistic (Celce-Murcia *et al.*, 1996), and provide experimental evidence which shows that both of them are equally effective in the phonetic training of Polish teenagers. We report on an experiment in which two groups of learners were taught English pronunciation in two different ways for a period of several months. Group A did a lot of 'listen and repeat' tasks and phonetic drills without any explicit theoretical instruction, while in Group B the focus was on form, i.e. developing pupils' metacompetence and raising their phonological awareness (followed by some production exercises). It turned out that in both cases we could observe a similar, comparable degree of improvement in pronunciation. This shows that both approaches under discussion are effective and deserve to be employed in the language classroom. Moreover, if each of them employed separately brings good results, it is to be expected that combining them in the course of phonetic training will be even more fruitful.

A.3.2.4 Multisensory training

Various authors (e.g. Bukowski, 2003; Celce-Murcia *et al.*, 1996; Wrembel, 2010) suggest that effective pronunciation teaching should incorporate a multisensory approach to phonetic training to cater for the needs of those students who learn faster and remember things better when an appeal is made to several different channels of perception and not just one.

According to specialists, while each of us employs all modalities to some extent, we have one dominant learning mode and one subsidiary mode. Thus, there are visual, auditory and kinaesthetic/tactile learners. Visual learners need to see something in order to understand and remember it. Typically they have to take notes and write everything down. Auditory learners activate mainly their aural channel so they have to hear what they are to learn. Oral lectures and recordings appeal to them far more than written materials. Finally, kinaesthetic/tactile students' learning is largely enhanced through body movement and a sense of touch.

While there are no statistics as to how frequently different modalities are used,[7] the very fact that we all employ more than one of them might be responsible for the frequent ineffectiveness of 'listen and repeat' tasks, since they rely on our ears and appeal only to one modality, which is not always our strongest.[8] To aid learners who represent different types of dominant modalities, the teacher should try to use not only imitation activities, but a larger variety of instructional procedures that appeal to different senses.[9] As argued by Sankey et al. (2010: 854), 'students engaged in learning that incorporates multimodal designs, on average, outperform students who learn using traditional approaches with single modes'.

Thus, visual learners need different kinds of visual support, such as charts, diagrams, pictures, films and colours. The instructor should make sure that there are some visual aids in the classroom such as, for example, sound charts or, if possible, simplified articulatory diagrams. Moreover, visual learners benefit greatly from the use of phonemic transcription in which symbols can be accompanied by drawings of animals or objects in whose names a given sound is found, e.g. a picture of a bee symbolizing [i:], a cat standing for the vowel [æ] or a snake representing a fricative consonant [s]. Students can be asked to suggest their own examples of words which they associate with particular English sounds and make their own individualized illustrated cards with phonetic symbols. It is also useful to assign different colours to various sounds. Phonetically difficult and commonly mispronounced words, both in their orthographic and phonemically transcribed forms, can be placed on corkboards. According to Bukowski (2003), instead of correcting students' pronunciation errors orally, the teacher can flash an appropriate colour card or a card with a drawing or a phonetic symbol on it so that the learners will self-correct themselves. Using a mirror to see the visible articulators is also recommended.

Modern technology (see Section A.3.5.4) offers many other ways of visualizing speech. Articulation-related aids, such as animations of speech organs, palatograms and electropalatograms, display articulators (e.g. lips, tongue, velum, vocal cords) and show how they function in speech production. There are also computer programs and internet sources which offer visual representations of various aspects of prosody such as intonation contours, stress patterns and duration of sounds. Acoustics-related aids allow their users to see some properties of the acoustic speech signal in the form of oscillograms and spectrograms of different speech units (e.g. syllables, words or sentences) and can be used to facilitate advanced learners' understanding of many aspects of L2 pronunciation (see, for example, Gonet, 2014). They require, however, familiarity with the basics of acoustic phonetics and can only be used by those instructors that have received an appropriate training in it.

Kinaesthetic/tactile learners require physical involvement in the process of learning, i.e. a lot of body movement (kinaesthetic learners) and reinforcement through the sense of touch (tactile learners). Both can be provided by various hand signals, e.g. indicating vowel length by two hands with a large space between them for long vowels and a small space for short vowels or tracing intonational contours with arms or fingers. Much body movement can be provided by games, acting out poems, dialogues and scenes from plays and films as well as by any manipulative activities that employ various objects which students can be asked either to bring to the classroom or to make themselves. They should be encouraged to feel some parts of the vocal tract involved in the articulation of sounds. For example, the distinction between voiced and voiceless consonants can be simply demonstrated by asking learners to press two fingers against their neck inside which the larynx is situated and to pronounce sounds like /sss/ and /zzz/ interchangeably to feel the vibrations of the vocal folds or their absence. Numerous other suggestions of phonetic activities particularly suited to kinaesthetic/tactile learners can be found in Celce-Murcia *et al.* (1996).

Auditory learners rely mainly on auditory input in the form of spoken utterances, recordings of various kinds and the teacher's oral explanations. In other words, they learn mostly 'by ear' and are happy to do the tasks summarized in the section devoted to auditory training. As argued by Bukowski (2003), auditory learners enjoy making their own recordings and comparing them with samples of native English pronunciation. According to Celce-Murcia *et al.* (1996), they benefit greatly from the use of a mnemonic device called a memory peg, in which various speech sounds are remembered through their association with extralinguistic sounds. For example, imagining the sound of a buzzing insect can help students to produce /z/ or the hissing of a snake can be helpful in articulating /s/.

Various cross-modal activities, meant to complement traditional auditory training and to enhance learners' auditory memory and production skills, have been suggested by some scholars (e.g. Celce-Murcia *et al.*, 1996; Fraser, 2004; Wrembel, 2010). They encourage learners to associate sounds with tastes, textures, sizes, colours, body movements and even emotions. For instance, Wrembel (2010) applies colour terminology to sounds and proposes a coloured English vowel chart based on experimentally established sound-colour correspondences. She also proposes developing kinaesthetic representations of L2 sounds.

Bukowski (2003), in order to examine the learning style of 29 secondary school pupils (aged 17–18), carried out a test (the Learning Styles Modality Preference Inventory) and established that 41% of them displayed a marked preference for visual learning, 27% for kinaesthetic/tactile learning and only

13% had the strongest auditory mode. The remaining students scored the same number of points in two modalities, i.e. visual-kinaesthetic and auditory-kinaesthetic. The study of the subsidiary modes representing the second strongest dominance in learning has shown that all visual students had the kinaesthetic subsidiary mode and almost all kinaesthetic learners were secondarily visual. Auditory students had different subsidiary learning styles.

If the above data turn out to be similar for other groups of students as well, this means that in current pronunciation instruction there is too much emphasis on auditory learning with a considerable neglect of appeal to the visual and kinaesthetic modalities, far more frequently employed than the former one. This conclusion concerning the dominance of visual learning over auditory learning is further supported by the fact which has been mentioned several times throughout this book, namely of the powerful impact of the written form of English on EFL learners' pronunciation. On the one hand, it stems undoubtedly from their insufficient exposure to spoken English but, on the other hand, from the strength of the visual, i.e. written input.

It seems that limiting phonetic training to 'listen and repeat' activities follows from many teachers' conviction that pronunciation by its very nature must be learned through frequent aural exposure to speech, coupled with numerous repetitions, as with the case of young children acquiring the sound system of their native language. While this is undoubtedly true, it should also be remembered that in the process of language acquisition, different channels of perception are activated. A child is often shown an object, a person or an animal while its name is being pronounced, which means associating sequences of sounds not only with their meaning, but also with certain visual images (*Look at this little white doggie! Can you see this big red thing? It's a bus.*). Smaller objects are often handed to the child together with an appropriate term or the child is asked to do something with them (*Here's your teddy bear. Bring me your car. Build a big tower.*). Thus, acquiring the meaning of words and their pronunciation (verbs in particular), is often connected with various physical activities and body movements, which means kinaesthetic learning. To sum up, native language acquisition involves auditory, visual and kinaesthetic channels as well as, obviously, the cognitive processing of information. Evidently, if similar mechanisms are involved in L2 learning, this fact must be taken into consideration in designing L2 teaching processes including pronunciation training.

It should be noted that the pronunciation teaching techniques discussed in the following section cater for the needs of students with different learning styles. Ear training is particularly beneficial for auditory learners, phonemic transcription appeals primarily to visual students, while games and drama-related activities are ideally suited to the kinaesthetic learning style. Since in all instances the formation of the English sound system in the learners' minds should be aimed at, various cognitively based activities like introducing elements of phonology or games which raise language awareness are also advocated here. Thus, ideally, all the techniques presented in this chapter should be employed in the course of holistic phonetic training. As argued by Sankey *et al.* (2010), multimodal learning brings a number of benefits which include:

(1)   making complex information easier to comprehend;
(2)   deeper processing of information;
(3)   maintaining learner attention by making the information more attractive and motivating.

It is also possible, of course, for teachers to design simple phonetic activities which incorporate several kinds of multisensory reinforcement, meant to benefit different types of learners at the same time. Below, we offer some suggestions for phonetic activities which appeal to various senses and are particularly well suited for younger learners. Their obvious assets lie in the fact that they do not require any particular equipment, they can be adjusted to a phonetic issue that needs to be practised and they break the routine of typical pronunciation classes.

Take the regular past tense forms. First we can ask students to prepare several slips of paper with /t/, /d/ and /ɪd/ written on them.

t	d	ɪd

Other paper slips should contain different regular verbs ending in a variety of consonants and vowels, e.g.:

want, work, mend, pick, die, love, join, wash, watch, judge, hope, rob, sail, enjoy,
jump, shout, pull, push, paint, lie, care, look, clean, tolerate, guess, move, seem

In one activity the teacher can read the past tense forms of such verbs and the students' task is to match the verbs with the appropriate endings by putting paper slips from the two sets together. Then the correct forms should be repeated by the students' (chorally and individually). In another exercise a similar task can be carried out without, however, the teacher providing the past tense forms. In this case students should the select the appropriate paper slips from both sets and read the inflected verbs aloud. Finally, the teacher produces a sentence in the present tense with some verbs from the pool and indicates a student who is supposed to change it into the past tense, at the same time showing the slip with the ending to the rest of the class, e.g.:

Teacher: *I pull and push very hard.*   **Student:** *She pulled and pushed very hard.*

Teacher: *I mend and paint it all day.*   **Student:** *She mended and painted it all day.*

Teacher: *I jump and shout*   **Student:** *She jumped and*
when I'm happy.   *shouted when she was happy.*

Note that the activities proposed above include auditory as well as visual input, but also manipulation of paper slips and some movement. If the students are willing to get even more physically involved, they can express the contents of the verbs through movement. Similar activities can be carried out with present tense verb forms and different realizations of the -(e)s suffix.

Multisensory reinforcement can be employed to practise various other phonetic elements of English. For instance, a set of bisyllabic and trisyllabic words can be prepared by the teacher and copied onto separate slips of paper by the students. Below, we present some simple names of popular dishes and foods:

potato, lettuce, marmalade, pancake, tomato, beefsteak, cabbage, cauliflower, roastbeef, cornflakes, cucumber, sardines, sausages, vegetables, hamburger

Three numbers are placed on the table, which mean the following:

(1)   stress on the initial syllable
(2)   stress on the medial syllable
(3)   stress on the final syllable

In one version of this activity, the teacher provides the auditory input and reads an item from the list; students place the paper slip with it into the appropriate category, i.e. (1), (2) or (3). In another version students receive no prompts from the instructor, but do the placing task themselves and then take turns to read each word aloud. Of course, vocabulary items should be selected taking into account the current topics of the lessons and the learners' proficiency level. Students should also be encouraged to add their own examples to each of the lists.

To practise the falling intonation of wh- questions and the rising intonation of yes/no-questions, the following activity can be employed. The teacher prepares slips of paper with one question written on each of them, e.g.:

Where is your mother?   Why are you worried?   When will you go home?
Is this your teacher?   Are you tired?   Did you watch TV yesterday?

Two props must be prepared: something heavy, e.g. a weight or a piece of rock (to indicate falling intonation with an accompanying gesture of an arm with a heavy object going down), and something very light, e.g. a balloon (to indicate rising intonation with raising the arm holding the balloon). The teacher shows these gestures to students and explains their meaning using some examples. Then each learner draws a slip of paper with a question, chooses an appropriate prop and reads the question aloud with the gesture emphasizing its intonation. The whole group repeats the question and the next student is asked to present his/her question. A similar activity can be employed in the case of question tags and positive or negative responses to them depending on intonation. One student reads a sentence with a tag showing falling or rising intonation in the manner described above and another student provides an answer.

A game-like multimodal activity for practising the pronunciation of notoriously difficult interdental fricatives can be proposed. The teacher prepares cards with nouns containing these consonants which are familiar to the students, e.g.:

tooth ,mouth, throat, thumb, bath, maths, earth, thief, birthday, panther, month, mother, father, brother, feather, weather, clothes, theatre, thriller, south, north

A selected student is now supposed to present the content of a given item by means of gestures or drawings, but without any sounds. The remaining learners guess which word it is and then repeat it chorally and individually after the teacher, who at the same time shows the written version to them. Body movements and gestures can also be employed to express the meaning of such verbs as:

thank, think, throw, threaten, thread, bathe, breathe

or more difficult nouns like:

depth, length, width, breadth, strength, warmth, wealth, health

The next suggestion involves the use of phonemic transcription. Two sets of paper slips are prepared: one with the orthographic forms of words, the other with the same items in a transcribed version. The learners' task is to match the slips from both sets after hearing a given word pronounced by the teacher. More examples of multimodal activities are provided in the section below.

A.3.3 Selected Pronunciation Teaching Techniques

Recent years have brought a renewed interest in different techniques of teaching and learning L2 pronunciation. Not only have the traditional and well-known procedures been employed and further developed, such as, for example, ear-training, imitation, drilling, the use of phonetic transcription, articulatory descriptions and elements of contrastive phonetics, reading dialogues and acting out plays, reciting poems and singing songs, but a whole range of multifarious innovative methods of mastering the foreign sound patterns have been suggested. The latter include, for instance, pronunciation games, techniques taken from theatre arts, psychology and speech pathology, appeals to multisensory modes of learning, using multimedia and computer-assisted instruction, etc. (e.g. Celce-Murcia *et al.*, 1996; Hancock, 1995; Kelly, 2000; Wrembel, 2001, 2002).

With all these numerous older and newer procedures, an important question that emerges concerns their effectiveness. Which pronunciation teaching techniques are most efficient and useful? Which are particularly attractive for the learners? Which should be abandoned as unsatisfying and which should be employed to achieve the intended purposes? As pointed out by Moyer (2013: 7), 'the kinds of activities they [i.e. learners] are likely to encounter ... have not changed appreciably for decades, but little is known about how effective they are'.

In this section we do not intend to discuss all the types of techniques (for an excellent introduction, see, for example, Celce-Murcia *et al.*, 1996), but to focus on those of them which are, in our view, of particular importance to EFL learners, first of all in terms of their effectiveness, but also with regard to their attractiveness. While the former factor is of primary importance, the latter should also be taken into consideration since boring phonetic activities can discourage learners from working on their English pronunciation. It should also be remembered that, regardless of how exciting a given technique is, it stops being enjoyable if it is overused. Thus, we advocate the diversification of pronunciation activities, which should, as argued by Fraser (2006), be both learner friendly, but also teacher friendly.

As in the preceding sections, we will suggest a number of tasks and activities which can be employed in the pronunciation classroom. They are easy to prepare and carry out, with no need to use any specialized equipment. As a matter of fact, the majority of them require a blackboard, a piece of chalk and the teacher's willingness to change the everyday instruction routine.

A.3.3.1 Phonemic transcription

Throughout this book, and in Chapter 2 in particular, it has been pointed out that foreign learners, having a very limited exposure to spoken English, are particularly liable to be affected by its written form, with all its irregularities and idiosyncrasies. To overcome this powerful impact of English spelling on students' pronunciation two very useful tools are needed: phonemic transcription (also called phonemic or phonetic script[10]) and instruction in spelling-to-pronunciation rules (discussed in some detail in Chapter 2).

Pronunciation specialists seem to be unanimous in regarding phonemic transcription as an invaluable tool in teaching English phonetics to foreign learners. Its numerous advantages are discussed in various sources and are generally well known (e.g. Collins & Mees, 2003; Kelly, 2000; Lecumberri & Maidment, 2000; Tench, 1992, 2011; Underhill, 1994).

Thus, due to phonemic transcription, learners are made aware of differences between English spelling and pronunciation and can minimize the impact of the former on the latter. In other words, it allows them to avoid many cases of spelling pronunciation that are so frequent, as shown earlier, in learner English. As pointed out by Rogerson-Revell (2011: 243), phonemic script 'raises learners' awareness of the number of phonemes in English'. It also helps them to internalize the sound system of English. Moreover, the employment of special symbols makes students realize that sounds represented by them often differ from seemingly similar sounds found in their L1 (of course when different symbols are used). In short, phonemic script is an important tool in learners' cognitive phonological training. Another important advantage of using phonemic transcription is that it provides visual reinforcement of auditory input. As demonstrated in the preceding sections, a considerable number of people are visual learners and remember things better when they write them down. Phonemic script is also an invaluable aid in enhancing learner autonomy, particularly important in contemporary approaches to language teaching and learning (e.g. Benson, 2007), since it allows them to use dictionaries and learn the pronunciation of new words on their own.

It is also important to consider some consequences of not using phonemic script. In such cases learners have several options. The first of them is to try to remember the pronunciation of words and phrases. This is often problematic as our perception of L2 sounds is heavily influenced by L1 sounds and we might simply hear and remember a given form incorrectly. As shown in Chapter 2, learner English abounds in incorrectly remembered words. When our auditory memory fails us, the written version is usually resorted to, which results in spelling pronunciation.

The second possibility, commonly employed by learners who do not trust their memory and who do not know phonetic symbols, is to use their own quasi transcription in which the pronunciation of new words is recorded by means of L1 letters and letter sequences. In such instances, students convert sounds in English words into strings of L1 letters, later pronounced as L1 sounds. To illustrate this procedure, consider some 'transcriptions' I found in Camilla's (a girl who is a relative of mine, aged 9) English notebook. Her class had a lesson in which the teacher introduced names of some exotic animals. To make sure she would remember their pronunciation, Camilla added her own 'transcribed' forms, e.g. *camel* [kamel], *tiger* [tajger], *panther* [pemfer] and *chimp* [czimp].[11] Observe that the child's versions depart considerably from the correct forms in various ways. First of all, Camilla's 'transcriptions' suggest incorrectly that both English and Polish contain identical consonants and vowels. Secondly, apparently her perception of the above items was heavily influenced by the Polish sound system. For example, *panther* transcribed as [pemfer] shows that the ash vowel (absent in Polish) has been interpreted by her as the Polish mid front /e/ and the voiceless dental fricative (also absent in Polish) as a labiovelar fricative. The latter triggered place assimilation of the preceding nasal. The schwa vowel (absent in Polish) was heard by the child as Polish /e/; as noted by many specialists, without phonetic symbols, it is impossible to represent schwa in writing. The final /r/ was evidently induced by spelling. With this type of 'transcription' it is not surprising that Camilla's pronunciation reflected it rather closely.

To conclude, the teachers' failure to introduce and employ phonemic script regularly has serious negative consequences for learners' pronunciation since it enhances their use of L1 sounds and sound patterns.[12] Moreover, without this tool the powerful impact of English orthography cannot be successfully overcome.

In spite of these facts, phonemic transcription appears to be used reluctantly by many, if not the majority of English teachers, who find many faults with it. It is not only claimed to be time consuming and tedious to teach, but also unattractive, boring, difficult and thus discouraging for learners. According to Crookston (2001: 7):

> phonemic transcription seems to be virtually effortless for a small minority of students (...) However, as every teacher of phonemic transcription knows, the majority of learners, even the majority of successful learners require non-negligible effort to get to the point of being able to transcribe the 'citation forms' of, say, two-syllable words with a reasonable degree of accuracy.

Realizing these facts, EFL instructors, working under considerable time pressure and with syllabuses which, generally, establish priorities different from pronunciation teaching, tend to neglect this useful aid.

Another reason for most teachers' reluctance to employ phonemic transcription in the classroom seems to be their lack of familiarity with interesting techniques of introducing and practising it, which leads to a common, but largely ill-informed and erroneous view that phonemic script is extremely boring for students to learn (and for instructors to teach).[13] It should also be pointed out that general course books in English, which for many teachers represent an authority on what to teach and how to do it, tend to make very limited use of phonemic script since they often include a list of phonetic symbols in the introductory section and a list of transcribed vocabulary items at the end without, however, any attempt to teach book users how to use these symbols.

What seems to lie at the heart of the matter, however, is the teachers' lack of conviction that familiarity with phonemic transcription crucially facilitates the acquisition of proper English pronunciation. In other words, many language instructors appear to doubt whether the time and effort required to teach and learn phonemic script are well spent and indeed bring about the desired results. They generally seem to subscribe to views such as Abercrombie's (1949: 29) opinion that,[14] 'the use of phonetic symbols is a very valuable part of the phonetician's technique, but it is perfectly possible to teach pronunciation without making use of them, and it is also possible, and alas! quite common, to use phonetic symbols without succeeding in teaching pronunciation'. Clearly, the primary goal is learners' improved pronunciation of their L2, which is the only genuinely convincing argument in favour of not only teaching phonemic script but, in fact, using any other technique of phonetic instruction. In Section B.3.3 we present a study in which a group of teenage Polish learners was taught English pronunciation by means of a variety of techniques and then was asked to evaluate them in terms of their effectiveness and attractiveness. It is striking that phonemic script was assessed by the participants as the most effective technique which contributed significantly to the improvement of their pronunciation, although in terms of attractiveness it certainly was not the winner. These results suggest that the question is not whether to teach phonemic script or not, but how to teach it in an interesting and appealing way and how to convince learners that making this extra effort is really worthwhile. Below we provide some suggestions as to how it can be done.

When we asked several English instructors how they teach phonemic script, they told us that they presented a list of phonetic symbols to their students together with some words in which such sounds are found and asked learners to memorize them. This, however, seems to be a perfect way to discourage everyone, as a list of alien-looking and largely meaningless symbols is not only unexciting, but also fairly terrifying. Moreover, there is a huge difference between knowing transcription symbols and knowing how to use them. The latter skill requires much practice and no doubt providing students with a list of symbols cannot replace it.

In our view, the teacher should begin with an explanation as to why phonemic transcription is needed and should justify its use with some examples of words in which pronunciation departs drastically from the orthographic form, e.g. *enough, through, though,* where the same sequence of letters, i.e. <ough> is pronounced in three different ways. Students can also be given some new words in ordinary spelling in order for them to guess how they are pronounced. This can be done to demonstrate to them that such guesses are frequently incorrect and that a system of transcribing phonetic forms is needed to avoid serious mispronunciations. In brief, students must be in the first place motivated to learn phonemic script and see the gains achieved due to its use, as well as drawbacks of failing to do so. Put differently, it is essential to develop students' positive attitude towards this tool. Next, remembering the importance of visual reinforcement in learning, it is advisable to place the phonetic chart in the classroom for everyone to see and consult whenever necessary.

Transcription symbols should be introduced gradually, starting with the simplest ones, that is, those which are identical to ordinary letters of the Latin alphabet.[15] Thus, students should first become acquainted with the symbols corresponding to consonant letters, i.e. /p, b, m, t, d, k, g, f, v, s, z, h, l, r, w, j/, together with examples of simple words in which they appear, preferably with the segments in question in word-initial position, e.g. *pen, ball, make, ten, do, key,* etc. Next the new symbols must be learnt, i.e. those which denote interdentals /ð, Θ/, palatoalveolars /ʃ, ʒ, ʧ, ʤ/ and the velar nasal /ŋ/, which means only seven consonant symbols different from ordinary letters.[16]

First, some practice is needed in writing them in order for students to become familiar with the new shapes and to associate them with the sounds they represent. A simple game can be organized to add some fun to the learning process. Learners can be divided into several teams and given several minutes to write on a piece of paper as many words which contain a given sound as they can, for example, /ʧ/, /ŋ/ or /Θ/. The team that lists more examples than others is the winner. To make it a pronunciation practice, each word must be said aloud. This type of activity is also an excellent opportunity to study spelling and sound correspondences. Students can be asked to observe how, for instance, the interdental fricatives are spelled. If they represent a more advanced level of language proficiency, they can be given a list of words in which the digraph <th> is pronounced as [t], e.g. *Thames, thyme, Theresa, Thailand.*

A different version of this game can also be used in which the teacher writes the transcription symbol of a sound on the blackboard, for instance, of a palatoalveolar fricative. Each team is supposed to come up with a word with this consonant and write it on the blackboard (in ordinary spelling). The team that is unable to add a new example is eliminated and the game continues until the winner emerges. Alternatively, the same game can be played between individual students. Note that in the case of the velar nasal an excellent opportunity is created to demonstrate that this consonant is represented in spelling by the <nk> and <ng> digraphs and that <g> is not pronounced after angma in word-final position and before consonants. Pairs such as *think – thing, sink – sing, rink – ring* can be practised.

Vowel symbols are more difficult and have to be introduced gradually as well, with the focus on those symbols which are different from the letters of the alphabet. The 12 RP monophthongs (if RP is the accent model) should be further divided into smaller classes: for example, long and short vowels, front and back sounds. The same concerns diphthongs which should be taught after all vowel symbols have become familiar to students. Again similar games as in the case of consonants can be employed to make learning more enjoyable. The teacher can, of course, use different activities, suitable for a particular learner group. For example, he/she can pronounce an English word and ask students to answer some questions in writing by using an appropriate transcription symbol, e.g.:

What symbol represents the vowel in *bad*?
What symbol represents the vowel in *bed*?
What symbol represents the vowel in *bit*?

In all cases, care should be taken to retain a close link between practising transcription symbols and the skill of pronouncing them.

A nice way of teaching transcription symbols to younger learners has been suggested to me by a student of mine, a primary school teacher. To make them less alien, she asked children (aged 8) to come up with names for the 'strange' symbols. They proposed 'a (little) flower' for the ash vowel (/æ/), 'a (little) tent' for wedge (/ʌ/), 'a (little) column' for the short high vowel (/ɪ/), 'upside down e' for schwa (/ə/), 'a flower pot' for the short high back vowel (/ʊ/), 'a snake' for the consonant in *shoe* (/ʃ/) and 'an n with a little tail' for angma (/ŋ/). According to the teacher, children used these names enthusiastically and remembered the symbols with names much better than those without them.

Another game-like multimodal activity involving transcription symbols consists of placing each of them on a separate piece of paper. Students draw one of them and compose a sentence with as many occurrences of a given sound as they can think of. Next each participant reads the prepared sentence to the others who are supposed to say which sound is meant. The proper transcription symbol is then shown to all the learners. Some possible sentences are provided below:

A black cat sat on a mat and saw a sad rat. What sound am I? (/æ/)
Drink this milk, silly little Jill. What sound am I? (/ɪ/)
Go home, Joe, and show Joan your boat. What sound am I? (/əʊ/)

Once all the symbols have been learnt, more complex activities can be employed. The simplest of them is to write some transcribed words on the blackboard, ask students to pronounce them aloud and then write them in ordinary spelling. The items ought to be simple at first and then more difficult and should, of course, belong to the vocabulary already familiar to the students. This type of activity can also be developed into a game. One team places a transcribed word on the blackboard and other competitors are supposed to supply the orthographic form. A reverse course of action can be taken, but emphasis should be placed on developing learners' ability to pronounce transcribed forms rather than transcribing written items. An interesting type of exercise is the use of transcription crossword puzzles which can be taken, for example, from Hancock's (1995) book, after the teacher makes sure that all the items are known to the learners.

Several activities can be carried out with the use of cards with transcription symbols written on them. A set of them can be made by each student and brought to the class (or made in it). In a simple task the teacher places several symbols in a random order on the blackboard, asking learners to form an English word (or words) out of them (e.g. /p, l., m, æ/ – /læmp/, /t, m, iː, s, r/ – /striːm/). In a more complex exercise the teacher gives the learners sets of identical cards with phonetic symbols. The task is to form as many transcribed words as they can out of the supplied symbols, e.g. /t, p, n, m, s, l, r, ʃ, ɪ, iː, eɪ, aʊ, e/ – /ʃɪp, reɪn, pet, pen, meɪn, lɪp, seɪm, aʊt, siːm, ʃeɪm, sliːp, ten, naʊ, ɪt/. The team which comes up with the largest number of items is the winner.

A different activity involves preparing two sets of words: the first one contains orthographic forms, the second their transcribed versions. The students' task is to match pairs of items. Another exercise, particularly useful in eliminating fossilized forms, consists of making a short list of well-known words that tend to be mispronounced, together with their transcribed forms which, however, contain some errors. Students are asked to indicate these errors and correct them. Below we present several such examples.

sister /siːster/   mother /mʌver/   something /sʌmsiŋk/   half /haːlf/   dead /diːd/

Alternatively, a list of words presented to students can contain some correctly and some incorrectly transcribed items with the task of telling them apart.

An important element of training in phonemic script is the use of dictionaries. If some copies are available in the classroom, the teacher might write a few words on the blackboard and ask the learners to find their transcribed versions to be copied and then pronounced aloud. Alternatively, a similar task can be given to students as homework and repeated several times in order to show them how useful phonemic script is and how much independence from the teacher it can ensure.

After the one-word stage the instructor can proceed to use transcribed phrases and sentences, which is particularly useful in introducing weak forms as well as changes that occur in connected speech. Numerous useful ideas as to how this can be done are provided by Lecumberri and Maidment (2000).

Several additional comments are necessary in connection with transcription training. The first of them concerns an appropriate moment to introduce phonemic script. On the one hand, the earlier learners are familiarized with it, the sooner their habit of using transcription will be formed. On the other hand, it seems that at the beginning stages of language learning it might be too heavy a burden to place on learners, particularly young ones. The teacher should consider all the pros and cons before making a decision.

Secondly, it is important to decide on the degree to which phonemic script should be mastered. It seems that for the majority of learners it is sufficient to be able to copy transcribed forms (from the blackboard or a dictionary) and to pronounce them correctly (passive knowledge of transcription) without the need to transcribe words from hearing (active knowledge), which is much more difficult and in most cases unnecessary.

Finally, it cannot be assumed that once learnt, phonemic script will be used properly. Occasional practice in transcribing is needed from time to time. It is also important to employ phonemic script regularly and consistently, particularly while introducing new vocabulary, even if a given word or a phrase seems phonetically simple. What matters here is forming in learners the habit of transcribing all new items. This idea has been nicely expressed by a teenager who participated in our study summarized in B.3.3: 'At first it was difficult to learn all those strange symbols, but now I cannot imagine learning a new word without transcribing it – it has become a habit with me.'

A.3.3.2 Songs, poems and elements of drama

A popular way of enhancing students' involvement in language learning is to employ a variety of authentic materials, such as songs and poems, in the classroom, the use of which makes phonetic training more attractive to many learners. Other useful materials are supplied by the so-called phonetic trivia, usually based on pronunciation puns, found in various advertisements and commercials as well as on the internet (e.g. Sobkowiak, 2003).

Songs and music are of particular appeal to young people who find it very interesting to learn the lyrics of their favourite songs. Needless to say, this provides an excellent opportunity to do some vocabulary work, to practise listening comprehension and pronunciation as well. Thus, students can listen to a song trying to understand as much as possible. Then they should practise the pronunciation of whole phrases found in the lyrics. Finally, they can sing along together with the recorded performer. What should be taken into account, however, is that various performers use accents different from the one adopted for our teaching purposes. Therefore, the teacher must be prepared to provide suitable comments about accent differences as well as on the frequent use of slang or substandard grammar in such materials. This means that activities with songs must be carefully prepared beforehand.

The selection of songs to listen to and/or to learn can also be made by the teacher in order to draw students' attention to some aspects of English pronunciation. For instance, the following fragment of a well-known Beatles song, *Close your eyes and I'll kiss you, tomorrow I'll miss you*, illustrates well the palatalization of alveolars before the palatal glide of the pronoun *you*. A Christmas carol, 'Twelve Days of Christmas', can be used to practise the interdental fricatives present in the ordinal numbers, e.g. *on the third, fourth, fifth, sixth, seventh, eighth, ninth, tenth, eleventh, twelfth day of Christmas*.

Memorizing and reciting short English poems, such as limericks, also provides good pronunciation practice and a nice distraction from the ordinary classroom routine. There are many advantages to using them: they are brief, rhythmic and therefore memorable. As observed by Vaughan-Rees (1992: 47), people remember poems for years: 'it may have something to do with the inherent memorability of verse, especially when allied to a strong, rhythmic beat. [...] Wise language teachers, whatever the language, take advantage of the universal appeal of rhyme and rhythm.' The teacher can organize a poetry reciting competition, asking each student to memorize a short English poem to be presented in the classroom. The winner is then selected (either by the instructor or by all the students), with good pronunciation being the most important criterion of evaluation.

Nevertheless, while authentic materials are no doubt valuable, they are not always suitable for phonetics classes. Vaughan-Rees (1992: 51–52) points out that, 'one problem is that the syllables which are stressed in verse and song are not necessarily those which would be stressed in natural speech' and adds that 'raps, like limericks, often exhibit a cavalier attitude towards stress placement'. Moreover, such materials often contain non-standard forms, which might confuse the learners (especially beginners) and require additional explanation from the teacher. Finally, since they are not written specifically for the purposes of practising pronunciation, songs and poems usually require control over many different aspects of phonetics. While this is advantageous for advanced students (in natural speech one does have to control all the pronunciation features), it may be too difficult for those representing lower levels of language proficiency.

For these reasons I decided to write with my students some short poems which centre on a single English sound (a vowel or a consonant). I wanted them to focus on mastering some selected features of English pronunciation without having to worry about too many phonetic issues. To make the task more attractive, we tried to create poems that would be humorous in nature, knowing that humour is always appreciated and fosters the learning process. We followed Brown's (1994: 266) guidelines for successful drills, who suggests that they should be kept short, simple (one point at a time), 'snappy' and limited to one aspect of language (phonetic or grammatical).

Below, I present some of the 'sound poems' that have been written by us. Although they are unlikely to win any literary prizes, they can be useful as pronunciation practice material (more such poems are found in Szpyra-Kozłowska & Bukowski, 2006).

A **h**airy **h**amster called **H**ugh
Once **h**id **h**imself in a stew.
He **h**ad a **h**orrible **h**unch
They might **h**ave **h**im for lunch.

A **Ch**inese **ch**ess **ch**ampion Lee **Ch**oo
Chose for lun**ch** **Ch**eddar **ch**eese to **ch**ew.

Sergeant **J**ones and **G**eneral Ran**g**er
Were once in **g**enuine dan**g**er
When in the sava**g**e **j**ungle they met
A stran**g**e **J**apanese **j**umbo **j**et.

My very best friend named Ben
Couldn't tell how to count to ten.

Then **ch**icken, **ch**ips and **ch**ocolate cake
All for the **ch**ampionship's sake.

'I b**e**t it is all in my h**ea**d,
I just can't g**e**t it out', he s**ai**d.

A b**eau**tiful girl named S**ue**
Wanted to have something n**ew**
So she bought a kangar**oo**
And got herself a h**u**ge tatt**oo**.

A j**o**lly bulld**o**g named M**o**p
Was sp**o**tted once in a sh**o**p
Shouting, 'I w**a**nt s**au**sage and n**o**t
Those disgusting h**o**t-d**o**gs I've g**o**t.'

Writing simple poems like the ones above is possible only with advanced students whose lexical and grammatical knowledge is sufficient for tasks of this kind. We can even organize a competition in which learners form several teams, each writing a poem devoted to a particular vowel or consonant. The best, most amusing ones are then selected as winners. Of course writing poems is only the first step and reciting them aloud with the correct pronunciation should constitute the next and far more important stage. Finally, they can be placed on a corkboard for visual reinforcement.

With less advanced students simpler creative tasks can be employed. For instance, pronunciation practice proper can be preceded by an activity in which learners are asked to collect as many words as they can that contain a given sound, e.g. an interdental fricative:

Voiced: *the, they, this, there, these, those, with, mother, father, brother, rather, weather, without bother, them, their, either, clothes*
Voiceless: *think, thing, bath, birthday, something, thief, healthy, mouth, thousand, both, thank, thin, three, third, tooth, mouth, north, thriller*

The next task consists of writing sentences which contain as many such words as possible, e.g.:

His **mother, father** and **brother** gave him **three things** for his **thirtieth birthday**.
I **think this thin thief with** bad **teeth** was not as **healthy** as he **thought**.

The most interesting sentences are then selected for oral practice.

Our students' phonetic training can also be made more efficient and attractive by the use of elements of drama in the classroom. Drama techniques in foreign language teaching enjoy quite a long tradition and their advantages have often been pointed out (e.g. Archibald, 1992). It has been observed that due to drama activities students become not only more fluent and competent in a foreign language, but also more creative, imaginative and self-confident. Teachers using such techniques have also been noted to benefit from them by becoming more committed to their work and by treating students as individuals to a greater extent than other language instructors.

It is important to clarify at the outset that introducing elements of drama does not necessarily imply staging a three-act theatre play with costumes, props, music and lighting, but can take various less time-consuming and technically simpler forms which involve role-playing, such as, for example, acting out a poem, a conversation, scenes from well-known films, dialogues written by the students or the teacher and improvisations of various kinds. As a matter of fact, any type of public delivery of a text (self-created or written by someone else) with elements of acting, use of movement, space and props can be assigned to this category.

There is no doubt that elements of drama can also be seen as a useful tool for the improvement of learners' pronunciation, with respect to both fluency and accuracy. In Section B.3.4 we demonstrate empirically how employing elements of drama helped a group of adult learners with poor English pronunciation to make considerable phonetic progress. Moreover, such activities also aid students to overcome their natural fear of using a foreign language in public. As observed by Celce-Murcia *et al.* (1996: 308):

> the rationale underlying the use of drama in the general language classroom extends to its use in teaching pronunciation – namely, that the context provided by the dramatic situation and the emotional involvement occasioned by drama foster communicative competence [...]. There is evidence that psychological factors are at work (e.g. increased empathy and self-esteem along with a decreased sensitivity to rejection) that enable students to transcend the normal limits of their fluency and accuracy, leading to more fluid and comprehensible speech, especially in the realms of intonation and inflection.

As emphasized by Archibald (1992), students performing on the stage must learn to speak loudly in order to be heard, clearly, i.e. with proper articulation, to be understood and in a variety of tones to keep the audience interested. These features of good pronunciation are, according to the author, often maintained by them off the stage as well. Thus, in Archibald's view, drama techniques help learners to develop natural and confident speech.

Another beneficial aspect of drama activities is that they make pronunciation learning more enjoyable and help to break the common boring routine of phonetic drills. It should also be observed that memorizing a passage and rehearsing it aloud many times is, in fact, a form of a repetition drill, much more interesting, however, than the usual tedious 'listen and repeat' procedure. Undoubtedly, elements of drama can enrich pronunciation classes, particularly because they are usually associated with fun and not so much with learning. As with ready-made texts learners do not have to concentrate on grammar and vocabulary, but can focus exclusively on pronunciation, drama activities provide the teacher with plenty of opportunities to diagnose students' pronunciation problems and to devise remedial procedures.

Rehearsals are excellent for both teacher correction and peer correction of pronunciation errors.

It is also worth pointing out that the use of drama in pronunciation training combines two important aspects of the process: individual work (rehearsing at home) with group work (rehearsing on stage). Thus, it fosters both students' responsibility for their learning process and promotes group cooperation and mutual feedback. Finally, drama-based activities provide an excellent opportunity for employing multisensory modes in the pronunciation class. Observe that acting involves not only visual and auditory channels but, through body movement and the use of props, also provides kinaesthetic and tactile reinforcement.

Thus, drama activities bring considerable benefits to pronunciation teaching. Despite this fact, they are not employed by language instructors as often as they deserve. Many teachers are reluctant to use them because they feel most comfortable with the traditional course book and recording-based tasks, and are sceptical of the efficiency of more innovative techniques, probably due to the education they have received themselves. Most of them are either unfamiliar with drama-based activities or do not see themselves in the role of drama coaches.

As for the students, not all of them are willing to participate in drama because of their shyness, poor pronunciation and/or lack of confidence in their own acting abilities. This observation is supported by Archibald (1992), who notes that the fear factor for a new drama user is hard to overcome. Moreover, as with all language teaching/learning techniques, there are not any that would suit all types of teachers and learners. This view finds support in Kelly's (2000) opinion, who claims that only those teachers who feel confident in using drama should do so, bearing in mind that many students balk at the idea of performing publicly.

A.3.3.3 Phonetic games

Most people, particularly young ones, enjoy playing games as they appeal to their competitive nature and a need for some of the excitement they inevitably bring. This fact can be used in the process of pronunciation teaching to make it less tedious and more attractive, just like employing songs, poems and drama discussed in the previous section. Many such materials, for example, Hancock's (1995) photocopiable *Pronunciation Games* or Hewings' (2004) *Pronunciation Practice Activities* have been published. Various other sources are also full of ingenious ideas for phonetic versions of traditional and well-known games such as Bingo, Hangman or Snakes and Ladders, phonetic crosswords, etc.

Ready-made materials, however, are not without some problems. First of all, they are not always available as in poorer countries funds for books and other teaching aids are always limited. Secondly, some games require props, e.g. special boards, drawings or cards of different kinds, which might discourage less artistically (or technically) minded instructors. Finally, the vocabulary and grammatical structures included in them might be inappropriate for a given group of learners, i.e. they can be either too easy or too difficult. For these reasons, in what follows we intend to encourage teachers to create their own games, suited to their learners' proficiency level, phonetic needs, age and interests. Some proposals have already been presented in the preceding sections. Below we offer several suggestions for simple games which can be used in the classroom without any complicated preparations and with different learners. We claim no originality here as similar proposals have been made in other sources as well, usually as raising phonetic awareness tasks. We are of the opinion that in a game-like form such activities are more appealing to learners, require more involvement from them and are therefore more effective. Of course, each of them should be followed by pronunciation practice of the included material. Since in this book the focus on words is advocated, most of the games show how we can tie pronunciation in with vocabulary work. Observe also that in many cases we can do a given task either as an ordinary phonetic activity to be carried out by learners or as a competitive game to be played by individual students or by teams.

Game 1

Take the names of months. First practise their pronunciation with the class. Next ask the participants to indicate those words which are characterized by the features listed below. Those of them who provide a correct answer score a point. Then all the points are added and the winner is indicated.

Which months:
(a) *contain the /r/ sound?*
(b) *contain affricates (/tʃ, ʤ/)?*
(c) *contain a long vowel (e.g. /a:/, /u:/ and /o:/)?*
(d) *contain a diphthong (e.g. /eɪ/)?*
(e) *have more than two syllables?*
(f) *have stress on the initial syllable?*
(g) *have stress on the final syllable?*

You can play this game with other types of vocabulary items which are introduced during the lessons.

Game 2

This is a version of the previous game. Here, however, instead of providing students with a set of words to study, you can ask them to think of their own examples with the required phonetic features. Each correct example scores a point. The winner is the person or team with the highest score, of course. Each of the supplied items must be pronounced aloud and corrected, if necessary.

List as many names of animals/foods/plants/countries as you can which:
(a) *start with /p, t/ or /k/*
(b) *contain the /æ/ vowel, as in cat*
(c) *start with two consonants*
(d) *end with two consonants*
(e) *contain the /aɪ/ diphthong, as in tiger*
(f) *contain /ŋ/, as in monkey*
(g) *contain /ʃ/, as in shark*

Game 3
Write several words on the blackboard. The students' task is to come up with as many items as they can which rhyme with the provided examples. In this way many minimal pairs will be formed which can then be employed in pronunciation practice, e.g.:

Supply as many words as you can which rhyme with the following items:
(a) *take (make, bake, lake)*
(b) *my (lie, why, tie)*
(c) *write (bite, kite, sight)*
(d) *cat (mat, bat, fat)*
(e) *pill (Bill, fill, till)*
(f) *get (set, let, met)*
(g) *go (slow, throw, show)*

Game 4
Write several words frequently mispronounced by your students on the blackboard and ask them to group these items according to the specified phonetic feature. Below I list several words frequently mispronounced by Polish learners (Sobkowiak, 1996):

won't, half, bull, world, sweater, nurse, soup, palm, worse, examine, purple, stomach, comfortable, damage, Turner, sweat, muscle, support, turkey, doubt, glove, comb, image, worst, oven, broad, circuit, surface, model, occur, salmon

Which of these words contains:
(a) /ʌ/
(b) /ɜː/
(c) /æ/
(d) /aɪ/

(e)   /iː/
(f)   /eɪ/
(g)   end in two consonants‹

As always, pronunciation practice of these items should follow.

Game 5

For learners who are familiar with phonemic transcription we can suggest an activity which also involves commonly mispronounced words. We can make a list of several such items in their orthographic form and two pronunciation versions: a correct one and an incorrect one. The task requires pointing out the proper phonetic forms which should then be practised.

Which forms given below are correct?
(a)   *climb* /klaɪm/ or /klaɪmb/‹
(b)   *foreign* /ˈfɒrɪn/ or /fɒˈreɪn/‹
(c)   *delicate* /ˈdelɪkeɪt/ or /ˈdelɪkət/‹
(d)   *event* /ɪˈvent/ or /ˈiːvent/‹
(e)   *broad* /brəʊd/ or /brɔːd/‹
(f)   *captain* /kæptn/ or /kæpteɪn/‹
(g)   *half* /haːlf/ or /haːf/‹

Game 6

In this activity learners are requested to provide examples which fulfil the specified requirements. Some answers are given below, but many other options are also possible.

Give examples of:
(a)   a word which starts with a long vowel and ends in a short one (e.g. *army, Easter*)
(b)   a word with two short vowels (e.g. *happy, mother*)
(c)   a word with three short vowels (e.g. *cinema, elephant*)
(d)   a word which starts with three consonants (e.g. *stranger, student*)
(e)   a word which starts and ends in two consonants (e.g. *plums, treats, slipped*)
(f)   a word which consists of two syllables and has final stress (e.g. *decide, police*)
(g)   a word which consists of three syllables and has initial stress (e.g. *Africa, government*)

Game 7

In this task learners are supposed to find common pronunciation features in the supplied sets of examples. In many cases several alternative correct answers are possible.

What pronunciation feature(s) do the following sets of words have in common?

(a)   *decide, propose, admit* (e.g. their final syllables are stressed)
(b)   *sister, doctor, comma* (they end in the same vowel)
(c)   *know, write, psychology* (the first letter is not pronounced)
(d)   *meet, team, scene* (they contain the same vowel)
(e)   *bomb, sing, damn* (the final consonant letters are not pronounced)
(f)   *match, chain, picture* (they contain the same consonant)
(g)   *long, bring, doing* (they all end in the same consonant)

Game 8

Below, we propose a few activities which can be carried out by drawing simple tables on the blackboard (or in the notebooks) and asking students to fill in the blank cells. In the first of them a sentence is provided and the task consists of counting the number of specific sounds which occur in it.

Buyers are always unhappy about higher prices before Christmas.

How many sounds listed below are found in this sentence?	
/r/	
/aɪ/	
/z/	
/s/	
/ɪ/	
/h/	
/p/	
/j/	

Game 9

This is another activity meant to eliminate frequently mispronounced words. Several items are provided in their orthographic form. Next to them there is a statement referring to their pronunciation. The students' task is to decide whether it is true or false.

Indicate whether statements given below are true or false:

Word	Statement	True or false?
lamb	/b/ is not pronounced	
steak	pronounced with /iː/	
Thames	pronounced with /Θ/	
waiting	no /k/ or /g/ at the end	
vegetable	pronounced with /eɪ/	

Word	Statement	True or false?
computer	has initial stress	
bass	pronounced with /eɪ/	
aren't	has two syllables	
nurse	pronounced with /ʌ/	
police	pronounced with /i:/ in the second syllable	

Game 10

Draw the following table on the blackboard. The students' task is to fill in all the cells as quickly as possible.

Give examples of words which fulfil the specified requirements:

	They consist of two syllables	They contain three syllables and have initial stress	They contain /æ/ or /ɑ:/	They contain /ʃ/, /ʒ/, /tʃ/ or /dʒ/
first names				
countries				
professions				
pieces of clothing				
colours				
fruits				
vegetables				
plants				

Activities such as the ones suggested above can be employed in the classroom when there is some time available and a need arises for some break from ordinary routine. The teacher can simply have a file with such materials at hand and use them whenever required. Of course their contents should be adjusted to the learners' level of language proficiency and the phonetic issues which are particularly relevant for them.

A.3.3.4 Using technology in pronunciation training

It is difficult to imagine contemporary pronunciation training without employing some instructional technology, starting from simple recordings of authentic English speech and ending with sophisticated commercial computer programs and internet websites devoted to articulatory and acoustic phonetics. As they are presented in numerous sources and some of them have been briefly introduced in the preceding sections, below we will concentrate on selected aspects of this issue with the focus on the language laboratory (LL) and its role in pronunciation teaching and learning.

The story of the use of technology in pronunciation teaching consists of a series of periods in which enchantment alternates with disillusion. During the audiolingual era, with its theoretical foundation in behavioural psychology, it was assumed that habit formation was the basis of language learning. This meant that repetition and drills, as mentioned earlier, constituted the core of this approach. As pointed out by Celce-Murcia *et al.* (1996: 311):

> nowhere during this era was instructional technology more heralded as an avenue for improving the skills of language learners than in the domain of pronunciation instruction, since it was felt that learners with enough exposure to and imitation of native models of pronunciation would be able to 'mimic' or correctly produce the targeted item. The audiotape recorder and its favoured environment – the language laboratory – were the medium and setting of choice for such learning to occur.

LLs, in spite of their high cost, were installed in every major teaching institution, also in less affluent countries, such as Poland, since it was believed that success in foreign language learning crucially depended on them. The LL was a symbol of high teaching standards and its effectiveness was taken for granted. As noted by Warschauer and Meskill (2000: 303), 'language programmes were enchanted by promises of magic through technology'.

Nevertheless, the magic did not turn out to be long lasting and the usefulness of the audio-based laboratory soon started to be questioned. As observed by Celce-Murcia *et al.* (1996), disenchantment with the audiolingual method meant that the LL fell into disfavour. It was claimed that language training in the lab environment brought disappointing results. Moreover, 'the methods and materials were felt to be passé, to have limited applications, and to be tedious and unstimulating' (Celce-Murcia *et al.*, 1996: 311). Warschauer and Meskill (2000: 303) attribute this phenomenon to the excessive use of much-dreaded repetition drills and maintain that: 'by the late 1970s, the audiolingual method fell into disrepute, at least in part due to poor results achieved from expensive language laboratories. Whether in the lab or in the classroom, repetitive drills which focused only on language form and ignored communicative meaning achieved poor results.'

Another factor which has contributed to the gradual decline of a typical LL with an audio console and student listening booths was the development of new types of instructional technology which have provided new, attractive tools for teaching language skills, including pronunciation. First the video was added, then satellite receivers. Finally, computers connected to the internet were introduced into the lab, which became modern language media centres. As argued by Celce-Murcia *et al.* (1996: 312), 'in its updated version, the language lab is again serving a serious pedagogical purpose, particularly as it relates to the teaching of pronunciation'.

Let us then consider the major strengths of pronunciation classes in the lab, discussed in detail by Szpyra-Kozłowska *et al.* (2006).

- **Acoustics:** Due to the use of headphones the LL provides all students, no matter where they are seated, with excellent technical conditions and an equal opportunity to hear the teacher and the recording clearly, which is not possible in an ordinary classroom.
- **Efficiency:** In a lab students can work all the time, with no breaks when the teacher communicates with an individual learner, whereas in a classroom one student interacts with the instructor while others only listen. Within a single laboratory session many learners can get feedback from the teacher, which makes efficient use of teaching time.
- **Privacy:** The lab provides an uninhibiting, sheltered environment for pronunciation practice which reduces the level of fear and embarrassment of shy and sensitive students, who are not intimidated by being corrected in front of other learners.
- **Attention:** The LL, with its listening booths and no visual and other distractors, permits all students to focus on their task, which increases their concentration and attention span.
- **Amount of practice:** The lab is ideally suited for a large amount of pronunciation practice, involving mimicry and repetition in particular, and getting instantaneous feedback from the teacher, impossible or difficult to implement in a classroom.
- **Access to native speech:** The lab provides access to different kinds of authentic audio material and many samples of native speech in all its varieties (e.g. dialect, register and sex) to study and/or imitate.
- **Individualization and self-pacing:** Many labs allow students to work on their assignments at a pace suited to their ability level. They can be given different, individualized tasks, record their own speech and compare it with the model.

Let us now turn to the discussion of the major weaknesses of the lab and the most frequent types of criticism levelled against it.

- **Intimidation:** Some learners feel that the lab, with its console, headphones, microphones and other equipment is an intimidating and unfriendly place.
- **Isolation:** By being placed in separate booths and talking through headphones some learners complain of feeling isolated. In the most extreme

cases they accuse the lab of creating a prison-like atmosphere, with the listening booths resembling prison cells.

- **Loss of contact between teacher and class:** It is often claimed that the lab is an obstacle to a good personal relationship between the teacher and the students. The teacher at the console is often isolated from the students by panes of glass and has limited visual contact with them.
- **Limitation of perception:** In the traditional lab only the learners' auditory channel is activated without the benefit of other kinds of support (e.g. visual or kinaesthetic). The focus on the ear ignores the needs of students with other modes of learning.
- **Ineffectiveness:** Listen-and-repeat drills in the lab are tedious, boring, unstimulating and ineffective. As observed by Evans (1976: 110), 'unrelieved repetition can sap the enthusiasm of even the most highly motivated student, so that his responses become mechanical and lethargic'.

Closer scrutiny of the above criticism reveals that most of it is directed not so much against the lab itself, but against its improper use. The isolation of the teacher and the learners does indeed occur in the lab but, as noted by Lee (1976: 199), 'the isolation is temporary, and it may well be that some language-learning has to be non-social in order to support the social role'. In fact, the sheltered environment of a student booth is often seen as one of the assets of the lab (see the list of advantages). It should also be added that in newer types of the LL there are no separate booths enclosing the learner on three sides, and the teacher and students are readily visible to each other.

Phonetic drills might be boring and ineffective if they are the only types of pronunciation activities used. As argued in the previous pages, such exercises should constitute only part of phonetic instruction, supplemented and enriched with a whole variety of other tasks for learners to perform. If classes in the lab are uninteresting, it is not the fault of the LL, but of either the tape or unvarying, monotonous exercises proposed by the teacher. Lee (1976: 200) rightly observes that boredom can be generated by many factors and 'students can fall asleep as readily over a dull textbook as over a dull tape'.

Intimidation of students by the lab and its equipment can be decreased or even eliminated if students are introduced to it gradually by being shown around, told how it works and by being given time to get familiarized with the whole set-up before starting to work. In other words, they should be convinced that the lab is their ally in pronunciation training and is a friendly environment in which to do so.

Summing up, it appears that the lab, and its modernized, improved version in particular, offers many different phonodidactic options and has numerous assets while its alleged drawbacks can be minimized or even eliminated. The following guidelines for the use of the LL can be offered, which can make pronunciation teaching and learning both effective and enjoyable.

(1)   The lab is not a method of teaching, but a tool which can be used in a variety of ways. It should be regarded as a complementary instructional aid, employed together with other methods of pronunciation instruction.
(2)   As often argued, effective classes in the lab should last no more than 20–25 minutes. After that learners' attention and concentration drops considerably.
(3)   If possible, labs should be technically upgraded on a regular basis to allow students to benefit from different types of instructional technology.
(4)   Varied, interesting audiotape materials of high technical quality should be employed in lab sessions. They should allow the teacher to use a variety of different activities, by no means limited to listen-and-repeat drills.
(5)   Phonetic drills can, and should, be used in the lab under the following conditions (Evans, 1976: 111):
   (a)   they must contain a limited amount of repetition, but this should be varied so that wherever possible the student is given tasks of a non-mechanical nature;
   (b)   they must develop the skill of reproducing patterns and sounds in a non-imitative situation;
   (c)   they must aim to develop skills which will stand the test of situations outside the LL.
(6)   Teachers must be well prepared to operate the lab equipment properly. In many cases various interesting uses of the lab are made impossible due to their technical ignorance and fear of the unknown. It must be remembered that lab classes do not mean less, but more work for the instructors.
(7)   The equipment in the lab must be maintained properly by qualified technicians, who should be able to instruct the teachers as to how to operate it.
(8)   Ideally, students should also have access to the lab for individual work and should be able to use some of the recordings on a library basis.

If no LL is available, good use can be made of other technological advances, computer technology and the internet in particular. We will discuss them in the following section.

A.3.4 Pronunciation Learning Outside the Classroom

As mentioned in other parts of this book, in EFL contexts learners usually do not have many opportunities to practise their English outside the classroom. Since the instruction time must be devoted to many different issues, pronunciation training is bound to be fairly limited. Therefore, to obtain the desired results, the teacher should encourage students to work on their pronunciation at home. Encouragement alone may not be sufficient, however, and the instructor must convince learners that it is not only necessary, but also easy to carry out, and show them how it can be done. Recall that, as argued in Section A.3.2.2, in EFL contexts one of the major principles is maximization of phonetic input which requires phonetic training to be continued after the classes.

It should be added that in contemporary approaches to language teaching much importance is attached to developing learner autonomy in the sense of instilling in students responsibility for their language learning not only in the classroom, but also outside it, when the instructor is not nearby to help them with language problems. In other words, students have to be told again and again that their success in achieving good English pronunciation largely depends on the amount of work they put into it on their own.

The question that arises is whether pronunciation can be learnt without the teacher's presence and direct guidance. It seems that in the initial stages of language education autonomous pronunciation work must be limited mainly to some forms of auditory training. Thus, beginners should regularly listen to various recordings, mostly those employed in the classroom and accompanying their course books, with very clear guidelines as to what exactly they are supposed to do with them. These can be, for example, different carefully specified sound discrimination and noticing tasks. At more advanced levels learners' receptive skills should be developed with samples of different English accents provided for students to listen to (see Section A.3.2.2).

Students can, of course, try to do 'listen and repeat' exercises, but they will generally be unable to assess whether their own pronunciation is good enough.[17] This observation finds support in the study presented in Section B.3.3, in which teenage secondary school learners in their evaluation of 10 different types of phonetic activities assigned the lowest scores to pronunciation work at home, both in terms of effectiveness and attractiveness, with the following typical comment: 'I'm afraid of working on pronunciation on my own because I may learn things incorrectly.' This result also shows that in matters of pronunciation learner autonomy does not come by itself, but must be carefully and gradually trained.

Luckily, modern technology provides some means for developing students' phonetic autonomy. Thus, all learners should be encouraged to use electronic dictionaries, both for finding the pronunciation of new words and for checking how already known items are properly pronounced in order to eliminate incorrect, fossilized forms. The teacher should demonstrate how such dictionaries work and devise several practice sessions. For example, some words, known to be phonetically difficult, can be written on the blackboard. The students' task is to find their pronunciation in an electronic dictionary and repeat the items several times. Next the teacher can point to some words on the board and ask learners to pronounce them to find out whether they have been remembered correctly. For homework, a list of lexical items can be given to students to be prepared in a similar way.

With intermediate and advanced students other forms of teacher-independent phonetic training can also be employed. For instance, they can record their own utterances and then listen to them, focusing on one selected pronunciation feature. The teacher should indicate which areas of pronunciation the student should work on. For example, for speakers of an L1 with no quantity distinctions among vowels it is very difficult to learn to produce long vowels of appropriate duration. In such instances, a useful homework assignment is to give students a short passage to practise reading at home, paying particular attention to vowel length. A good idea might be to make long vowels excessively long at first. Learners can record themselves reading the passage and then analyse it with respect to vowel length. Then the next recording should be prepared with an attempt to improve on the preceding version. Finally, both recordings should be compared in order to see whether some progress has been made. Of course, if necessary, the whole procedure can be repeated. Other features of English pronunciation can be practised in a similar fashion, conducive to developing in learners the ability to self-monitor their phonetic performance.

More advanced students can select an audiobook, choose a passage of 10–15 sentences and learn to reproduce it as faithfully as possible. As audiobooks are usually recorded by actors with excellent elocution and standard pronunciation and represent a high technical quality with no background noise, they provide an appropriate auditory input for learners, who can focus on imitating the reader without other distractors. With visual learners in mind, a written copy of the passage would be useful so that two channels of perception could be activated. Kinaesthetic learners should prepare action-packed passages which can then be performed with props, gestures and body movement. Students may also prepare at home some scenes or dialogues in pairs, preferably based on some recorded material.

Nevertheless, there is no doubt that there are computer programs and specialized internet pages which provide a much-needed modern aid in autonomous pronunciation training. Computer-assisted language learning (CALL) and within it computer-assisted pronunciation teaching (CAPT) are fast-developing areas with many ideas and interesting multimedia materials for teacher-independent phonetic practice. To this purpose, some commercially available programs can be employed, such as, for instance, Handke (2001) or Cauldwell (2003). Such aids, however, are not always easy to obtain and are associated with additional costs. What can be recommended to students are numerous pronunciation materials which are available free of charge on many internet pages, the addresses of which can be found in various sources (e.g.

Rogerson-Revell, 2011). They are not included here because by the time the book has been published, many of them will have disappeared.

According to Rogerson-Revell (2011: 261), CAPT has several important assets:

- it is tireless and patient;
- it can provide repetitively consistent speech models;
- it can provide a variety of voices;
- it can encourage learner autonomy;
- it enables visual as well as audio input and feedback.

Levis (2007: 184) also argues that the use of computers is almost ideally suited to learning pronunciation skills. He claims that: 'Computers can provide individualized instruction, frequent practice through listening discrimination and focused repetition exercises, and automatic visual support that demonstrates to learners how closely their own pronunciation approximates model utterances.'

Nevertheless, as pointed out by many pronunciation specialists, computer-based materials, although quite impressive, are not always pedagogically sound and suffer from many shortcomings in terms of interactivity and the feedback they provide. Kaltenboeck (2005: 21) argues that: 'one of the limitations of the computer at present is in the area of evaluative feedback to spoken language production. Despite its various feedback possibilities (...), machine-based evaluation of a user's recording is still largely unsatisfactory.' He further adds that: 'software all too often pretends to the role of a tutor without being able to respond as effectively as a human expert. It seems necessary therefore not to overrate the possibilities of the computer and treat it as a tool rather than an "expert tutor"'. Munro and Derwing (1995: 390) are also critical of the quality of such materials, claiming that 'if computer software could actually provide useful, individualized feedback to learners on their pronunciation, the teacher's burden would be dramatically reduced' and add that this has not happened so far. Levis (2007: 185) agrees, 'despite this great promise, effective commercial CAPT applications are less innovative either in pedagogy or use of computer technology than one might expect'. These critical comments suggest that computer programs and web pages devoted to pronunciation should be carefully examined by the instructor before they are recommended to students. Some training in their use should be carried out in the classroom so that learners know exactly what to do when they work on their own.

A.3.5 Providing Feedback

It is largely uncontroversial that in pronunciation training one of the most important teachers' tasks is providing feedback to learners, which can take different forms. Below we discuss some of them briefly, focusing on one of its most basic types, i.e. error correction.

First of all, instructors must realize that learning the pronunciation of another language is an enormous challenge that requires from them much patience, understanding and full support of the learners' endeavours. This means that emphasis should be put on their pronunciation successes rather than failures, at least in the initial stages of instruction. The teacher should thus praise students' phonetic achievements and encourage them to continue working on their English pronunciation. Moreover, as proved by research (e.g. Baran-Łucarz, 2011, 2013), phonetic training brings the best results when it is carried out in a friendly, relaxed, stress-free atmosphere in which the anxiety level is relatively low. The best approach, in our view, is to present learning English pronunciation to students as a complex, but very important and exciting task to tackle, a task which is difficult, but which can be accomplished successfully by all students. It can be likened to doing sports; the more we train, the better results we achieve. Nevertheless, just as only very few sportsmen become Olympic champions, few learners manage to acquire native-like pronunciation, which does not mean that somewhat worse results are worthless.

At more advanced levels each learner ought to be informed explicitly about how good (or bad) their pronunciation is, which areas of phonetics require special attention from them and how much progress they have made within a certain period of time, e.g. a semester. To do that properly, the student's pronunciation should be recorded regularly and assessed by the instructor. This, however, is very difficult to accomplish in the case of school teachers who frequently have hundreds of students to teach. We are, of course, fully aware that recording and analyzing students' phonetic performance means placing an extra burden on the teacher and may often be unrealistic, but it should be realized that EFL learners, who rarely have a chance to converse in English outside the class, are generally not capable of assessing whether their pronunciation is good or bad. As a matter of fact, in the school context students usually judge the quality of their pronunciation on the basis of their marks, as shown by their comments ('My pronunciation must be good because my marks in English are good').

This brings us to the issue of assessing students' pronunciation, necessary, as argued in Section A.3.1, if they are to regard it as an important component of language, the quality of which should constantly be improved. While assessment of pronunciation is not easy and can be carried out in different ways (see, for example, Szpyra-Kozłowska et al., 2005), it requires approaching each learner individually. This can best be accomplished if their pronunciation progress is recorded regularly. It is also needed in order to diagnose specific students' problems and to devise an appropriate remedial course of action.

In fact, teachers must be made aware of the fact that effective pronunciation training cannot be limited to group work only, but must address individual students' problems and abilities. Unfortunately, phonetically talented learners,[18] being every teacher's pride and joy, are usually outnumbered by those whose pronunciation fails to progress as planned. In Szpyra-Kozłowska *et al.* (2008) we present a project, termed the English Pronunciation Clinic, in which several very low-level phonetic achievers have undergone a special 'treatment' based on individual tutorials. In all instances the 'patients' made remarkable, and in some cases even spectacular, progress proving that phonetically hopeless cases are quite rare. This approach, however, is extremely time consuming for teachers and we cannot expect it to be commonly used.

A simpler type of feedback is provided by phonetic error correction, frequently employed by language teachers. It has been approached from a variety of theoretical perspectives. On the one hand, advocates of the teaching methods stemming from behaviourism maintain that every instance of an error should be immediately corrected as it is feared that the lack of reaction could lead to the reinforcement of incorrect forms. At the other extreme lies a conviction that since errors constitute an unavoidable part of the learning process, correction is unnecessary and even counterproductive. Thus, in the natural approach it is entirely excluded in the belief that improvement will occur without it. The communicative method represents the middle ground between these two extremes. Here emphasis is placed on fluency and communicative effectiveness, which entails a different attitude to error correction; namely, teachers are advised to be selective in their treatment of errors, focusing only on those that seriously affect communication. Therefore, they are expected to carry out an instantaneous analysis of a student's error in order to decide whether it should be corrected or not.

The latter approach can be generally recommended although it is not devoid of certain problems since the same type of inaccuracy might be regarded by some instructors as serious enough to require intervention, while others will consider it irrelevant. What is necessary is a set of pronunciation priorities (and some common sense) to provide the necessary criteria for evaluating error gravity. Moreover, after hearing the same types of errors for years, many teachers, who understand their students' English well, might become insensitive to various inaccuracies and decide not to correct them.

The question of timing is also relevant, with basically two types of options: on-the-spot and delayed correction. The choice depends on the aim of the activity in which students are engaged at the time when an error occurred. It is claimed that when fluency and communication are the primary objectives, delayed correction is more appropriate than interrupting the learner in mid-sentence. However, if the focus is on accuracy or when it is apparent that the student seeks immediate correction because otherwise they would not be able to convey an intended message, instantaneous error treatment is advised.

A significant issue relates to the person of the corrector. Although traditionally it is viewed as solely the teacher's duty, in fact correction may work equally well when this responsibility is delegated to other co-learners. Thus, there are three strategies depending on who assumes the role of the corrector:

- teacher correction – when the teacher corrects the students,
- peer correction – when the correct form is elicited from another learner,
- self-correction – when the correct form is elicited from the learner who committed the error.

Which of these strategies should be used to provide corrective feedback in a particular situation is a complex issue depending on a number of factors, such as the educational context, the learning and teaching styles of the participants, students' and instructors' personalities and the nature of the error. For instance, an experiment carried out by Szpyra-Kozłowska *et al.* (2004) demonstrates that what works best with Polish teenage pupils is teacher correction of pronunciation errors while peer correction is ineffective, which results from their reliance on teachers' professional competence and authority, denied to other students.

There are many ways in which phonetic error correction can be done. The first step involves indicating the mispronunciation. This can be done verbally by the teacher, who either provides the correct form or elicits it from the learner or other students. It is important for the person who has made an error to repeat the proper version in order to remember it. Correction can also be non-verbal, carried out by means of mime, gestures or other signals and signs previously agreed on (e.g. coloured cards). Silent correction through non-verbal signalling is less intrusive and is particularly useful for self-correction.

Apart from those techniques in which correction is executed overtly, there are also implicit ways of error treatment. One of them is zero correction in which the teacher notes down the errors that later serve as the basis for pronunciation work in future classes. Another strategy for providing implicit corrective feedback can take the form of the teacher's commentary referring to the learner's erroneous utterance. Instead of directly pointing to the error, the teacher can join in the conversation and, showing their interest, use a paraphrase of the student's words in which the correct form should be included. In order to ensure the greater effectiveness of this procedure, the teacher may even repeat the correct string several times in their commentary (Komorowska, 1989; Pawlak, 2004).

In brief, correcting students' mispronunciations can take different forms which should be employed in phonodidactics in order for teachers to select those which suit them and their students best and bring the desired results. In Section B.3.4 we present an experiment meant to examine the effectiveness of two methods of phonetic error correction: correction of selected inaccuracies versus correction of all phonetic errors. Both of them resulted in the participants' improved pronunciation, while in the control group in which no corrective feedback was provided no phonetic progress took place.

A.3.6 Problems with Pronunciation Teaching Materials

Nowadays an English pronunciation teacher is in the fairly comfortable situation of having a variety of textbooks, manuals and collections of phonetic activities, usually accompanied by appropriate recordings, to choose from to meet course requirements and satisfy their learners' needs. As pointed out in the preceding sections, many interesting materials are also offered by commercially available computer software as well as by numerous multimedia pronunciation courses found in the internet.

While there are undoubtedly many valuable sources for phonetic practice (several of them have been mentioned in this book), EFL teachers must be made aware of the fact that not all of them are appropriate for their students. Derwing and Munro (2005: 389) are also of the opinion that teachers 'may rely too heavily on pronunciation textbooks and software without regard for their own students' problems'. They point out that this strategy does not work since most materials have been designed without reference to pronunciation research findings and are not suited to all learners. This means that before any such materials are used, they should be carefully and critically examined. As this issue generally fails to be addressed in books devoted to phonetic instruction, it will be discussed here in some detail.

First of all, it should be emphatically stated that the majority of general course books in English contain a very limited phonetic component and are therefore insufficient for proper pronunciation training. This is an important issue since many teachers tend to rely exclusively on the course books and closely follow the activities found in them. Simply, they often assume that such books are written by professionals who know perfectly well how to devise an appropriate pronunciation teaching syllabus, properly integrated with lexical and grammatical issues. It should be remembered, however, that first of all course book writers are rarely also pronunciation specialists. Secondly and most importantly, they address their works to international learners, without catering for the needs of specific EFL students.

Thus, if a course book is meant to form the basis for pronunciation training, in selecting it the following criteria should be taken into account:

- **Number of phonetic activities:** If they constitute less than 10% of all tasks, we can conclude that they are insufficient in number and should be supplemented by additional sources.

- **Types of pronunciation activities:** In this case we should evaluate the quality and diversity of phonetic tasks. Many course books offer only a few types of activities, e.g. sound discrimination and imitation exercises. As argued earlier, pronunciation activities should be attractive to learners to enhance their interest in this aspect of language.
- **Elements of English phonetics covered by the book:** If the course consists of several parts, meant for learners of different levels of language proficiency, we should expect it to cover all the major areas of pronunciation, both segmental and suprasegmental.
- **Arrangement of phonetic material:** Since, in our view, a foreign sound system, in order to be mastered, should be cognitively processed by learners, a clear, logical arrangement of pronunciation issues with a justified set of priorities is very important as it facilitates system formation. Teachers should therefore examine whether the course book organizes the phonetic material according to some well-defined principles or offers a set of randomly ordered tasks. Moreover, as a principle of effective learning is repetition, a recursive approach in which once introduced issues must be returned to many times should be adopted.
- **Satisfying students' pronunciation needs:** Instructors should enquire whether a course book pays sufficient attention to the phonetic issues which are particularly relevant for their learners. For example, as demonstrated in Chapter 2, Polish learners require more training in segmental than in suprasegmental problems. Therefore, a book which focuses on intonation and marginalizes segments will not be appropriate for them.
- **Phonemic transcription:** As argued in Section A.3.6.1, phonemic transcription is an important tool for eliminating many phonetic errors, particularly in EFL contexts. Teachers can therefore examine whether a given course book employs phonetic script and whether it does so consistently and systematically.

An analysis of 25 sets of such course books (all published in Great Britain),[19] which took into account the above criteria, has shown that they differ strikingly in the amount and quality of phonetic material. The absolute winner has turned out to be *New Headway*, due to a separate booklet devoted entirely to pronunciation. Other titles to be recommended because of their appropriate treatment of phonetic issues include *Matters, Lifelines, Reward, Wavelength, Inside Out, Go* and *English File*. In the remaining books under analysis phonetic instruction is marginalized.

Many teachers use textbooks which prepare students for international language examinations, such as, for instance, those organized by the University of Cambridge Examinations Syndicate, which are taken by thousands of EFL learners in many countries. Szpyra-Kozłowska (2003) analyzed the phonetic component of 65 such books, advertised as teaching all the language skills needed to successfully pass the following examinations: First

Certificate in English, Certificate in Advanced English and Certificate of Proficiency in English. The study has shown that out of 65 publications subject to scrutiny 51 contained no phonetic component at all and only 14 comprised some pronunciation activities, usually limited to several tasks, with hundreds of exercises devoted to other aspects of English.[20]

Thus, the analysis of the phonetic component of many general course books and language examination materials leads to the conclusion that the majority of them cannot be regarded as providing sufficient pronunciation practice and, if used, must be supplemented with additional resources. Such publications as well as software are abundant. As mentioned in Chapter 1, their usefulness for EFL learners, however, can often be questioned. Below we discuss some of their problematic aspects of which EFL teachers should be made aware.

Pronunciation practice materials designed for international learners usually suffer from a number of shortcomings when approached from an EFL perspective since, on the one hand, they supply too much or unnecessary information and, on the other hand, they are not detailed enough for specific L1 learners. Thus, a typical pronunciation manual (e.g. Baker, 1981; Ponsonby, 1982) introduces all the English phonemes one by one and then contrasts them with some other phonemes by means of minimal pair exercises. Then sounds are practised in single words and phrases or whole sentences, sometimes in longer passages. The point is that many languages share various sounds with English which do not need to be practised. Polish learners of English, for example, do not have to learn how to pronounce /m, p, b, f, v, k, g/ or how to contrast word-initial voiced-voiceless pairs of consonants, as in *fine – vine*. Nor do they need to differentiate between two liquids: /l/ and /r/. Of course, in such instances all that is needed is the selection of practice material and omitting irrelevant tasks. What is more problematic, however, is that such books fail to provide activities on phonetic problems specific for L1 learners. This means, in consequence, that if they follow such manuals closely and do all the exercises conscientiously, it will not help them to eliminate many serious pronunciation errors since such sources do not cater for their particular phonetic needs. For example, Poles and Germans need to practise the retention of obstruent voicing in word-final position, e.g. in *bad, judge* and *have*. Hungarians require practice in making the /w/ – /v/ distinction and the French need to suppress the deletion of the initial fricative in *happy, house* and *history*. To put it differently, phonetic manuals for international learners offer them both too much and too little. This means that only materials prepared with the specific L1 learners in mind can truly help them to improve their English pronunciation.

Realizing the problem that has just been discussed and in order to cater for the needs of learners from various countries, many publications include sections devoted to the major phonetic difficulties of students with different L1s (e.g. Avery & Ehrlich, 1992; Rogerson-Revell, 2012; Walker, 2011). Our examination of such materials concerning the pronunciation problems faced by Poles reveals, however, that all of them contain serious errors and omissions. A common case involves observations made on the basis of a limited body of data then incorrectly overgeneralized to the whole sound system.

Avery and Ehrlich (1992) claim, for instance, that Poles have difficulties with the articulation of the voiced labiodental fricative /v/ and tend to replace it with the labiovelar glide /w/. They often say *walley* (instead of *valley*). While such replacements do occur, they are not connected with Poles' inability to articulate /v/ since exactly the same sound appears in numerous Polish words, e.g. initially in *Warszawa* 'Warsaw', *wódka* 'vodka' and *wada* 'drawback'. As these examples show, the labiodental fricative is spelt in Polish as <w>. The letter <v> is absent in Polish words. The pronunciation of these two letters is sometimes confusing to Polish learners in less frequent words, such as *valley* or *village*, but never in more common *very*, *love* or *river*. This confusion, however, is spelling-based and has nothing to do with any articulatory difficulty.

The same incorrect information is repeated in other sources, for example in Rogerson-Revell (2011: 286), where it is maintained that Poles 'tend to substitute /v/ for /w/ (e.g. *vest* for *west*)'. In this book, however, even more serious errors can be noted. The author includes a chart with Polish consonants (Rogerson-Revell, 2011: 285), in which as many as five palatal consonants, the velar fricative and the labiovelar glide are omitted. This means that out of 28 consonantal phonemes of Polish, seven are missing. Moreover, the velar nasal, which is a contextual realization of the dental nasal before velar plosives, is surprisingly placed in the phoneme inventory.

Walker (2011), in his book devoted to teaching the pronunciation of English as a lingua franca, has adopted a slightly different way of approaching language-specific pronunciation difficulties in that, instead of relying on available written sources, he asked some linguists with different L1 backgrounds to prepare appropriate lists of phonetic problems. This, however, has not always been successful in that various inaccuracies can still be found in Walker's book, probably due to the fact that not all description providers are pronunciation specialists.[21]

Thus, in the Polish section some errors can be noted. For example, it is stated (Walker, 2011: 122) that 'Polish /z/ is the same as in English', which is not true since /s/ and /z/ have a different place of articulation in both languages; they are postdental in Polish and alveolar in English. On the previous page the following claim is made: 'Polish is notorious for its consonant clusters in all possible positions, so the English clusters are not a problem.' Again, this is incorrect since, as shown by Sobkowiak (1996) and argued in the preceding chapter, some English clusters, e.g. those involving interdentals and comprising sequences of liquids, are problematic for Poles. Furthermore, while the provided description repeats six times the same information about word-final devoicing of obstruents, it fails to mention just as frequent cases of obstruent assimilation in voicing whereby obstruent clusters must be uniform in voicing (either all voiced or all voiceless). This feature is carried over to Polish English in which *dog fights* and *doc fights*, *backspace* and *bag space* become homophonous, leading to possible intelligibility problems.

The reason why some details of Polish and Polish English pronunciation are discussed above is simple. As demonstrated, in many cases the provided descriptions contain important errors and omissions. It is only logical to assume that sections devoted to other varieties of foreign-accented English are not error free either. This means that many general books on pronunciation teaching do not always provide a reliable guidance for language teachers.

Pronunciation textbooks should also be scrutinized in terms of the quality of the provided activities. In Szpyra-Kozłowska (2006) selected phonetic explanations and instructions found in some pronunciation materials and their usefulness for the foreign learner are examined. We address there the question of whether theoretical descriptions and suggestions for production exercises based on them enclosed in the analyzed resources can indeed facilitate the acquisition of English pronunciation by foreigners, and Poles in particular. The materials under examination included three high-quality books: Cunningham and Bowler's (1999) *New Headway Pronunciation Course* (NHPC) – a unique publication, meant for students of four levels of language proficiency, and two phonetic resource books for teachers: Kelly's *How to Teach Pronunciation* (HTTP) and Hewings' *Pronunciation Practice Activities* (PPA).

While in what follows we shall centre on some problematic aspects of these and other similar publications, it should be clarified at the outset that our criticism is not meant to discredit them since these are undoubtedly valuable aids both for learners and teachers of English, as we argue elsewhere. Rather, our aim is to point to some recurrent types of weaknesses such materials often suffer from, of which their users, EFL teachers in particular, (and obviously the authors) should be made aware.

In order to avoid drawing conclusions based solely on the author's subjective observations, an attempt has been made to verify them by the data obtained from a questionnaire filled in by 10 experienced teachers of English (including secondary school, college and university teachers), 20 recordings of secondary school learners of English and a questionnaire administered to them.

Consider the selected examples of phonetic tasks provided below.

(1) 'Here is a list of technical words we use in this book. Use a bilingual dictionary to translate them:
consonant, contraction, flat, intonation, linking, phonemic, polite, pronunciation, rude, sentence, sound, spelling, stress, syllable, symbol, vowel, weak.' (NHPC Elementary: 5)

(2) 'A lot of English words are spelt with *th*. These letters are pronounced /Θ/ or /ð/. (...) To make these sounds, the tongue must touch the back of your teeth like this [a drawing]. If you have problems with the

sounds, put your finger in front of your mouth and touch it with your tongue, like this [a drawing]. With the sound /ð/ you use your voice. With /Θ/ you do not use your voice.' (NHPC Elementary: 23)

The problem posed by the above tasks is that they contain many phonetic terms which are inappropriate for beginners who struggle with basic vocabulary and grammar. The teachers that have been consulted do not consider it desirable to introduce such linguistic jargon at early stages of teaching English and regard it as putting an unnecessary extra burden on the learners. The problem is a complex one as it is not possible to discuss sound articulation, either orally or in writing, without using some phonetic terminology which is, however, too difficult for beginners. Apparently, in this respect phonetic instructions in learners' L1s are far more useful.

The activities below, also meant for beginners, present a different type of difficulty.

(3) 'Underline the vowel sounds in these words: *fall, learn, way, road.* Does your language have the same vowel sounds? Underline the consonant clusters in these words: *space, play, climb, strong.* Does your language have the same consonant clusters?' (PPA: 24)

(4) 'How good is your English pronunciation? Circle your answer: 1 = high, 5 = low

vowels	1 2 3 4 5
consonants	1 2 3 4 5
consonant clusters (e.g. cl-, fr-)	1 2 3 4 5
word stress (e.g. aGO, FOLLow)	1 2 3 4 5
intonation (e.g. Yes↘ Yes↗)	1 2 3 4 5

Note any particular problems you have with English

vowels ....

consonants ....

consonant clusters ....

word stress ....

intonation ....,'

(PPA: 26)

(5) 'Identifying good English pronunciation. Students choose the person in the group with best English pronunciation. At the end of the activity the teacher asks why they have chosen particular students as having "better" pronunciation. What is it about these students' pronunciation they particularly like?' (PPA: 31).

In the first of these tasks learners are asked to compare sounds of English with the sounds of their native language. In the second of them, they are to assess the quality of their own English pronunciation and in the third one other students' pronunciation. Thus, they are either language awareness tasks which call for some knowledge of two sound systems or require the ability to assess one's own and other people's pronunciation. Expecting beginners, particularly young learners who constitute the majority in this group, to complete such tasks is clearly unrealistic. As mentioned earlier, even university students, near-graduates of English departments and proficient speakers of this language are often unable to self-assess their own pronunciation objectively and accurately. This claim is supported by the following teachers' comments: 'Lower-level learners may not have sufficient phonetic awareness to assess their own pronunciation.' 'This task requires theoretical phonetic knowledge of both languages which students don't have.'

To verify the validity of our objections to the above activities, we asked 20 Polish teenagers, pre-intermediate and intermediate learners of English to do some of them. First, they were to carry out task (4), i.e. to indicate the major problems they have with English vowels, consonants, consonant clusters, word stress and intonation. The most frequent answers were as follows: 'I don't know', 'I have no problems' and 'I often don't know how to read some letters'. Apparently, the participants were unable to provide more specific answers to this question.

Next the students were asked to indicate the person in their class who has best English pronunciation and state what they particularly liked about it, as required by task (5). Here are some typical opinions:

'Magda, because she speaks very fast.'
'Daria, because she speaks loudly.'
'Iza. I like her voice. It sounds nice.'
'Daria, because I can understand what she says.'

Clearly, all the comments are very general, impressionistic in character and lack any phonetic details which, apparently, the pupils were unable to provide.

These results give solid support to the correctness of the claim that non-advanced students possess neither sufficient language awareness of their own mother tongue and the foreign language they are learning, nor the ability to assess their own and other students' pronunciation to be able to do activities such as those quoted above.

We have also analyzed the content of some phonetic instructions provided in the books under examination in terms of their phonetic accuracy and pedagogical usefulness for foreign learners. All the authors of pronunciation materials provide some suggestions meant to help students produce English sounds correctly. They try to do that in a learner-friendly manner, offering explanations that can easily be understood and followed. One of the popular techniques is to make use of onomatopoeic words, i.e. items which imitate sounds produced by animals, humans and forces of nature.

Let us examine several examples of tasks involving onomatopoeic expressions in which students are asked to produce real-world sounds in order to learn English consonants and vowels.

(a) 'A noise you make if you want someone to be quiet.' (HTTP: 56)
(b) 'Make a bleating sound, like a lamb.' (Ponsonby, 1982: 76)
(c) 'The "something horrible" sound. Make and hold the sound, curl your upper lip, and pretend to look at something nasty. Look in the litter bin, if there is one at hand.' (HTTP: 38)
(d) 'Pretend not to hear someone and make this sound.' (HTTP: 39)
(e) 'The "Friday afternoon" sound. Relax your whole body, slump your shoulders, relax your face and mouth, and make this sound, as though completely exhausted.' (HTTP: 38)
(f) 'Make a sound as if you've heard something surprising, or some interesting gossip.' (HTTP: 39)

The problem with these activities is that sounds uttered in the above situations are not universal, but language-specific, i.e. conventionalized, which means that they differ from language to language. In other words, as pointed out by Trask (1995: 14), 'onomatopoeic items exhibit a great deal of arbitrariness in their forms (. . .) and have to be learned individually, just like ordinary words'. The quoted tasks can only confuse the learners in whose mother tongue such expressions are not the same as in English.

Table 3.2 juxtaposes the intended English sounds and typical Polish, Hungarian and Cuban Spanish responses to the provided situations. Evidently, the provided instructions are fairly useless for Poles, Hungarians and Cubans, who either employ different conventionalized items (sometimes several of them) from the English or do not use any particular fixed expressions in the situations mentioned in the tasks.

Let us now examine some further examples:

(a) 'The "shut your finger in the door" sound. Pretend to do this and make the sound while pulling a "pained" expression.' (HTTP: 39)
(b) 'Produce the sound that doctors ask you to make when they want to look at your throat.' (PPA: 43)
(c) 'The "holding the baby" sound. Place your arms as though holding a baby and make this sound.' (HTTP: 38)
(d) 'Produce the noise you would make if you were trying to steam up a mirror by breathing on it.' (PPA: 65)
(e) 'A noise a snake makes.' (HTTP: 38)

In these instances, Polish, Hungarian and Cuban Spanish sounds are often, although not always, similar to those found in English responses, but not identical (Table 3.3). For example, even if doctors often ask their patients

Table 3.2 Selected onomatopoeic expressions in English, Polish, Hungarian and Cuban Spanish (1)

Instruction	Intended English sounds	Sounds made by Poles	Sounds made by Hungarians	Sounds made by Cubans
(a) The 'be quiet' sound	/ʃʃʃ/	ciiii [tɕi:]/psst	csit [tʃit]	/ʃʃʃ/
(b) The lamb's bleating sound	/æ/	bee/mee	mé [me:]	[bee]
(c) The 'something horrible' sound	/ɜ:/	fe!/fuj! [fuj]	fuj! [fuj]	[ba]!
(d) The 'say it again' sound	/eɪ/	hmm? [xm:]/ coo? [tsoo] 'what?'	hogy? [xodʲ][a] 'how'/mit? 'what?'	[e:] (with rising intonation)
(e) The 'Friday afternoon' sound	/ə/	uff	áh! [a:x], óh! [o:x]	uff
(f) The 'something surprising' sound	/u:/	ooo!/oh! [ox]/ coo? [tsoo] 'what?'	óh? [o:x] (with rising intonation)	wow! (borrowing from English)

Note: [a]The final consonant is a palatal plosive.

Table 3.3 Selected onomatopoeic expressions in English, Polish, Hungarian and Cuban Spanish (2)

Instruction	Intended English sounds	Sounds made by Poles	Sounds made by Hungarians	Sounds made by Cubans
(a) The 'shut your finger in the door' sound	/aʊ/	auć! [awtɕ]/ au [aw]/aua [aʲwa]	oj!	uj!
(b) The sound doctors ask you to make	/a:/	aaa (low central)	é! [e:]	aaa! (low front centralized)
(c) The 'holding the baby' sound	/a:/	aaa (low central)	tente, tente	aaa (as above)
(d) The 'steaming up a mirror' sound	/h/	huu [xu:]/hu hu [xuxu] (velar fricative)	huu [xu:] (velar fricative)	huu [xu:] (velar fricative)
(e) The 'snake' noise	/s/ (alveolar)	sss (postdental)	sss!(dental)	sss (alveolar)

with a sore throat to produce a low vowel, its realizations will be a back advanced sound in English, but a front (centralized) vowel in Polish and Spanish. When steaming up a mirror, native speakers of English will employ the glottal fricative, but Poles, Hungarians and Cubans will use a velar spirant. The following high back vowels are not the same either.

Not only will Polish, Hungarian and Cuban students not learn how to pronounce English sounds correctly if they follow the above instructions, but they may be led into believing that these languages contain identical consonants and vowels, which in most cases is not true.

A common procedure adopted by many authors involves providing simplified articulatory descriptions of English sounds, often coupled with drawings of head cross-sections. They are claimed to be particularly useful for those learners who want to work on their pronunciation on their own without the benefit of a teacher's guidance.[22] The question that arises is whether such descriptions can indeed help foreign learners in mastering the sounds of English. To find an answer, several passages dealing with sound production taken from the books under investigation have been analyzed by a group of English teachers who then commented on their phonodidactic value. Moreover, in order to examine the usefulness of such descriptions, some secondary school pupils representing the intermediate level of proficiency were asked to follow the instructions provided. The sounds they produced were then recorded by their English teacher.[23] In what follows we discuss just a few selected cases which concern sounds known to be problematic for Polish learners (for a fuller discussion and more examples, see Szpyra-Kozłowska, 2006).

Consider the following quotations.

> The sound /ʤ/ is made with the two sounds /d/ and /ʒ/. First say /d/. Then say /ʒ/. Repeat each sound quickly until you say the two sounds together. You use your voice. Feel your throat vibrate when you say it. To make the sound /ʧ/, first say /t/. Then say /ʃ/. Repeat each sound quickly until you say the two sounds together. (NHPC. Elementary: 33 & 51)

The respondents were unanimous in claiming that the above instruction is both phonetically inaccurate and of no use to Polish students. English palatoalveolar affricates are not sequences of sounds, but single segments which involve two articulatory gestures (that of a complete closure followed by its gradual release with accompanying friction). Moreover, as in Polish sequences of plosives and fricatives are commonplace (e.g. in *drzewo* /d-ževo/ 'tree', *trzy* /t-ši/ 'three'), Polish learners tend to pronounce the two segments separately regardless of the tempo of speech. This was confirmed by the pupils' recordings, all of whom produced sequences of plosives and alveolar fricatives instead of the expected affricates.

Below we present another instruction which is also meant to help learners pronounce English affricates.

> If students have special problems with /tʃ/, ask them to shape the mouth as if they were going to produce /t/. Then to push the lips forward and round them; flatten the tongue a little against the top of the mouth; build up pressure in the mouth and release it suddenly. To produce /dʒ/, do the same but with less pressure, making sure that the sound is voiced. (PPA: 63)

This instruction was found by the teachers to be very difficult to follow, because of both its phrasing and the complexity of the whole series of articulatory gestures required of students. It seems that the authors of such instructions often appear to ignore the fact that phonetically untrained persons do not have full control of their speech organs and cannot easily follow the provided advice. This reasoning finds full support in the recordings that were made; the participants produced a dental plosive followed by some fricative sound, most frequently labiodental /f/. In some instances, due to the requirement of lip rounding, a sequence /tu/ (or even /tfu/) was uttered. In none of the cases was the ultimate result close to the expected English palatoalveolar affricates.

Finally, we shall consider some instructions concerning the pronunciation of vowels. Detailed descriptions do not work well here as vowel articulation is difficult to self-inspect. Therefore the authors resort to a fairly imprecise type of advice, e.g.:

> To make the sound /e/, open your mouth and smile. /e/ is a short sound. To make the sound /æ/, open your mouth and don't smile so much. /æ/ is a short sound.
> To make the sound /ʌ/, keep your mouth open but don't smile at all. /ʌ/ is a short sound. (NHPC Pre-Intermediate: 42)

The teachers participating in our study were all sceptical about the usefulness of these instructions, mostly because of their lack of precision. It was pointed out that they made no reference to tongue positioning and that remarks on the degree of lip rounding and spreading were too vague ('What does it mean "to smile"? How wide should a smile be? How high in the mouth should the tongue be?'). They also observed that many of these descriptions could just as well be used to introduce Polish or Spanish vowels as they were so general.

In order to find out whether such descriptions work, we asked several students to follow the instructions concerning vowels. The obtained results, however, left much to be desired. In fact, the pupils found the advice to smile or not to smile too much rather confusing, and it distracted them from the task of articulating vowels. The resulting sounds bore little resemblance to the intended English segments and were, generally, realizations of Polish /e/ and /a/.

In this section we have analyzed selected types of phonetic activities present in some recent pronunciation teaching materials and found them frequently inadequate in several respects. First, they often employ phonetic terminology and comprise language awareness tasks which are too difficult for the lower-level learners they are often meant for. Secondly, such publications make use of simplified articulatory descriptions, which although learner friendly, are frequently inaccurate, imprecise and do not result in the production of appropriate sounds. Finally, some of the examined activities refer to specifically English onomatopoeic forms and are of little or no use for foreign learners in whose native languages different expressions are employed. In brief, the usefulness of the tasks under consideration can be seriously questioned. It is important to add that many other pronunciation teaching materials which have not been scrutinized here suffer from similar shortcomings. Thus, the cases described above seem to be typical rather than exceptional, and further problematic activities are not difficult to find. Pronunciation teachers should therefore carefully examine the activities suggested in various sources to make sure they are adequate and suitable for their learners.

The majority of the problems with pronunciation materials outlined in this section stem from the fact that they mean to accomplish the impossible – to cater for the needs of all learners of English, both ESL and EFL students, speakers of a variety of native languages, who have diversified pronunciation difficulties. It is like suggesting one universal type of, say, facial cream, good for everyone. As we know perfectly well, face cream users have different complexions and different skin types, and what works for some of them might not work for others.

The conclusion is evident – appropriate pronunciation practice materials should be prepared with specific users in mind, covering the major areas of phonetic interference from the L1 on English. When available, they should be employed in phonetic instruction.[24] If not, general sources should be made use of, supplemented, however, with additional materials dealing with the pronunciation problems of specific EFL learners.

Part B

Several experimental studies presented in this part deal with various pronunciation teaching techniques. First, in Section B.3.1 we compare the intuitive-imitative and analytic-linguistic approaches and Section B.3.2 examines several methods of phonetic instruction in terms of their effectiveness and attractiveness to teenage Polish learners. Next, Section B.3.3 provides some evidence for the usefulness of employing elements of drama and in Section B.3.4 we argue for the necessity of phonetic error correction.

B.3.1 Motor Training Versus Cognitive Training

Stasiak and Szpyra-Kozłowska (2003) carried out a small-scale experiment in order to examine the effectiveness of two approaches to pronunciation teaching, one based on 'listen and repeat' activities and phonetic drills (intuitive-imitative) and the other involving explicit instruction (analytic-linguistic or cognitive).

The experiment took place in a Polish secondary school and lasted five months. It was carried out during regular English classes taught by one of the experimenters. Forty-five participants, divided into three groups (A, B and C), each consisting of 15 students, aged 17, of both sexes took part in it. They represent the pre-intermediate level, both in terms of their general level of English proficiency and pronunciation.

Out of each class, five randomly selected students were recorded having being asked to read a short diagnostic passage of 16 sentences. Next the experimental five-month period of teaching pronunciation began. After five months the same 15 participants were re-recorded while reading the same passage as before. Each recording was analyzed auditorily by the experimenters with respect to the following aspects of English phonetics:

- word linking and fluency;
- vowel length;
- the interdental fricatives;
- the velar nasal (without the following velar plosive, e.g. in *sing*);
- the post-alveolar approximant;
- /æ/;
- strong and weak forms;
- aspiration;
- word-final devoicing of obstruents.

It is worth adding that all the above phonetic features of English were introduced and briefly dealt with during the language course previous to the experiment.

The three experimental groups were taught English pronunciation in three different ways, specified below.

Group A: Special attention was paid to pronunciation teaching, with emphasis put mainly on aural exposure to the recorded phonetic material, followed by imitation and drilling, without any explicit instruction.

Group B: Special attention was paid to pronunciation teaching, with emphasis put mostly on explicit phonetic instruction and the use of phonemic script. For example, students were presented with head cross-sections illustrating different places of consonant articulation in English and Polish, given instructions how to position speech organs in the production of selected English sounds and provided with information on the major differences between Polish and English phonetics. Each new lexical item was introduced together with its transcribed form of which knowledge was then required. Imitation of teacher's pronunciation was employed, but it was kept to a minimum.

Group C: No special emphasis was placed on pronunciation teaching. The basic school curriculum in English was followed and phonetic activities were limited to those provided in the course book and the accompanying CD.

The pupils in Groups A and B were engaged in 55 pronunciation tasks altogether, lasting approximately 8 minutes per lesson. Pronunciation activities in Groups A and B focused on the aspects of English phonetics enumerated above.

Table 3.4 summarises the analysis of the recordings both before and after the experiment in all three groups. The provided figures refer to the percentage of correctly pronounced features.[25] Before the experiment, all the participants failed to pronounce properly various elements of English phonetics. For

Table 3.4 Experimental results: Effectiveness of two approaches to phonetic instruction

Problematic pronunciation areas	Before the experiment	After the experiment		
		Group A (intuitive-imitative approach)	Group B (linguistic-analytic approach)	Group C (control group)
Devoicing word-final obstruents	0%	20%	20%	0%
The velar nasal	0%	60%	20%	0%
Vowel length	0%	0%	0%	0%
The interdental fricatives	0%	40%	40%	0%
/æ/	0%	0%	0%	0%
Aspiration	0%	0%	0%	0%
Strong and weak forms	0%	0%	0%	0%
Word linking and fluency	27%	60%	80%	40%
The post-alveolar approximant	80%	100%	100%	80%

instance, each student fully devoiced word-final voiced obstruents, pronounced the word-final velar nasal with the following velar plosive, failed to make a systematic distinction between long and short vowels, replaced the interdental fricatives with the dental plosives /t, d/ or the labiodental fricatives /f, v/, substituted the vowel ash with /e/ or /a/, and failed to aspirate voiceless plosives and use weak forms.

The post-experimental recordings show some improvement in the learners' pronunciation, the degree of which, however, varies greatly depending on the group. In Groups A and B some advancement has been observed in the following six areas: the pronunciation of the postalveolar approximant (20% in both groups), the velar nasal (60% in Group A and 20% in Group B) and the interdental fricatives (40% in Groups A and B), voicing of word-final obstruents (20% in Groups A and B), word linking and fluency (33% in Group A and 53% in Group B). No improvement, however, occurred with respect to vowel length, the vowel ash, aspiration and the use of weak forms. To sum up, phonetic progress in Groups A (19.2%) and B (17%) was virtually the same. These data allow us to draw a tentative conclusion that the employment of these two approaches brings similar results. Moreover, while in most cases the improvement in the learners' phonetic performance was observed in the same areas of pronunciation, some interesting differences could be noted as well. Explicit instruction has turned out to be more effective in teaching the pronunciation of the velar nasal, while 'listen-and-repeat' tasks have brought better results in improving students' word linking and fluency. Thus, both methods of phonodidactic instruction have proved to be equally effective with regard to some aspects of pronunciation, while in some instances one of them has been more beneficial than the other. Consequently, they both deserve a place in the language classroom, but their use must depend on the type of phonetic problem. Moreover, if each of them employed separately leads to students' improved phonetic performance, a combination of these approaches is bound to produce even better results.

As anticipated, the negligence in the teaching of English phonetics produced virtually no progress in Group C (1.4%). There is only one pronunciation area where some improvement (13%) was observed, i.e. in word linking and fluency. An obvious conclusion is that pronunciation training limited to phonetic tasks included in the course books is clearly insufficient and must be complemented with additional activities.

B.3.2 Effectiveness Versus Attractiveness of Pronunciation Teaching Activities

As shown in Section A.3.3, numerous ways of teaching L2 pronunciation have been suggested by specialists. While the effectiveness of many of them still remains to be tested, an important issue is also that of their attractiveness to learners. Ideally, phonetic activities should be both effective and attractive, but this ideal is certainly difficult to attain as some of them are not very exciting but produce the desired results, while others provide great fun, but bring no particular progress in learners' pronunciation.

In order to examine this issue, Stasiak and Szpyra-Kozłowska (2003b) carried out an experiment with 50 Polish secondary school students, aged 16–17, representing the pre-intermediate to intermediate level of English proficiency, who were taught English pronunciation for four months by means of 10 different types of activities. After the experimental period the participants were asked to complete an anonymous questionnaire in which they evaluated their phonetic training.

Below we describe briefly all the types of phonetic activities which were used in the experiment.

Repeating after the tape

After listening to a recorded passage, students were asked to repeat selected words, phrases and sentences, first chorally, then individually, paying particular attention to the pronunciation of sounds, proper word and sentence stress, fluency, rhythm and intonation.

Imitating the teacher

This was the most frequently used type of activity. During almost every lesson students repeated after the teacher various English sounds, words, phrases and whole sentences. Both choral and individual repetition was employed.

Phonetic drills

Phonetic drills involved numerous repetitions (of the recorded material and the teacher) of selected sounds, sound sequences, words, phrases and sentences until the teacher decided that the quality of the students' pronunciation was satisfactory.

Minimal pairs

Activities with minimal pairs were used mainly to make students realize the fact that frequently mispronouncing a single sound leads to a change in a word's meaning. Thus, they were asked to repeat words such as, e.g. *pin – ping – pink, sin – sing – sink*. Moreover, minimal pairs appeared in sound discrimination activities.

Phonemic transcription

Phonemic transcription, introduced prior to the experiment, was employed in every lesson whenever new vocabulary was introduced. Each new item was transcribed by the teacher on the blackboard and students copied these forms into their notebooks. Frequently whole difficult phrases and sentences, e.g. tongue twisters, were transcribed. Needless to say, the pronunciation of all transcribed items was then practised.

Songs

Several British and American songs, all current pop hits, well-known and well-liked by the students, were practised during the lessons. After listening to a song, its lyrics were explained, with particular emphasis being placed on pronunciation. A frequently employed activity involved providing students with the lyrics with some words missing which they were expected to supply upon listening to it. In another task different lines were placed on separate strips of paper to be then placed in the right order. Finally, the students sang the songs and the teacher corrected their pronunciation errors.

Dialogues

Several dialogues taken from teenagers' magazines and recorded by native speakers of English were used. They contained language typical of young people, with colloquial vocabulary and simple grammar, and many features of connected speech (contractions, assimilations and elisions).

At first, students focused on comprehension of the dialogues and their vocabulary. Next, their task was to reproduce them as faithfully as possible, paying particular attention to pronunciation accuracy. In fact, they were asked to act them out, using appropriate facial expressions, gestures and body movement, as in a theatrical performance.

Tongue twisters and limericks

Many tongue twisters and limericks were employed to practise some difficult sounds and sound combinations. After explanations concerning the meaning of new vocabulary items and comments on particular phonetic issues which appeared in the material, the students were asked to repeat them, first chorally and then individually.

Pronunciation games

The games employed by the teacher came mainly from Hancock's (1995) book. In one task, for example, students had to join pairs of words which contained the same vowel or began with the same consonant. Another game involved finding the way out of a phonetic maze which comprised words beginning and ending in a vowel. The solution required indicating the appropriate linking element (one of the glides or /r/). Other games concerned rhythm and intonation.

Working on pronunciation at home

As part of their homework assignments, students were asked to do the following tasks:

- looking up the pronunciation of new words in a dictionary and repeating them aloud;
- using electronic dictionaries to find the pronunciation of new words and repeating them after the recording;

- reading aloud passages taken from the course book;
- recording these passages and analyzing one's own pronunciation.

After five months of the phonetic training described above, the participants were requested to complete a questionnaire, meant to evaluate the attractiveness and effectiveness of the employed pronunciation activities.

First we asked the participants to assess the attractiveness of the 10 techniques on a scale from 1 to 6, where 1 = very unattractive and 6 = very attractive. Table 3.5 presents mean evaluations supplied by the students. The table shows that teenagers enjoy learning English pronunciation through songs, acting out dialogues, tongue twisters and limericks, that is, activities which require some emotional involvement and/or humour. An interesting result is a high place for phonemic transcription, commonly regarded as rather tedious and boring. At the bottom of the list there are different types of 'listen and repeat' activities, all of which involve mechanical imitation of the model. The participants strongly dislike working on pronunciation on their own at home.

Next the students were to indicate their favourite type of phonetic activity and to justify their opinion. Songs, dialogues, tongue twisters, limericks and phonetic games were the most frequent choices, in agreement with the data in Table 3.5. Below we quote some typical comments.

Songs

- *I learn words in the lyrics very quickly and remember them easily.*
- *I try to pronounce words exactly the way a singer does.*
- *Due to songs I finally understood what all these weak forms are about.*

Dialogues

- *I like dialogues because I can learn many slang words and expressions from them.*
- *Dialogues motivate me to learn pronunciation.*
- *I like pretending I'm a British person and pronounce sentences like the British do.*

Table 3.5 Attractiveness of 10 phonetic activities: Students' evaluations

Ranking	Type of activity	Mean score
1	Songs	5.0
2	Dialogues	4.8
3	Tongue twisters and limericks	4.4
4	Phonemic transcription	3.8
5	Phonetic games	3.0
6	Repeating after the tape	2.7
7	Imitating the teacher	2.7
8	Minimal pairs	2.2
9	Phonetic drills	1.7
10	Working on pronunciation at home	1.6

Tongue twisters and limericks
- *I learn quickly things which are amusing.*
- *I try to pronounce properly every word in them.*
- *If I can learn to pronounce such difficult things as tongue twisters, ordinary sentences will be much easier.*

These comments indicate that teenagers learn English pronunciation willingly in a stress-free, relaxed and informal atmosphere created by such activities as singing songs or reciting limericks, which depart from more routine school tasks. Moreover, they point to various advantages of such activities, for example, the ease of memorizing new vocabulary, both its meaning and pronunciation.

Let us now examine the least attractive ways of learning English pronunciation. As shown in Table 3.5, repeating after the tape, imitating the teacher's pronunciation, minimal pairs and phonetic drills have been evaluated most negatively. As in all these cases the students' comments were very similar, we present some of them jointly below.

Phonetic drills, repeating after the tape and the teacher, minimal pairs
- *They are monotonous and boring.*
- *I hate repeating the same things over and over again.*
- *They discourage me from learning pronunciation.*

According to the presented comments, Polish teenage learners dislike monotonous, mechanical and repetitive activities which do not motivate them to learn the language.

The second part of the questionnaire was devoted to eliciting learners' judgements on the effectiveness of various pronunciation teaching activities. They were requested to evaluate the 10 types of techniques in terms of their effectiveness, using the same scale from 1 to 6 (where 1= very ineffective; 6 = very effective). The results are provided in Table 3.6.

The participants consider phonemic script the most effective technique of pronunciation teaching/learning. They justified this view in the following fashion:

- *Thanks to phonemic transcription I can learn the pronunciation of new words at home.*
- *Whenever I have doubts how to pronounce a given word, I can always check it in a dictionary.*
- *Phonetic symbols made me realize differences between spelling and pronunciation.*
- *Ever since I've learnt phonemic transcription, I make fewer pronunciation errors.*
- *At first it was difficult to learn all those strange symbols, but now I cannot imagine learning a new word without transcribing it – it has become a habit with me.*

Table 3.6 Effectiveness of 10 phonetic activities: Students' evaluations

Ranking	Type of activity	Mean score
1	Phonemic transcription	5.0
2	Songs	4.8
3	Imitating teacher's pronunciation	4.5
4	Dialogues	4.4
5	Tongue twisters and limericks	4.1
6	Phonetic games	3.4
7	Repeating after the tape	2.8
8	Minimal pairs	2.2
9	Phonetic drills	2.0
10	Working on pronunciation at home	1.7

Thus, students observe that thanks to phonemic transcription they have become more independent of their teacher as now they can consult a dictionary in matters of pronunciation whenever needed. Phonemic script has also allowed them to eliminate many fossilized and spelling-dependent errors. The final comment is particularly interesting; here a student admits that learning phonetic symbols was quite a challenge, but it was well worth the effort. This result of our study clearly shows that in the case of EFL learners phonemic script, frequently neglected by many teachers, should constitute one of the major pronunciation teaching techniques. Other highly valued activities include learning songs, dialogues, tongue twisters and limericks; similar arguments for these have been provided as those quoted earlier.

Let us now pass on to the activities regarded by the students to be the least effective. They include repeating after the tape, minimal pairs, phonetic drills and working on one's pronunciation at home, all of which scored below 3 points. In all the cases similar and fairly general comments were given:

- *These are boring activities and I don't think I benefit much from them.*
- *Instead of motivating me to learn pronunciation, they demotivate me.*
- *I quickly forget the pronunciation of words learnt in this way.*

Apparently, the participants dislike purely mechanical activities and do not believe in their effectiveness.

It is also interesting to examine some typical comments on working on pronunciation at home, which occupies the lowest position in both rankings:

- *I'm afraid of working on pronunciation on my own because I may learn things incorrectly.*
- *I cannot learn pronunciation on my own because no one corrects me.*
- *Speaking to myself with no one to listen and correct me makes no sense.*

Such remarks clearly indicate that at this stage of advancement students have little trust in their ability to learn pronunciation without the teacher's guidance and constant feedback.

Finally, we should like to examine briefly the relationship between the attractiveness and effectiveness of the 10 types of examined pronunciation activities which emerged from our study. A comparison of Tables 3.4 and 3.5 shows numerous similarities between the two rankings. Thus, the use of songs, dialogues, tongue twisters and limericks is considered to be both attractive and effective. The participants assess negatively repeating after the tape, minimal pairs, phonetic drills and working on one's pronunciation at home, as neither interesting nor bringing positive results. This means that, generally, students are of the opinion that only enjoyable activities can be effective.

Let us now focus on the major differences between the two evaluations. What is perhaps particularly striking is the top position of phonemic transcription, viewed by the participants as the most effective technique, which is, at the same time, of medium attractiveness. It is also interesting to note that of the 'listen and repeat' activities, imitating the teacher's pronunciation is considered the third most effective type of activity, which remains in contrast to repeating after the tape, regarded as neither attractive nor effective. The latter result supports the claim that pronunciation is acquired not only 'through the ears', but also through other senses. In other words, audio recordings provide only auditory input whereas the teacher, with his/her facial expressions, gestures and other types of body language, supplies visual reinforcement to the phonetic material. Moreover, in the classroom learners can observe the instructor's lips and jaw movements, which also enhances pronunciation learning.

A final comment is that the presented data reflect only the participants' subjective opinions and cannot be viewed as an objective assessment of the phonodidactic value of the analyzed types of activities. Thus, more objective measurements are needed to study their effectiveness. On closer scrutiny it might turn out that tasks considered boring do, in fact, improve learners' pronunciation while those regarded as very interesting bring negligible progress. On the other hand, we cannot ignore learners' attitudes towards phonetic training and should try to employ activities which fulfil both criteria: that of effectiveness and that of attractiveness. In other words, it is important for our students to be convinced that what we are offering them as teachers is of appropriate quality as well as interesting. Only then can they feel motivated to work hard on their pronunciation.

B.3.3 Employing Elements of Drama

In order to examine the effectiveness of drama techniques in pronunciation training, Szpyra-Kozłowska and Bukowski (2006) carried out a small-scale experiment, termed the English Pronunciation Theatre. It took place in a teacher training college, attended by adult learners wishing to become teachers of English. Twelve of them, aged between 24 and 42, of both sexes, volunteered to take part in the performance to be later presented to the remaining college students. In terms of English proficiency, they were intermediate learners with rather poor English pronunciation.

Five students with serious pronunciation problems were selected for the purposes of the experiment. They were individually recorded while reading a diagnostic passage which was not available to them during the experiment. Each participant was given several lines to memorize. These were mostly humorous monologues and dialogues, written by the students themselves, delivered by ghosts of some famous British historical figures, such as Queen Victoria, and more recent celebrities, e.g. Princess Diana, who came to the college Christmas Party with some messages for the audience. Then the weekly rehearsals, of approximately 60–90 minutes each, began and lasted for about eight weeks. Apart from the usual aspects of a theatrical performance, such as costumes, props, lighting and, of course, acting, during the rehearsals particular attention was paid to the quality of the actors' pronunciation. The performance was presented to the college audience before Christmas and was a great success.

About two weeks later, five students selected earlier were re-recorded while reading the same diagnostic passage. All the recordings were then evaluated holistically by three raters, all experienced phonetics teachers, using a scale from 1 to 5, where 1 denoted very poor pronunciation and 5 very good pronunciation. It should be added that the judges were not informed which recordings were made prior to the rehearsals and which after the performance. The results are presented in Table 3.7. This table demonstrates that all the participants received higher scores for their post-experimental recordings than for the pre-experimental ones. Thus, Student 1 improved by half a point, while in the remaining cases the progress equalled one point, which corresponds to one mark. Student 5 made the greatest progress of the five – 1.17.

Thus, the implementation of one type of drama technique, i.e. rehearsing and then acting out monologues, resulted in a marked progress in the

Table 3.7 Experimental results

Student	Recording 1 (mean score)	Recording 2 (mean score)	Progress
1	1.00	1.50	0.50
2	1.33	2.33	1.00
3	2.00	3.00	1.00
4	2.33	3.33	1.00
5	2.66	3.83	1.17

participants' pronunciation. What deserves emphasizing is the fact that, although the designed activities focused on specific texts only, an overall improvement in the students' pronunciation was observed. The results of this study demonstrate that employing elements of drama in pronunciation teaching not only makes this process more diversified and attractive, but also brings about the desired effects.

B.3.4   Phonetic Error Correction

In order to examine the impact of various types of phonetic error correction on the quality of students' pronunciation, several experiments involving Polish secondary school learners were carried out by Szpyra-Kozłowska *et al.* (2004). Below, one of them is briefly discussed.

The goal of the study was to compare the effectiveness of two approaches to correcting phonetic errors: one in which the teacher reacts to mispronunciations of selected features of English and the other in which all major errors are responded to. The participants were three groups (A, B and C) of approximately 19 students each, aged 18, of both sexes. They represent the pre-intermediate to intermediate level of proficiency.

Before the experiment, out of each group 10 randomly chosen pupils were recorded while reading a short diagnostic passage. Next the experimental two-month period of teaching began, in the course of which the following aspects of English phonetics were given special attention in all three groups:

- word stress;
- the palatoalveolar fricatives and affricates;
- the interdental fricatives;
- the vowels: /iː/, /ɪ/ and /ɜː/.

Three different approaches to the issue of error correction have been adopted in the three groups participating in the experiment. The students in Group A were given no special corrective feedback. In Group B those errors were corrected which mainly involved the features listed above. In Group C all major pronunciation errors were pointed out to the learners. Two months later the previously selected students were re-recorded while rereading the same passage, to which they did not have access during the experimental period. All recordings were assessed auditorily by three experienced phoneticians. The results obtained in both recording sessions are summarised in Table 3.8.

Let us analyse these data for each of the experimental groups.

- **Group A** (no correction): In Group A no significant improvement in the students' pronunciation could be observed (about 4% decrease of errors). They made some progress with regard to the vowels /ɜː/, /iː/ and word stress (6–7%).

Table 3.8 Error correction: Experimental results

Feature	Before experiment % Errors			After experiment % Errors			Decrease in errors (%)		
	Group A	Group B	Group C	Group A	Group B	Group C	Group A	Group B	Group C
Word stress	63	70	87	57	33	38	6	37	49
/ʃ/, /ʒ/, /tʃ/, /dʒ/	95	92	100	95	82	77	0	10	23
'th'	69	58	75	66	37	55	3	21	20
/iː/	58	67	87	52	32	38	6	35	49
/ɪ/	51	63	60	49	36	32	2	27	28
/ɜː/	50	76	81	43	36	37	7	40	44
Total means	**64.3**	**71**	**81.6**	**60.3**	**42.6**	**46.1**	**4**	**28.4**	**35.5**

- **Group B** (correction of selected features): In this group the overall decrease of errors amounted to 28.4%. Just like in the previous group the greatest progress concerned the vowels /ɜ:/, /i:/ and word stress, in which cases a 36–41% drop in errors was noted. The pronunciation of palatoalveolars and interdental fricatives improved less markedly (11% and 21%, respectively).
- **Group C** (correction of all errors): The greatest improvement in the subjects' pronunciation was observed in Group C, where the total mean decline in the number of errors reached 35.5%. The same regularities as in the previous two cases occurred here as well. Thus, much progress was made in the quality of /i:/ and /ɜ:/, and the placement of proper word stress (44% and 50%). As before, the pronunciation of the palatoalveolars and interdental fricatives was most resistant to change.[26]

The results of the experiment demonstrate that the greatest decrease in the number of errors was observed in Group C in which the most intensive correction of all major pronunciation inaccuracies was executed. This may lead to a tentative conclusion that the more frequently error correction is employed in the classroom and the more often the students' attention is drawn to phonetic problems, the easier it is for them to improve their English pronunciation. A somewhat less marked progress took place in Group B, where only selected types of errors were subject to the teacher's intervention. Finally, negligible improvement was observed in Group A, in which phonetics was taught, but pronunciation errors remained uncorrected. To conclude, even if the experimental data require further empirical support, they leave no doubt that phonetic error correction contributes significantly to the improvement of learners' pronunciation.

In this part of the book we provided some empirical evidence for the effectiveness of various pronunciation teaching activities showing that their use brings about progress in learners' pronunciation. Evidently, if pronunciation is taught regularly, regardless of the employed techniques, learners' phonetic performance will slowly but steadily improve. If phonetic training is neglected in the mistaken belief that students will pick up good pronunciation as they develop other language skills, no satisfactory results can be achieved.

Notes

(1)   Many learners, particularly children, enjoy phonetic drills, particularly when done chorally, as they resemble many verbal activities employed in kindergarten and early school education.

(2)   An interesting and important question is whether training-induced changes in the articulatory setting are only short lasting or can become long lasting as well. Empirical evidence is needed to clarify this point.

(3)   The similarity is only partial since ESL students can engage in conversations with native speakers, which is rarely possible in EFL contexts.

(4)   This division is somewhat artificial as the borderline between phonetics and phonology is difficult if not impossible to draw (see, for example, Cyran & Szpyra-Kozłowska, 2014, a volume of papers devoted to this issue).

(5)   This approach does not mean that that we deny the value of implicit learning which, according to Williams (2005: 269), 'occurs without intention to learn and without awareness of what has been learned'. Some experiments have shown that learners are capable of generalizing form-meaning connections without explicit training. More studies, however, are needed, as argued by Williams, to find out what can and what cannot be learned implicitly, to examine factors that make some individuals more successful implicit learners than others and to help us understand the nature of unconscious learning mechanisms and their relationship to memory and attention.

(6)   This generalization cannot, however, be extended to all affixed forms as in some of them geminates do occur, e.g. *u[nn]ecessary, no[nn]ative, mea[nn]ess, sou[ll]ess*.

(7)   It is estimated that over 60% of us use different learning modes (multimodal learning), which means that unimodal learners are in the minority.

(8)   As observed by some researchers (e.g. Lowie, 2011), and pointed out by the anonymous reviewer, since second language learning is a dynamic process, the learning style preferences of individual students can change with time and even on task.

(9)   Ideally, tests should be carried out to define individual students' learning styles. This is not, however, a realistic requirement. Moreover, as is often argued, learners benefit from strengthening their weaker modalities.

(10)   The term 'phonetic transcription' is inaccurate since it usually contains phonemes and does not include subphonemic (allophonic) features such as aspiration, vowel clipping, etc.

(11)   <cz> is a digraph which represents the Polish voiceless postalveolar affricate.

(12)   As pointed out by the anonymous reviewer, developing quasi transcriptions by learners can be viewed as a valuable learning tool and a type of a pupil-initiated approach to pronunciation learning. As such, it can be regarded as a self-driven and personally significant learning experience. In our view, however, the negative effects of using quasi transcriptions outweigh their alleged advantages.

(13)   Various researches (e.g. Ciszewski, 2004; Hancock, 1995; Tench, 2011) have demonstrated that there are many interesting and attractive ways of teaching phonetic transcription.

(14)   Quotation after Brown (1992: 8).

(15)   A certain problem is created by the existence of various transcription systems. We are in favour of using the IPA symbols, as they are the most frequently employed, for example in pronunciation dictionaries. Students should be warned, however, that different symbols may be found in various sources.

(16)   Depending on the learners' L1, there might be a need to introduce more symbols. For example, Polish students must learn that the letter <w>, which in their mother tongue represents the voiced labiovelar fricative, is a transcription symbol of the labiovelar semivowel and that <v>, which is not used in the Polish alphabet (except for some borrowings), stands for the voiced labiovelar fricative.

(17)   As a matter of fact, even at quite advanced levels of language proficiency, the ability to self-assess one's own pronunciation is fairly low, as shown by Nowacka's (2008) study involving university students of English.

(18)   On phonetic talent see, for example, Gonet (2006) and Jilka (2009).

(19)   It has been carried out by me and a team of my collaborators. Each series consisted of several parts, all of which, i.e. the whole packages, were examined. They are listed in Chapter 1.

(20)   This is particularly surprising in view of the fact that in these examinations 20% of the points are assigned to speaking skills, a quarter of which, i.e. 5%, is given for

pronunciation. The expectation thus is that at least 5% of all tasks should be devoted to pronunciation, which is not supported by the facts.

(21) As a matter of fact, no information is provided concerning the qualifications of description providers.

(22) The intermediate and upper-intermediate parts of the *New Headway Pronunciation Course* are claimed to be 'ideal for self-study' (book covers).

(23) It is important to add that, before the recording, the teacher made sure that the subjects were familiar with all the technical terms and understood the instructions.

(24) This does not mean that all locally published sources are adequate; unfortunately many of them are almost exact copies of the materials for international learners and fail to address specific L1 students' needs.

(25) It has to be noted that the phonetic realization of a given phonetic aspect by the pupils was far from being consistent, with instances of their proper pronunciation in some items and incorrect renditions in other cases. A phonetic feature was considered to be realized correctly if this occurred in at least 70% of the tokens.

(26) It should be pointed out that the obtained data concern short-term improvement in the participants' pronunciation of selected features. It is to be expected that long-term improvement will be considerably smaller.

4 Concluding Remarks

Teaching and learning the pronunciation of another language is an enormous challenge for all the parties involved, both teachers and learners, particularly when it takes place in a country in which it is not spoken on a daily basis. English is no exception to this rule. It might even be claimed that, in view of its global spread, its numerous native and non-native varieties and the major controversies surrounding the appropriateness of different pronunciation models, all evidenced in the previous pages of this book, the challenge of achieving an adequate mastery of the English sound system is undoubtedly greater than ever before. As the traditional assumptions and principles of EFL pronunciation instruction have frequently been questioned and various alternative proposals have been offered, the confusion of teachers and learners who are aware of this turmoil must be inevitable. This book is meant to provide some necessary help and guidance to all those who want to keep abreast of recent developments in the area of English practical phonetics and particularly to EFL instructors who care about improving their teaching skills.

Nevertheless, familiarity with theoretical discussions and controversies, while important and valuable in itself, is insufficient for achieving a phonodidactic success. We have also argued that principled and informed decisions concerning specific aspects of pronunciation instruction cannot be made solely on the basis of teachers' intuition and teaching experience (the value of which is, of course, undeniable), but must be grounded in solid empirical research. In other words, classroom-oriented studies are needed in order to provide instructors with reliable information on numerous important issues, such as, for instance, the acquisition of L2 phonetics by different learner groups, the perception of foreign-accented English by native and non-native speakers of this language or the effectiveness of various instructional procedures. In Parts B of each chapter we have summarized several such studies carried out by the author and her collaborators with mainly Polish participants (but also with subjects of several other nationalities) in order to provide empirical evidence for some of the theoretical claims made in Parts A as well as in order to demonstrate what relevant research should be like. It should be added that, if such research has not been done in many EFL contexts or its results are not easily available, teachers themselves are encouraged to conduct some simple informal tests and/or small-scale experiments to verify the validity of their various assumptions and instructional decisions, such as, for instance, administering short questionnaires meant to examine learners' views on English accent models (see Section B.1.2) or on the effectiveness and attractiveness of pronunciation teaching techniques (see Section B.3.2), carrying out brief tests to identify phonetically difficult words for a given learner group (see Section B.2.2).

The above reasoning implies that up-to-date pronunciation instruction should be based on considerations of both some global and local issues, that is, on some globally relevant problems and discussions, such as the choice of an accent model, principles of L2 pronunciation acquisition or general phonetic priorities, which should, however, take into account the local context in which language teaching and learning takes place and its local participants. It is combining these two perspectives that constitutes the major organizational principle of this book.

In this chapter we intend to sum up briefly the major claims made in the preceding pages by indicating those areas of modern English phonodidactics directed at foreign learners that deserve particular attention from EFL pronunciation instructors, in our presentation following largely the arrangement of the earlier chapters.

Before the L2 teaching process begins, several preliminary issues concerning pronunciation, established in previous research, must be considered in some detail. They include the following general points:

- **Pronunciation is an important component of language without which no efficient oral communication is possible.** It must be taught to L2 learners because poor pronunciation often leads to misunderstandings and communication breakdowns and causes listeners' unfavourable judgements of speakers' personal characteristics (e.g. their intelligence, education, personal integrity and social attractiveness). On the other hand, good pronunciation of the L2 is an important asset which improves the speaker's communicative efficiency, creates favourable personality impressions and provides foreign learners with confidence to speak their L2 and engage in conversations with other speakers of that language.
- Despite its unquestionable importance, **pronunciation teaching often tends to be neglected and marginalized in ELT** as the most difficult aspect of English to teach in instructed settings, due to a frequent focus on written language examinations (the 'washback effect') and usually poor quality of the phonetic training of prospective EFL teachers. If teacher trainees are insufficiently instructed in this area and if their English pronunciation is poor, they will not give due attention to their students' phonetic training.
- As argued by many specialists, **the traditional goal of achieving native-like pronunciation is both unrealistic and unnecessary** for

the overwhelming majority of EFL learners and, as such, should be abandoned in favour of **a more appropriate and attainable goal of striving for pronunciation which is comfortably intelligible** (requires no particular effort to understand) to English-speaking interlocutors, both native and non-native.

An important issue that has to be settled prior to the commencement of EFL instruction concerns the complex and controversial question of selecting an appropriate pronunciation model for learners. Teachers should be aware of the following global and local problems involved in making the right decision:

- **The traditional EFL approach** which is native speaker-centred in that it views communication with native speakers as the major objective of the teaching/learning process and involves strict adherence to native accent models and native cultural norms can be considered outdated and no longer adequate for numerous foreign learners who regard English mainly as a means of international communication between non-native speakers.
- **An alternative approach, known as ELF**, with the LFC as its pronunciation agenda, has been proposed as better suited for the purposes of effective international communication. It disregards native norms of correctness and is meant to ensure the mutual intelligibility of its users who, due to it, can focus on the most important and learnable aspects of English pronunciation, use non-native English without feelings of inferiority and express their national identity.
- **The concepts of ELF and the LFC are controversial**, however, and have raised much criticism concerning, among other things, their insufficient empirical foundation and programmatic character, eliminating native speakers of English as participants of international communication, their lack of clearly defined pronunciation models and various inconsistencies found in the LFC.
- In this book, **the concept of NELF (Native English as a Lingua Franca)** has been proposed as an alternative to the previous two approaches. According to it, for pragmatic reasons a (standard) native accent model should be selected to be employed for communication with both native and non-native speakers, with the focus on those features which are essential for achieving comfortable intelligibility. This approach adopts native norms of linguistic correctness, but includes both native and non-native sociocultural norms. Learners are bilingual and bicultural and English is a carrier of international culture.
- **If a native accent model is adopted, it should satisfy several important criteria.** It should be a standard variety, intelligible to many international users of English, which provides learners with increased

chances of an educational and professional career, for which teaching resources are easily available and used by EFL teachers. The two varieties which fulfil these criteria best are RP and GA, but in making an appropriate decision the local teaching/learning context must be taken into account.

Having decided on the approach to pronunciation teaching (EFL, ELF or NELF) and an accent model, teachers must also consider several additional, but also important issues:

- EFL teachers should be aware of **significant differences in pronunciation teaching and learning in EFL and ESL contexts**, which in many sources devoted to pronunciation instruction are treated incorrectly as the same phenomenon. Such important differences concern, among other things, the setting (instructed versus naturalistic), types of learning (explicit versus implicit), the quantity and quality of the auditory input (limited versus unlimited), and cannot be ignored as they have a considerable impact on various aspects of pronunciation teaching and learning.
- In order to teach English pronunciation effectively, language teachers should examine **the major features of the local context** and become familiar with other determinants of phonetic instruction which include **the educational context** (e.g. national language policy, teacher preparation, curriculum, materials, teaching/learning facilities) as well as a variety of **learner-related factors** (e.g. age, motivation, language aptitude, cognitive and learning styles) and **teacher-related factors** (e.g. teacher preparation, attitude to L2 pronunciation, quality of teachers' English pronunciation and their involvement in phonetic instruction).

The choice of an appropriate pronunciation model and familiarity with the major factors, both global and local, which affect the teaching/learning process must be accompanied by establishing the phonetic priorities for EFL learners needed to achieve comfortable intelligibility in communication with other users of English, an issue considered in much detail in Chapter 2, the most important aspects of which are repeated below.

- **Pronunciation priorities research focuses on identifying the phonetic features of English crucial for achieving intelligibility** whose determinants include numerous speaker-related, listener-related and context-related factors. As many of them are involved in a single act of communication, the impact of specific features is often difficult to establish in an unambiguous way.
- The presented analysis of **several proposals for pronunciation priorities**, i.e. **Jenkins's (2000) Lingua Franca Core**, **Cruttenden's (2008) Amalgam English** and **International English**, and **Collins and**

Mees' (2003) pronunciation Error Ranking, demonstrates that they contain many conflicting claims and suffer from other significant short-comings, mainly because of insufficient empirical support for the role and significance of specific phonetic features.

- In spite of numerous differences between the presented proposals and lack of clarity concerning the importance of many aspects of English phonetics, it appears that the majority of scholars involved in phonetic priorities research appear to agree with **the need to prioritize the following areas of English pronunciation**:
  - preserving consonant clusters, particularly in word-initial position;
  - preserving the fortis-lenis distinction (expressed in various ways, e.g. through voicing, aspiration (in the case of plosives) or vowel length);
  - rhotic pronunciation allowed;
  - preserving consonantal contrasts with a high functional load;
  - approximations of consonants allowed (of a slightly different place of articulation);
  - preserving vocalic contrasts with a high functional load;
  - preserving the phonemic distinction between long and short vowels;
  - proper placement of word stress;
  - proper placement of nuclear stress.
- **These 'global' priorities** can be regarded as general guidelines for EFL pronunciation teaching, but **must be made more specific ('local') for various L1 learner groups** in the course of intelligibility research which examines in more detail the phonetic properties of L1-accented English and their communicative impact.
- In this book it has been argued that **phonetic priorities should involve not only selected segmental and suprasegmental features, but also the pronunciation of whole words** which are prone to be mis-pronounced by many EFL learners and which considerably diminish the intelligibility of their English speech. Several types of such phonetically difficult items have been isolated, namely:
  - local errors;
  - phonetic 'false friends';
  - words prone to be mis-stressed;
  - longer words.
- Moreover, in the case of EFL learners, exposed to written English more frequently than to spoken English, **special attention should be given to orthography-induced errors and to instruction concerning English spelling-to-sound correspondences. Reducing the impact of the written form of English on learners' pronunciation** should thus be viewed as one of the teaching priorities.

An important aspect of the discussion on pronunciation priorities for EFL learners concerns the 'segmentals versus suprasegmentals' debate, which deals with the communicative importance of these two aspects of English phonetics and their instructional sequencing. The following points should be considered in connection with this controversy.

- While **in the traditional approaches to pronunciation instruction segmentals occupied a central position,** starting from the 1990s a **shift of emphasis** could be observed **from segments to prosody** due to many empirical studies which have argued for the primary role of suprasegmentals and the secondary place of consonants and vowels in safeguarding intelligibility.
- This means **a current dominance**, evidenced in numerous pronunciation teaching materials, **of the 'top down' view in which instruction starts from training in suprasegmentals and proceeds to segmentals** over the traditional 'bottom-up' approach in which this order is reversed.
- In recent years, however, mostly under the influence of the concept of ELF (and the pronunciation priorities put forward in the LFC) with its claims concerning the vital role of segments and a negligible contribution of prosody to intelligibility in international communication via English, **another shift in pedagogical practices can be noted towards prioritizing segments over suprasegmentals** and a return to 'bottom-up' instruction.
- In this book it is argued that neither of these two perspectives can be considered fully adequate as **phonetic priorities cannot be established for all learners of different linguistic backgrounds, but must be specified for each L1 on the basis of the phonetic distance between the L1 and L2, coupled with empirical research into the role of individual phonetic features in safeguarding intelligibility**. Moreover, the issue is not always whether these are all segmentals or all suprasegmentals that should be prioritized, but which particular segmental and prosodic aspects should be targeted in phonetic instruction.

After discussing the major problems involved in the question of what to teach with respect to pronunciation, in Chapter 3 we turned to the issue of how to do it effectively in a manner which is both learner-friendly and teacher-friendly. The major features of the approach to phonetic instruction advocated in this book can be characterized as follows:

- The teacher's basic and essential task, without which no phonetic instruction can succeed, is **to develop in learners a genuine and deep concern for good English pronunciation**. This can be done in a variety of ways, e.g. by explaining to them the importance of proper pronunciation for successful communication, carrying out phonetic practice and assessing students' progress regularly, approaching their pronunciation problems individually and showing active involvement in phonetic instruction.

- To compensate for the insufficient exposure of EFL learners to natural spoken English, the instructor should follow **the principle of the maximization of phonetic input** or **learners' immersion in English speech**, both in the language classroom and outside it. This means using every opportunity to expose them to spoken English, both recorded and direct.
- **A holistic multimodal approach to phonetic instruction** should be adopted, which involves the development of new motor habits (needed for the proper perception and production of foreign sounds and prosodies), work on the formation of the L2's sound system in the learner's mind and employing different kinds of multisensory reinforcement. In other words, effective pronunciation instruction should develop in EFL learners 'sounds in the body' and 'sounds in the mind' and include four components:
  - articulatory training;
  - auditory training;
  - cognitive phonetic and phonological training;
  - multisensory training.

The four components of a holistic multimodal approach to pronunciation teaching and learning can be briefly characterized as follows:

- **Articulatory training**, aimed at the formation of new motor habits, requires some amount of drilling, followed, however, by communicatively oriented activities in which the drilled items are employed in a variety of meaningful contexts. An important part of articulatory training consists of developing in learners native-like articulatory setting, which helps them to improve the quality of their English pronunciation.
- **Auditory training**, needed to foster learners' comprehension of spoken English as well as their phonetic progress, should initially involve a variety of basic tasks such as, for instance, sound discrimination, noticing various phonetic features of the L2 and noticing differences between sounds and prosodic patterns of the L1 and L2. At more advanced levels, students' receptive skills should be practised in order to enhance their comprehension of different accents of English, both native and non-native, standard and non-standard.
- **Cognitive phonetic and phonological training**, which should complement articulatory and auditory training, is meant to enhance learners' understanding of the basics of L1 and L2 phonetics and phonology through developing their phonetic metacompetence and raising their phonological awareness. It involves providing students with explicit information on selected aspects of L2 and L1 sound articulation and

prosodic properties, comparing L1 and L2 sound systems (contrastive analysis), discussing particularly important aspects of phonetic and phonological interference from the L1 on the L2. Learners can also get acquainted with various elements of the phonological system of the L2, such as phonotactic constraints and some phonological processes, and compare them with those of their L1. A problem-solving approach to these issues is advocated as beneficial for internalizing theoretical knowledge. This type of training is particularly important in the case of adult learners who need to understand what they are required to do.

- **Multisensory training**, which caters for the needs of students with different learning modalities (auditory, visual, tactile and kinaesthetic), and complements other types of instruction. It activates various channels of perception in the course of holistic phonetic training and integrates auditory, visual, tactile and kinaesthetic learning by employing different kinds of multisensory reinforcement. Due to it multimodal learners acquire L2 pronunciation more easily and faster as it allows for better comprehension and deeper processing of information. Moreover, it makes phonetic training more attractive and motivating to students.

An important element of pronunciation teaching is **the selection and use of effective techniques** and activities which are also attractive to learners. In EFL contexts, the following instructional procedures can be recommended as particularly useful:

- **phonemic transcription**, which is particularly helpful in overcoming the powerful impact of English spelling on pronunciation and aids in the cognitive process of L2 sound system formation in the learner's mind;
- **songs, poems and elements of drama**, which allow for an attractive and seemingly 'effortless' acquisition of pronunciation, immersion in English sounds and multisensory learning;
- **phonetic games**, which add a commonly well-liked element of competition to pronunciation learning and enhance L2 sound system formation through the problem-solving approach;
- **using technology** (internet sources in particular), which increases the amount of authentic phonetic input, fosters learner autonomy and adds to the attractiveness of the learning process.

Finally, we have drawn the readers' attention to several other issues of considerable relevance to successful phonetic instruction in EFL settings.

- In EFL contexts with a limited exposure to spoken English, **pronunciation learning should be continued outside the classroom**. The teacher should encourage students to work on improving their English pronunciation at home and to self-monitor their phonetic progress, show them how to do it properly and familiarize them with appropriate techniques and resources.

- One of the most important **teacher's tasks is to provide feedback to learners** on their pronunciation problems, which can take different forms, e.g. error correction, assessing students' pronunciation and phonetic progress regularly, catering for individual learners' problems and needs.
- The success of phonetic instruction largely depends on **the selection of good quality pronunciation teaching materials**. The teacher should examine the phonetic component of general course books, taking into account the number and types of pronunciation tasks, elements of English phonetics covered by the book, and their arrangement and suitability for a particular group of students. Special care should be taken in the choice of additional sources, many of which contain various errors and inaccuracies, and are not suitable for all L1 learners.

The issues signalled in this chapter and developed in greater detail throughout this book are obviously only a selection of the problems relevant to modern EFL pronunciation instruction. The choice has been made by the author, guided by her subjective judgements and interests, and was additionally influenced by the limits on book length imposed by the publisher. This means that many interesting and important questions have not been addressed here at all or have been treated only in a cursory fashion such as, for instance, pronunciation testing and assessment, integrating phonetic instruction with other components of language within a communicative framework, working with exceptionally talented learners as well as those who are low phonetic achievers, and the phenomenon of more and more frequent cases of multilinguality, i.e. one person learning several languages (L2, L3, ...) and the consequences of this fact for their acquisition of these languages' pronunciation (see, for example, Jarvis & Pavlenko, 2008; Marx & Melhorn, 2010). What deserves more attention is also the specificity of phonetic instruction aimed at different age groups and, of course, at learners of various L1 backgrounds. While an attempt has been made by the author to maintain a balance between global and local issues in English pronunciation instruction, the Polish bias has been unavoidable. After all, it is not always easy to maintain the global and local perspective at the same time. We do hope, however, that many readers of different nationalities will find in these pages much of interest to them and directly relevant to their experience of EFL pronunciation teaching and learning.

References

Abelin, A. and Boyd, S. (2000) Voice quality, foreign accent and attitudes of speakers. *Proceedings of FONETIK 2000* (pp. 21–24). Skövde: Hogskolan & Skovde.

Abercrombie, D. (1949) Teaching pronunciation. *English Language Teaching* 3, 113–122.

Anderson-Hsieh, J., Johnson, R. and Koehler, K. (1992) The relationship between native speaker judgements of nonnative pronunciation and deviance in segmentals, prosody, and syllable structure. *Language Learning* 42, 529–555.

Archibald, A. (1992) Developing natural and confident speech: Drama techniques in the pronunciation classroom. In P. Avery and S. Ehrlich (eds) *Teaching American English Pronunciation* (pp. 221–228). Oxford: Oxford University Press.

Archibald, A., Cogo, A. and Jenkins, J. (eds) (2011) *Latest Trends in ELF Research*. Newcastle Upon Tyne: Cambridge Scholars Publishing.

Avery, P. and Ehrlich, S. (1992) *Teaching American English Pronunciation*. Oxford: Oxford University Press.

Baker, A. (1981) *Ship or Sheep?* Cambridge: Cambridge University Press.

Baran-Łucarz, M. (2006) Prosto w oczy – fonetyka jako 'Michałek' na studiach filologicznych? In W. Sobkowiak and E. Waniek-Klimczak (eds) *Dydaktyka fonetyki języka obcego* 8 (pp. 7–17). Konin: Wydawnictwo PWSZ.

Baran-Łucarz, M. (2011) The relationship between language anxiety and the actual and perceived levels of FL pronunciation. *Studies in Second Language Learning and Teaching* 1 (4), 491–514.

Baran-Łucarz, M. (2013) Phonetics learning anxiety – results of a preliminary study. *Research in Language* 11 (1), 57–79.

Bassetti, B. (2006) Orthographic input and phonological representations in learners of Chinese as a foreign language. *Written Language and Literacy* 9 (1), 95–114.

Bassetti, B. (2008) Orthographic input and second language phonology. In T. Piske and M. Young-Scholten (eds) *Input Matters in SLA* (pp. 191–206). Bristol: Multilingual Matters.

Benson, P. (2007) Autonomy in language teaching and learning. *Language Teaching* 40, 21–40.

Blanco, M., Gayoso, E. and Carrillo, M. (2001) Analytical training for the teaching of EFL in primary school. See http://www.phon.ucl.ac.uk/home/johnm/ptlc2001/pdf/murcia.pdf (accessed 26 September 2014).

Brown, A. (1988) Functional load and the teaching of pronunciation. *TESOL Quarterly* 22 (4), 593–606.

Brown, A. (ed.) (1992) *Approaches to Pronunciation Teaching*. London: Macmillan.

Brown, H.D. (1994) *Teaching by Principles. An Interactive Approach to Language Pedagogy*. London: Prentice Hall.

Bryła-Cruz, A. (2013) English, Scottish and Irish listeners' perception of Polish-accented English. A comparative study. Unpublished PhD dissertation, UMCS, Lublin.

Bukowski, D. (2003) Multisensory modes in teaching and learning phonetics – a few practical suggestions. In W. Sobkowiak and E. Waniek-Klimczak (eds) *Dydaktyka fonetyki języka obcego* 5 (pp. 11–29). Płock: Wydawnictwo PWSZ.

Cauldwell, R. (2003) *Streaming Speech: Listening and Pronunciation for Advanced Learners of English* [CD-ROM]. Birmingham: Speechinaction.

Celce-Murcia, M., Brinton, D.M. and Goodwin, J. (1996) *Teaching Pronunciation: A Reference for Teachers of English to Speakers of Other Languages.* Cambridge: Cambridge University Press.

Cenoz, J. and García-Lecumberri, L. (1999) The effect of training on the discrimination of English vowels. *International Review of Applied Linguistics* 37, 261–275.

Ciszewski, T. (2004) Transkrypcja fonetyczna. Mity i uprzedzenia. In W. Sobkowiak and E. Waniek-Klimczak (eds) *Dydaktyka fonetyki języka obcego* 4 (pp. 28–34). Konin: Wydawnictwo PWSZ.

Collins, B. and Mees, I.M. (1995) Approaches to articulatory setting in foreign language teaching. In J.W. Lewis (ed.) *Studies in General and English Phonetics* (pp. 415–424). London: Routledge.

Collins, B. and Mees, I.M. (2003) *Practical Phonetics and Phonology.* London & New York: Routledge.

Crookston, I. (2001) Alphabetic literacy and practical phonetics teaching: Some preliminary connections. In J.A. Maidment and E. Estebas-Vilaplana (eds) *Proceedings of the Phonetics Teaching and Learning Conference* (pp. 7–10). London: Royal Holloway College, University of London.

Cruttenden, A. (2008) *Gimson's Pronunciation of English* (7th edn). London: Hodder Education.

Crystal, D. (1995) *The Cambridge Encyclopedia of Language.* Cambridge: Cambridge University Press.

Crystal, D. (1997) *English as a Global Language.* Cambridge: Cambridge University Press.

Cunningham, S. and Bowler, B. (1999) *New Headway Pronunciation Course.* Oxford: Oxford University Press.

Cunningham, U. (2010) Quality, quantity and intelligibility of vowels in Vietnamese-accented English. In E. Waniek-Klimczak (ed.) *Issues in Accents of English 2. Variability and Norm* (pp. 3–22). Newcastle Upon Tyne: Cambridge Scholars Publishing.

Cyran, E. and Szpyra-Kozłowska, J. (eds) (2014) *Crossing Phonetics–Phonology Lines.* Newcastle Upon Tyne: Cambridge Scholars Publishing.

Dalton, Ch. and Seidlhofer, B. (1994) *Pronunciation.* Oxford: Oxford University Press.

da Silva, R.S. (2011) Priorities in pronunciation teaching. *IATEFL Pronunciation Special Interest Group Newsletter* NN. See http://hancockmcdonald.com (accessed 26 September 2014).

Derwing, T.M. and Munro, M.J. (2005) Second language accent and pronunciation teaching: A research-based approach. *TESOL Quarterly* 39 (3), 379–397.

Derwing, T. and Rossiter, M. (2003) The effects of pronunciation instruction on the accuracy, fluency and complexity of L2 accented speech. *Applied Language Learning* 13, 1–18.

Derwing, T.M., Munro, M.J. and Wiebe, C. (1997) Pronunciation instruction for 'fossilized' learners: Can it help? *Applied Language Learning* 8 (2), 217–235.

Dickerson, W. (1983) The role of formal rules in pronunciation instruction. In J. Handscombe, R. Orem and B. Taylor (eds) *On TESOL 83.* Washington, DC: TESOL.

Doel, R. van den. (2006) How friendly are the natives? An evaluation of native speaker judgements of foreign-accented British and American English. Ph.D. dissertation. University of Utrecht.

Dziubalska-Kołaczyk, K. (2002) Conscious competence of performance as a key to teaching English. In E. Waniek-Klimczak and J. Melia (eds) *Accents and Speech in English* (pp. 97–106). Frankfurt: Peter Lang.

Dziubalska-Kołaczyk, K. and Przedlacka, J. (eds) (2005) *English Pronunciation Models: A Changing Scene.* Bern: Peter Lang.

Dziubalska-Kołaczyk, K., Balas, A., Schwartz, G. and Rojczyk, A. (2013) Teaching to suppress L1 processes in L2. *Proceedings of PTLC 2013* (pp. 35–38). London: University College London.

Elliot, A.R. (1995) Foreign language phonology: Field independence, attitude and the success of formal instruction in Spanish pronunciation. *Modern Language Journal* 79 (4), 530–542.

Erdener, V.D. and Burnham, D.K. (2005) The role of audiovisual speech and orthographic information in nonnative speech production. *Language Learning* 55 (2), 191–228.

Evans, L. (1976) The use of the language laboratory for phonetics at advanced levels of English learning. *Language Learning* 20 (1), 109–125.

Fayer, J.M. and Krasinsky, E. (1987) Native and non-native judgements of intelligibility and irritation. *Language Learning* 37 (3), 313–326.

Field, J. (2005) Intelligibility and the listener: The role of lexical stress. *TESOL Quarterly* 39 (3), 399–423.

Firth, S. (1992) Pronunciation syllabus design: A question of focus. In P. Avery and S. Ehrlich (eds) *Teaching American English Pronunciation* (pp. 173–181). Oxford: Oxford University Press.

Flege, J.E., Munro, M.J. and MacKay, I.R.A. (1995) Factors affecting strength of perceived foreign accent in a second language. *Journal of the Acoustical Society of America* 97, 3125–3134.

Frankiewicz, J., Gonet, W. and Szpyra-Kozłowska, J. (2002) Aspekty fonetyki angielskiej nauczane w polskich szkołach średnich. In Sobkowiak, W. and Waniek-Klimczak, E. (eds) *Dydaktyka fonetyki języka obcego*. Płock: Wydawnictwo PWSZ, 9–27.

Fraser, H. (2004) Constraining abstractness: Phonological representation in the light of colour terms. *Cognitive Linguistics* 15, 239–288.

Fraser, H. (2006) *Teaching Pronunciation: A Handbook for Teachers and Trainers*. See http://helenfraser.com.au/downloads/HF%20Handbook.pdf (accessed 26 September 2014).

Friedrich, P. (2003) English in Argentina: Attitudes of MBA students. *World Englishes* 22 (2), 173–184.

Gibbon, D. (2005) Afterword: Navigating pronunciation in search of the golden fleece. In K. Dziubalska-Kołaczyk and J. Przedlacka (eds) *English Pronunciation Models: A Changing Scene* (pp. 439–466). Bern: Peter Lang.

Gilbert, J.B. (1999) Six pronunciation priorities for the beginning student. *Speak Out!* 25. See www.associates.iatefl.org/pages/materials/tskills18pdf (accessed 26 September 2014).

Gilbert, J.B. (2008) *Teaching Pronunciation. Using the Prosody Pyramid*. Cambridge: Cambridge University Press.

Gimson, A.C. (1994) *An Introduction to the Pronunciation of English*. London: Edward Arnold.

Goh, C. (2009) Perspectives on spoken grammar. *ELT Journal* 63 (4), 303–312.

Gonet, W. (2006) Success in the acquisition of English phonetics by Poles (a pilot study). In W. Sobkowiak and E. Waniek-Klimczak (eds) *Dydaktyka fonetyki języka obcego* 8 (pp. 70–88). Konin: Wydawnictwo PWSZ.

Gonet, W. (2014) Speech visualization as an aid in teaching/learning the pronunciation of the release stage of English plosives. In J. Szpyra-Kozłowska, E. Guz, P. Steinbrich and R. Święciński (eds) *Recent Developments in Applied Phonetics* (pp. 79–113). Lublin: Catholic University of John Paul II Press.

Gonet, W. and Pietroń, G. (2004) The Polish tongue in the English ear. In W. Sobkowiak and E. Waniek-Klimczak (eds) *Zeszyty Naukowe PWSZ w Koninie* 1/204 (4), 56–65.

Graddol, D. (1999) The decline of the native speaker. *AILA Review* 13, 57–68.

Gut, U. (2009) *Non-Native Speech: A Corpus-Based Analysis*. Frankfurt am Mein: Peter Lang.

Hahn, L. and Watts, P. (2011) (Un)intelligibility tales. In J. Levis and K. LeVelle (eds) *Proceedings of the 2nd Pronunciation in Second Language Learning and Teaching Conference* (pp. 17–29). Ames, IA: Iowa State University.

Hancock, M. (1995) *Pronunciation Games*. Cambridge: Cambridge University Press.

Handke, J. (2001) *The Mouton Interactive Introduction to Phonetics and Phonology.* The Hague: Mouton de Gruyter.

Henderson, A., Frost, D., Tergujeff, E., *et al.* (2012) The English pronunciation teaching in Europe survey: Selected results. *Research in Language* 10 (1), 5–28.

Hewings, M. (2004) *Pronunciation Practice Activities.* Cambridge: Cambridge University Press.

Honikman, B. (1964) Articulatory settings. In D. Abercrombie (ed.) *In Honour of Daniel Jones* (pp. 77–84). London: Longman.

Hudson, R.A. (1980) *Sociolinguistics.* Cambridge: Cambridge University Press.

Hülmbauer, C. (2010) *English as a Lingua Franca between Correctness and Effectiveness: Shifting Constellations.* Saarbrücken: VDM (Verlag Dr Müller).

Hülmbauer, C., Böhringer, H. and Seildhofer, B. (2008) Introducing English as a lingua franca (ELF): Precursor and partner in intercultural communication. *Synergies Europe* 3, 25–36.

Janicka, K., Kul, M. and Weckwerth, J. (2005) Polish students' attitudes to native English accents as models for EFL pronunciation. In K. Dziubalska-Kołaczyk and J. Przedlacka (eds) *English Pronunciation Models: A Changing Scene* (pp. 251–292). Bern: Peter Lang.

Jarvis, S. and Pavlenko, A. (2008) *Crosslinguistic Influence in Language and Cognition.* London and New York: Routledge.

Jenkins, J. (2000) *The Phonology of English as an International Language.* Oxford: Oxford University Press.

Jenkins, J. (2006) Points of view and blind spots: ELF and SLA. *International Journal of Applied Linguistics* 16 (2), 137–162.

Jenkins, J. (2007) *English as a Lingua Franca: Attitude and Identity.* Oxford: Oxford University Press.

Jenkins, J. (2009) (Un)pleasant? (In)correct? (Un)intelligible? ELF speakers' perceptions of their accents. In A. Mauranen and E. Ranta (eds) *English as a Lingua Franca. Studies and Findings* (pp. 10–36). Newcastle Upon Tyne: Cambridge Scholars Publishing.

Jenkins, J. and Seidlhofer, B. (2001) Bringing Europe's lingua franca into the classroom. *The Guardian*, 19 April.

Jenner, B. (1989) Teaching pronunciation: The common core. *IATEFL PronSIG Newsletter* 1, 2–4.

Jenner, B. (1997) The English voice. In A. Brown (ed.) *Approaches to Pronunciation* Teaching (pp. 38–46). Hemel Hempstead: Prentice Hall International.

Jilka, M. (2009) Assessment of phonetic ability. In G. Dogil and S.M. Reiterer (eds) *Language Talent and Brain Activity* (pp. 17–66). Berlin and New York: Mouton de Gruyter.

Jones, R. and Evans, S. (1995) Teaching pronunciation through voice quality. *ELT Journal* 49, 244–251.

Kachru, B. (1986) *The Alchemy of English: The Spread, Functions and Models of Non-native Englishes.* Oxford: Pergamon Press.

Kalin, R. and Rayko, K. (1978) Discrimination in evaluative judgements against foreign-accented job candidates. *Psychological Reports* 43, 1203–1209.

Kaltenboeck, G. (2005) A multimedia approach to suprasegmentals: Using a CD-ROM for English intonation teaching. See http://www.phon.ucl.ac.uk/home/johnm/ptlc2001/pdf/kaltenboeck/pdf (accessed 26 September 2014).

Kaur, J. (2009) *English as a Lingua Franca: Co-constructing Understanding.* Saarbrücken: VDM (Verlag Dr Müller).

Kelly, G. (2000) *How to Teach Pronunciation.* Harlow: Longman.

Kendrick, H. (1997) Keep them talking! A project for improving students' L2 pronunciation. *System* 25, 545–560.

Kenworthy, J. (1987) *Teaching English Pronunciation.* London: Longman.

Komorowska, H. (1989) *Metodyka nauczania języków obcych.* Warszawa: WSiP.

Ladefoged, P. and Maddieson, I. (1996) *The Sounds of the World's Languages.* Oxford: Blackwell.

Lamb, M. (2004) Integrative motivation in a globalizing world. *System* 32 (1), 3–19.

Laver, J. (1980) *The Phonetic Description of Voice Quality.* Cambridge: Cambridge University Press.

Laver, J. (1994) *Principles of Phonetics.* Cambridge: Cambridge University Press.

Leather, J. and James, A. (1991) The acquisition of second language speech. *Studies in Second Language Acquisition* 13, 305–341.

Lecumberri, M.L.G. and Maidment, J.A. (2000) *English Transcription Course.* Cambridge: Cambridge University Press.

Lee, W.R. (1976) Language laboratories and the learning of foreign languages. *ELT Journal* 30 (3), 195–205.

Lev-Ari, S. and Keysar, B. (2010) Why don't we believe non-native speakers? The influence of accent on credibility. *Journal of Experimental Social Psychology* 46 (6), 1093–1096.

Levis, J. (2005) Changing contexts and shifting paradigms in pronunciation teaching. *TESOL Quarterly* 39 (3), 369–377.

Levis, J. (2007) Computer technology in teaching and researching pronunciation. *Annual Review of Applied Linguistics* 27, 184–202.

Levis, J. and Cortes, V. (2008) Minimal pairs in spoken corpora: Implications for pronunciation assessment and teaching. In C.A. Chapelle, Y.-R. Chung and J. Xu (eds) *Towards Adaptive CALL: Natural Language Processing for Diagnostic Language* Assessment (pp. 197–208). Ames, IA: Iowa State University.

Lindemann, S. (2002) Listening with an attitude: A model of native-speaker comprehension of nonnative speakers in the United States. *Language in Society* 31 (3), 419–441.

Lintunen, P. (2013) The effect of phonetic knowledge on evaluated pronunciation problems. In J. Przedlacka, J. Maidment and M. Ashby (eds) *Proceedings of Phonetics Teaching and Learning Conference* 2013, University College London (pp. 55–58).

Lippi-Green, R. (1997) *English with an Accent: Language, Ideology and Discrimination in the United States.* London: Routledge.

Lowie, W. (2011) The development of early L2 phonology: A dynamic approach. In M. Wrembel, M. Kul and K. Dziubalska-Kołaczyk (eds) *Achievements and Perspectives in SLA of Speech: New Sounds 2010* (Vol. 2) (pp. 137–148). Frankfurt: Peter Lang.

MacDonald, D., Yule, G. and Powers, M. (1994) Attempts to improve L2 pronunciation: The variable effects of different types of instruction. *Language Learning* 44, 75–100.

Majer, J. (2002) *Sick* or *seek?* Pedagogical phonology in teacher training. In E. Waniek-Klimczak and J. Melia (eds) *Accents and Speech in Teaching English Phonetics and Phonology* (pp. 153–176). Frankfurt: Peter Lang.

Mańczak-Wohlfeld, E. (2010) *Słownik zapożyczeń angielskich w polszczyźnie.* Warszawa: PWN.

Marx, N. and Melhorn, G. (2010) Pushing the positive: Encouraging phonological transfer from L2 to L3. *International Journal of Multilingualism* 7 (1), 4–18.

Matsuda, A. (2003) The ownership of English in Japanese secondary schools. *World Englishes* 22 (4), 483–496.

Mompean-Gonzales, J.A. (2003) Pedagogical tools for teaching articulatory setting. In M. Sole, D. Recasens and J. Romero (eds) *Proceedings of the 15th International Congress of Phonetic Sciences: Barcelona 2003* (pp. 1603–1606). Adelaide: Casual Productions.

Morley, J. (1991) The pronunciation component in teaching English to speakers of other languages. *TESOL Quarterly* 25 (3), 481–519.

Moyer, A. (2004) *Age, Accent and Experience in Second Language Acquisition.* Clevedon: Multilingual Matters.

Moyer, A. (2013) *The Phenomenon of Non-native Speech.* Cambridge: Cambridge University Press.

Muñoz, C.Z. (2008) Symmetries and asymmetries of age effects in naturalistic and instructed L2 learning. *Applied Linguistics* 29 (4), 578–596.

Munro, M.J. (2003) A primer on accent discrimination in the Canadian context. *TESL Canada Journal* 20 (2), 38–51.

Munro, M.J. (2011) Intelligibility: Buzzword or buzzworthy? In J. Levis and K. LeVelle (eds) *Proceedings of the 2nd Pronunciation in Second Language Learning and Teaching Conference* (pp. 7–16). Ames, IA: Iowa State University.

Munro, M.J. and Derwing, T.M. (1995) Processing time, accent and comprehensibility in the perception of native and foreign-accented speech. *Language and Speech* 38, 289–306.

Munro, M.J. and Derwing, T.M. (1999) Foreign accent, comprehensibility and intelligibility in the speech of second language learners. *Language Learning* 49 (1), 285–310.

Munro, M.J., Derwing, T.M. and Sato, K. (2006) Salient accents, covert attitudes: Consciousness-raising for pre-service second language teachers. *Prospect* 21 (1), 67–79.

Nelson, C. (2012) Review of *English as a Lingua Franca: Attitude and Identity* by Jennifer Jenkins. See http://onlinelibrary.wiley.com/doi/10.1111/j.1467-971X.2011.01746.x/full (accessed 22 June 2014).

Nowacka, M. (2003) Analiza i ocena wymowy słuchaczy NKJO w Rzeszowie. *Zeszyt Naukowy Instytutu Neofilologii (2). Zeszyty Naukowe PWSZ w Koninie* 1/2003 (2), 46–55.

Nowacka, M. (2008) Phonetic attainment in university and college students of English. A study in the productive and receptive pronunciation skills. Unpublished PhD dissertation, UMCS, Lublin.

Pawlak, M. (2004) The role of error correction in teaching pronunciation. In W. Sobkowiak and E. Waniek-Klimczak (eds) *Dydaktyka fonetyki języka obcego* 4 (pp. 66–74). Konin: Wydawnictwo PWSZ.

Pawlak, M. (2010) Designing and piloting a tool for the measurement of the use of pronunciation learning strategies. *Research in Language* 8, 189–202.

Pennington, M. (1987) *Phonology in English Language Teaching. An International Approach.* London: Longman.

Ponsonby, M. (1982) *How Now, Brown Cow? A Course in the Pronunciation of English.* New York: Phoenix ELT.

Porzuczek, A. (2002) Problemy organizacji kursu fonetyki języka angielskiego. In W. Sobkowiak and E. Waniek-Klimczak (eds) *Dydaktyka fonetyki języka obcego* (pp. 91–100). Płock: Wydawnictwo PWSZ.

Porzuczek, A., Rojczyk, A. and Arabski, J. (2013) *Praktyczny kurs wymowy angielskiej dla Polaków.* Katowice: Wydawnictwo Uniwersytetu Śląskiego.

Purcell, E.T. and Suter, R.W. (1980) Predictors of pronunciation accuracy: A reexamination. *Language Learning* 30, 271–288.

Radomski, M. and Szpyra-Kozłowska, J. (2014) A pilot study on Poles' attitudes to foreign-accented Polish and its users. *Studies in Polish Linguistics* 9, 67–87.

Roach, P. (1991) *English Phonetics and Phonology.* Cambridge: Cambridge University Press.

Rogerson-Revell, P. (2011) *English Phonology and Pronunciation Teaching.* London and New York: Continuum.

Rojczyk, A. (2010) Preceding vowel duration as a clue to the consonant voicing contrast: Perception experiments with Polish-English bilinguals. In E. Waniek-Klimczak (ed.) *Issues in Accents of English 2. Variability and Norm* (pp. 341–360). Newcastle Upon Tyne: Cambridge Scholars Publishing.

Said, S.B. (2006) Attitudes towards accented speech: A comparative study of native and non-native speakers of American English. See http://www.personal.psu.edu/sbb170/MA%20Thesis.pdf (accessed 28 February 2014).

Sankey, M., Birch, D. and Gardiner, M. (2010) Engaging students through multimodal learning environments: The journey continues. *Ascilite 2010*, Sydney. See http://www.ascilite.org.au/conferences/sydney10/procs/Sankey-full.pdf (accessed 26 September 2014).

Scheuer, S. (2003) What to teach and what not to teach? Some reflections on the relative salience of L2 phonetic errors. In *Zeszyt Naukowy Instytutu Neofilologii* 1/2003 (2), 93–99.

Seidlhofer, B. (2011) *Understanding English as a Lingua Franca*. Oxford: Oxford University Press.

Setter, J. (2010) Theories and approaches in English pronunciation. See http://www.um.es/lacell/aesta/contenido/pdf/3/setter.pdf (accessed 26 September 2014).

Shockey, L. (2003) *The Sound Patterns of Spoken English*. Oxford: Blackwell.

Sipra A.M. (2013) Impact of English orthography on L2 acquisition. *English Language Teaching* 6 (3), 116–124.

Sobkowiak, W. (1996) *English Phonetics for Poles*. Poznań: Bene Nati.

Sobkowiak, W. (2003) Materiały ulotne jako źródło metakompetencji fonetycznej [Raising phonetic awareness through trivia]. In W. Sobkowiak and E. Waniek-Klimczak (eds) *Dydaktyka fonetyki języka obcego* 5 (pp. 151–166). Płock: Wydawnictwo PWSZ.

Sobkowiak, W. (2004) Phonetic difficulty index. In W. Sobkowiak and E. Waniek-Klimczak (eds) *Dydaktyka fonetyki języka obcego* 4 (pp. 102–107). Konin: Wydawnictwo PWSZ.

Stasiak, S. and Szpyra-Kozłowska, J. (2003a) The effectiveness of selected pronunciation teaching techniques. *Zeszyt Naukowy Instytutu Neofilologii. PWSZ w Koninie* 1 (2), 125–131.

Stasiak, S. and Szpyra-Kozłowska, J. (2003b) Atrakcyjność a efektywność technik nauczania wymowy. In W. Sobkowiak and E. Waniek-Klimczak (eds) *Dydaktyka fonetyki jśzyka obcego* 5 (pp. 167–180). Płock: Wydawnictwo PWSZ.

Stasiak, S. and Szpyra-Kozłowska, J. (2010) From focus on sounds to focus on words in English pronunciation instruction. *Research in Language* 8, 163–174.

Steinbrich, P. (2014) Phonetic accommodation in an EFL classroom setting: The case of NS teachers. In J. Szpyra-Kozłowska, E. Guz, P. Steinbrich and R. Święciński (eds) *Recent Developments in Applied Phonetics* (pp. 173–195). Lublin: Catholic University of John Paul II Press.

Swan, M. and Smith, B. (2001) *Learner English: A Teacher's Guide to Interference and Other Problems*. Cambridge: Cambridge University Press.

Święciński, R. (2004) Articulatory setting in Polish and its implications for teaching English pronunciation to Poles. *Zeszyty Naukowe PWSZ w Koninie* 1/2004 (4), 141–150.

Święciński, R. (2006) Teaching English articulatory setting features to Polish students of English – a study of phonation. In W. Sobkowiak and E. Waniek-Klimczak (eds) *Dydaktyka fonetyki języka obcego* 8 (pp. 203–215). Konin: Wydawnictwo PWSZ.

Szpyra-Kozłowska, J. (2003) Miejsce i rola fonetyki w międzynarodowych egzaminach Cambridge, TOEFL i TSE. In W. Sobkowiak and E. Waniek-Klimczak (eds) *Dydaktyka fonetyki języka obcego* 5 (pp. 181–191). Płock: Wydawnictwo PWSZ.

Szpyra-Kozłowska, J. (2004) Jaki model wymowy angielskiej? – dyskusji ciąg dalszy. *Zeszyty Naukowe Państwowej Wyższej Szkoły Zawodowej w Koninie* 1/2004 (4), 116–123.

Szpyra-Kozłowska, J. (2005a) LFC, phonetic universals and the Polish context. In K. Dziubalska-Kołaczyk and J. Przedlacka (eds) *English Pronunciation Models: A Changing Scene* (pp. 151–176). Bern: Peter Lang.

Szpyra-Kozłowska, J. (2005b) Intelligibility versus Polish accent in English. *Studia Phonetica Posnaniensia* 7, 59–73.

Szpyra-Kozłowska, J. (2006) Phonetic instructions in English pronunciation teaching materials – how useful are they? In W. Sobkowiak and E. Waniek-Klimczak (eds) *Dydaktyka fonetyki języka obcego* 8 (pp. 216–230). Konin: Wydawnictwo PWSZ.

Szpyra-Kozłowska, J. (2008) English pronunciation pedagogy in Poland – achievements, failures and future perspectives. In E. Waniek-Klimczak (ed.) *Issues in Accents of English* (pp. 212–234). Newcastle Upon Tyne: Cambridge Scholars Publishing.

Szpyra-Kozłowska, J. (2011) Phonetically difficult words in intermediate learners' English. In M. Pawlak, E. Waniek-Klimczak and J. Majer (eds) *Speaking in Contexts of Instructed Foreign Language Acquisition* (pp. 286–299). Clevedon: Multilingual Matters.

Szpyra-Kozłowska, J. (2012) Mispronounced lexical items in Polish English of advanced students. *Research in Language* 10, 243–256.

Szpyra-Kozłowska, J. (2013) On the irrelevance of sounds and prosody in foreign-accented English. In E. Waniek-Klimczak and L. Shockey (eds) *Teaching and Researching English Accents in Native and Non-native Speech* (pp. 15–29). Berlin and Heidelberg: Springer-Verlag.

Szpyra-Kozłowska, J. and Bukowski, D. (2006) Drama techniques in teaching phonetics – English Pronunciation Theatre. In W. Sobkowiak and E. Waniek-Klimczak (eds) *Dydaktyka fonetyki języka obcego* 8 (pp. 259–281). Płock: Wydawnictwo PWSZ.

Szpyra-Kozłowska, J. and Radomski, M. (2012) The perception of English-accented Polish – a pilot study. *Research in Language* 10, 97–110.

Szpyra-Kozłowska, J. and Sobkowiak, W. (2011) *Workbook in English Phonetics* (2nd edn). Lublin: Wydawnictwo UMCS.

Szpyra-Kozłowska, J. and Stasiak, S. (2004) Comprehension of RP and GA by intermediate Polish learners. *Zeszyty Naukowe PWSZ w Koninie* 1/2004 (4), 108–115.

Szpyra-Kozłowska, J., Chaber, I., Pietroń, G. and Stasiak, S. (2004) To correct or not to correct. A study in phonetic error correction. *Zeszyty Naukowe PWSZ w Koninie* 1/2004 (4), 124–132.

Szpyra-Kozłowska, J., Stadnicka, L. and Frankiewicz, J. (2005) Assessing assessment methods. On the validity and reliability of pronunciation tests in EFL. *Proceedings of Phonetics Teaching and Learning Conference 2005.* London: University College London.

Szpyra-Kozłowska, J., Frankiewicz, J. and Święciński, R. (2006) The language laboratory and modern pronunciation pedagogy. In W. Sobkowiak and E. Waniek-Klimczak (eds) *Dydaktyka fonetyki języka obcego* 8 (pp. 285–303). Płock: Wydawnictwo PWSZ.

Szpyra-Kozłowska, J., Czyżak, I. and Stasiak, S. (2008) English pronunciation clinic – the case of low phonetic achievers. In E. Waniek-Klimczak (ed.) *Issues in Accents of English.* Newcastle Upon Tyne: Cambridge Scholars Publishing.

Tench, P. (1992) Phonetic symbols in the dictionary and in the classroom. In A. Brown (ed.) *Approaches to Pronunciation Teaching* (pp. 90–102). London: Macmillan.

Tench, P. (2011) *Transcribing the Sound of English. A Phonetics Workbook for Words and Discourse.* Cambridge: Cambridge University Press.

Timmis, I. (2002) Native-speaker norms and international English: A classroom view. *ELT Journal* 56 (3), 240–249.

Trask, R.L. (1995) *Language: The Basics.* London and New York: Routledge.

Trudgill, P. (2005) Native-speaker segmental phonological models and the English Lingua Franca Core. In K. Dziubalska-Kołaczyk and J. Przedlacka (eds) *English Pronunciation Models: A Changing Scene* (pp. 77–98). Bern: Peter Lang.

Trudgill, P. and Hannah, J. (1994) *International English.* London: Edward Arnold.

Underhill, A. (1994) *Sound Foundations.* London: Macmillan.

Ur, P. (1984) *Teaching Listening Comprehension.* Cambridge: Cambridge University Press.

Ushioda, E. (2006) Language motivation in a reconfigured Europe: Access, identity, autonomy. *Journal of Multilingual and Multicultural Development* 27 (2), 148–161.

van den Doel, R. (2006) How friendly are the natives? An evaluation of native speaker judgements of foreign-accented British and American English. PhD dissertation, University of Utrecht, Utrecht.

Vaughan-Rees, M. (1992) Rhymes and rhythm. In A. Brown (ed.) *Approaches to Pronunciation Teaching* (pp. 47–56). London: Macmillan.

Walker, R. (2001) Pronunciation priorities, the Lingua Franca Core and monolingual groups. *Speak Out!* 18, 4–9.

Walker, R. (2011) *Teaching the Pronunciation of English as a Lingua Franca.* Oxford: Oxford University Press.

Waniek-Klimczak, E. (1997a) Context for teaching English phonetics and phonology at Polish universities and colleges: A survey. In E. Waniek-Klimczak (ed.) *Teaching English Phonetics and Phonology II* (pp. 5–17). Łódź: Wydawnictwo Uniwersytetu Łódzkiego.

Waniek-Klimczak, E. (ed.) (1997b) *Teaching English Phonetics and Phonology II.* Łódź: Wydawnictwo Uniwersytetu Łódzkiego.

Waniek-Klimczak, E. (2002) Akcent wyrazowy w nauczaniu języka angielskiego. In W. Sobkowiak and E. Waniek-Klimczak (eds) *Dydaktyka fonetyki języka obcego* (pp. 101–114). Płock: Wydawnictwo PWSZ.

Warschauer, M. and Meskill, C. (2000) Technology and second language learning. In J. Rosenthal (ed.) *Handbook of Undergraduate Second Language Education* (pp. 308–318). Mahwah, N: Lawrence Erlbaum.

Wells, J.C. (1982) *Accents of English.* Cassette. Cambridge: Cambridge University Press.

Wells, J.C. (1990) *Longman Pronunciation Dictionary.* Harlow: Longman.

Williams, J.N. (2005) Learning without awareness. *Studies in Second Language Acquisition* 27, 269–304.

Wrembel, M. (2001) Innovative approaches to the teaching of practical phonetics. *Proceedings of the Phonetics Teaching and Learning Conference PTLC2001* (pp. 63–66). London: University College London.

Wrembel, M. (2002) New perspectives on pronunciation teaching. In W. Sobkowiak and E. Waniek-Klimczak (eds) *Dydaktyka fonetyki języka obcego* (pp. 173–183). Płock: Wydawnictwo PWSZ.

Wrembel, M. (2005a) Phonological metacompetence in the acquisition of second language phonetics. Unpublished PhD dissertation, Adam Mickiewicz University, Poznań.

Wrembel, M. (2005b) Metacompetence-oriented model of phonological acquisition: Implications for the teaching and learning of second language pronunciation. *Proceedings of Phonetics Teaching and Learning Conference* (pp. 1–5). London: University College London.

Wrembel, M. (2010) Sound symbolism in foreign language phonological acquisition. *Research in Language* 8, 175–188.

Author Index

Abelin, A. 3, 46
Abercrombie, D. 7, 9, 174
Anderson-Hsieh, J. 111
Archilbald, A. 13, 64, 147, 180, 181, 182
Avery, P. 36, 65, 200, 201

Baker, A. 103, 200
Baran-Łucarz, M. 56, 195
Bassetti, B. 105, 107, 138
Benson, P. 172
Blanco, M. 157
Bowler, B. 202
Boyd, S. 3, 46
Brown, A. 101, 223
Brown, H.D. 179
Bryła-Cruz, A. 70, 79, 116, 117, 138
Burnham, D.K. 105
Bukowski, D. 164, 165, 166, 179

Cauldwell, R. 193
Celce-Murcia, M. vii, 5, 6, 36, 39, 40, 41,
        42, 63, 65, 95, 108, 143, 146, 147,
        164, 166, 171, 181, 188, 189
Cenoz, J. 39
Ciszewski, T. 223
Collins, B. x, 67, 69, 70, 77, 87–90, 101,
        150, 172, 228
Cortes, V. 69, 73
Crookston, I. 173
Cruttenden, A. ix, 31, 67, 77, 84–87, 101,
        102, 228
Crystal, D. 29, 63
Cunningham, S. 202
Cunningham, U. 15
Cyran, E. 223

Dalton, Ch. 70, 140
Derwing, T.M. vii, 5, 39, 46, 64, 66, 111,
        119, 136, 194, 198

Dickerson, W. 157
Doel, R. van den. 70, 76, 79, 101, 116
Dziubalska-Kołaczyk, K. vii, 13, 157

Ehrlich, S. 36, 65, 200, 201
Erdener, V.D. 105
Elliot, A.R. 5
Evans, L. 150, 191

Fayer, J.M. 47
Field, J. 67, 111, 137
Firth, S. 146
Flege, J.E. 41
Frankiewicz, J. 62
Fraser, H. 153, 157, 166, 171
Friedrich, P. 29

Gibbon, D. 83
Gilbert, J.B. 71, 100, 101, 108, 111,
        114–115
Gimson, A.C. 31, 83
Goh, C. 29
Gonet, W. 79, 80, 117, 138, 166, 223
Graddol, D. 64
Gut, U. 155

Hahn, L.D. 137
Hannah, J. 31
Hancock, M. 171, 182, 214, 223
Handke, J. 193
Henderson, A. 29, 55
Hewings, M. 5, 103, 108, 182, 202
Honikman, B. 147
Hudson, R.A. 32
Hülmbauer, C. 10, 21

James, A. 152
Janicka, K. 55

Jarvis, S. 233
Jenkins, J. vii, v, ix, 7, 9, 10, 13, 14, 21, 49,
    57, 64, 67, 70, 77–84, 101, 11, 228
Jenner, B. 9, 76, 81, 111, 147, 150
Jilka, M. 41, 223
Jones, R. 150

Kachru, B. 8
Kalin, R. 46
Kaltenboeck, G. 194
Kaur, J. 10
Kelly, G. 3, 5, 103, 108, 142, 143, 171, 172,
    182, 202
Kendrick, H. 39
Kenworthy, J. 65, 133, 134
Keysar, B. 46, 48
Komorowska, H. 197
Krasinsky, E. 47

Ladefoged, P. 79
Lamb, M. 27, 65
Laver, J. 79, 82, 148
Leather, J. 152
Lecumberri, M.L.G. 39, 172, 177
Lee, W.R. 190
Lev-Ari, S. 46, 48
Levis, J. vii, 69, 73, 194
Lindemann, S. 45
Lintunen, P. 139
Lippi-Green, R. 4, 45, 46
Lowie, W. 223

MacDonald, D. 39
Maddieson, I. 79
Maidment, J.A. 172, 177
Majer, J. 56, 139
Mańczak-Wohlfeld, E. 138
Marx, N. 233
Matsuda, A. 29
Mees, I.M. x, 67, 69, 70, 77, 87–90, 101,
    150, 172, 228
Melhorn, G. 233
Meskill, C. 188
Mompean-Gonzales, J.A. 147, 148, 150
Morley, J. 4, 39, 146
Moyer, A. 4, 41, 46, 153, 171
Munro, M.J. viii, 4, 5, 45, 46, 64, 66, 71,
    74, 111, 119, 123, 136, 137, 194, 198
Muñoz, C.Z. 34, 38, 65, 66

Nelson, C. 14
Nowacka, M. 7, 56, 81, 82, 151

Pavlenko, A. 233
Pawlak, M. 44, 197
Pennington, M. 39
Pietroń, G. 79, 80, 117, 138
Ponsonby, M. 91, 103, 200, 205
Porzuczek, A. 56, 142
Przedlacka, J. vii, 13
Purcell, E.T. 39

Radomski, M. 45, 113
Rayko, K. 46
Roach, P. 81, 82, 111
Rogerson-Revell, P. 31, 36, 41, 65, 66, 68,
    69, 70, 98, 102, 111, 143, 146, 172,
    194, 200, 201
Rojczyk, A. 139
Rossiter, M. 111

Said, S.B. 46, 48
Sankey, M. 165, 168
Scheuer, S. 91, 117, 138
Shockey, L. 104
Seidlhofer, B. 10, 12, 24, 64, 70, 140
Setter, J. 10, 21
da Silva, R.S. 115
Sipra, A.M. 108
Smith, B. 115, 138
Sobkowiak, W. 93, 94, 100, 103, 137, 163,
    178, 201
Stasiak, S. 32, 97, 103, 210, 213
Steinbrich, P. 65
Suter, R.W. 39
Swan, M. 115, 138
Szpyra-Kozłowska, J. viii, 5, 32, 45,
    49, 56, 77, 79, 92, 96, 97, 100,
    101, 103, 113, 116, 117, 118, 130,
    138, 139, 163, 179, 189, 195, 196,
    197, 199, 202, 207, 210, 213, 218,
    220, 223
Święciński, R. 148–150

Tench, P. 172, 223
Timmis, I. 29
Trask, R.L. 25, 205
Trudgill, P. 29, 31, 64, 137

Underhill, A. 172
Ur, P. 152
Ushioda, E. 65

Vaughan-Rees, M. 179

Walker, R. vii, 10, 11, 12, 13, 14, 17, 36, 57, 111, 137, 200, 201
Waniek-Klimczak, E. 55, 126
Warschauer, M. 188
Watts, P. 137

Wells, J.C. 81, 99, 161
Williams, J.N. 223
Wrembel, M. 147, 153, 157, 164, 166, 171

Yule, G

Subject Index

acceptability (pleasantness, degree of
annoyance/irritation) 47–48, 76, 97,
118, 119–120, 122, 133–136
accommodation 19–21, 26–27, 28, 64, 74
Amalgam English 77, 84–87, 88, 89,
101, 228
articulatory setting (voice quality) 74, 87,
137, 147–150, 222, 231
   English 149
   Polish 149
articulatory (motor) training 141,
145–150, 152, 164, 210, 231
aspiration 77, 80–81, 84, 85, 86, 88, 89,
90, 117, 131, 133, 134, 151, 163,
210–212, 229
attitudes to accented speech 3–4, 45–49,
142, 228
Audioligual Method (audioligualism) and
pronunciation 145, 188
auditory learners 164, 166, 167
auditory (ear) training 141, 150–152, 153,
164, 167, 170, 192, 231
Australian English 50, 53

basic (minimal) intelligibility 7–8, 71, 86
BBC English 9, 65
'bottom up' approach 110–117, 230

Caribbean English 79
Cockney 79, 80
cognitive training 141, 145, 153–164,
210, 231
   phonetic 145, 153, 154–157
   phonological 145, 153, 157–164, 172
comfortable (easy) intelligibility 7–8, 22,
25, 26, 67, 71, 85, 89, 227, 228
Communicative Method and
pronunciation 6, 63, 122, 141, 145,
146, 233

comprehensibility 47–48, 97, 118,
119–120, 122
Computer Assisted Language Learning
(CALL) 171, 193
Computer-Assisted Pronunciation
Teaching (CAPT) 193–194
connected speech changes 62, 63, 78, 88,
89, 104, 138, 151, 163, 177, 214
consonant clusters 77, 80, 85, 86, 87, 88,
89, 127–128, 160, 229
consonants
   interdental fricatives 21, 62, 63, 70,
77, 79–80, 81, 85, 86, 87, 88, 90, 92,
112, 113, 116, 117, 130, 133, 135,
136, 155, 170, 180, 201, 202–203,
210–212, 220
   velar nasal (angma) 77, 88, 116, 117,
130, 133, 135, 136, 175, 210–212
   palatoalveolars 14–15, 62, 77, 85, 88,
112, 117, 131, 134, 155, 159, 175,
207, 208, 220
   laterals 62, 77, 80, 81, 85, 86, 87, 88,
137, 162–163
   glides 86, 93, 94, 112, 158
   glottal fricative 77, 78, 84, 86, 87, 88,
93, 137, 158
   /r/ 76, 77, 78–79, 80, 86, 87, 88, 92,
131, 133, 135, 158
   /r/ - /l/ contrast 69–70, 86, 87, 88,
105, 129
   syllabic consonants 62, 87, 131, 163
Critical Period Hypothesis (CPH) 38

degree of annoyance/irritation see
acceptability
diphthongs 85, 86, 87, 95, 131, 133,
134, 175
drama in pronunciation training 141, 167,
170, 180–182, 218–220, 232

drills *see* phonetic drills
dropping of /h/ 85, 87

ear training *see* auditory training
EFL educational context 39–45, 228
EFL learner-related factors 41–42, 228
EFL teacher-related factors 42–44, 228
EFL vs ELF 8–23, 45, 111
EFL vs ESL 33–39, 105, 150, 228
English as a Foreign Language (EFL) 1,
    8–23, 23–29, 65, 222, 228
English as a Lingua Franca (ELF) 1, 8–23,
    23–29, 33–39, 49, 51–52, 54, 55, 65,
    142, 227, 228, 230
English as an International Language
    (EIL) 1, 9
English as a Second Language (ESL) 1,
    33–39, 65
English Language Teaching (ELT) 1, 6, 27,
    35, 226
error correction *see* phonetic error
    correction
Error Ranking (hierarchy of error) 69, 77,
    87–89, 101, 229
Estuary English 29, 80
Expanding Circle 9, 21

foreign-accentedness 47–48, 76, 97, 118,
    119–120, 122, 133–136
fortis-lenis distinction 82, 87, 88, 89, 229
functional load 69–70, 85, 86, 89, 90,
    91, 229

games *see* pronunciation games
gaps
    accidental 162
    systematic 162
geminates 161–162, 223
General American (GA) 9, 10, 24, 30, 32–33,
    49, 50, 51, 53, 54, 55, 78, 158, 228
Glaswegian English 30
global errors 92–97, 118–122, 229

hierarchy of error *see* Error Ranking

identity through accent 11, 12, 15, 18, 26,
    32, 227
inflectional suffixes *see* pronunciation of
    inflectional suffixes
Inner Circle 8, 10
International English 77, 84–87, 88, 89,
    101, 228

intonation 3, 63, 78, 83, 85, 87, 88, 89,
    90, 111, 112, 113, 114, 131, 133, 138,
    154, 169–170, 214
Irish English 50, 52–53

kinaesthetic/tactile learners 164, 166,
    167, 193

language aptitude (talent) 41–42, 44, 58,
    74, 75, 228
language laboratory in pronunciation
    training 188–191
learning styles 41, 44, 155, 156, 166–167,
    223, 228, 232
Lingua Franca Core (LFC) 1, 10, 11,
    13–14, 25, 64, 77–84, 84–89, 101,
    137, 227, 228, 230
Liverpool English 30
local errors 92–97, 118–122, 130, 229
long/longer words 57, 60, 102–103,
    128, 229

maximization of phonetic input 150–151,
    231
minimal pairs 72–74, 75, 91, 92, 108,
    109, 137, 145–146, 184, 200,
    214–218
mis-stressed words 100–102, 126–127,
    130, 132, 133, 135, 136, 229
morphological alternations 102,
    129–130
motivation 35, 36, 37, 41, 42, 44, 65, 228
    instrumental motivation 35, 37, 65
    integrative motivation 35, 37, 65
motor training *see* articulatory training
multisensory reinforcement 141, 145,
    168, 169, 232
multisensory training 164–170, 231, 232

Native English as a Lingua Franca (NELF)
    1, 23–29, 111–112, 227, 228
New Zealand English 30
nuclear (sentence) stress 62, 77, 88, 89,
    90, 112, 114, 229

onomatopoeic expressions 204–207
    in Cuban Spanish 205–207
    in English 205–207
    in Hungarian 205–207
    in Polish 205–207
Outer Circle 8–9
Oxford English 9

palatalization 62, 93, 131, 163
perception of accented speech *see*
    attitudes to accented speech
phonemic (phonetic) transcription
    (phonetic/phonemic script) 60,
    61–62, 63, 141, 171–178, 199, 213,
    223, 232
phonetically difficult words 67, 90–104,
    123–130, 143
phonetic drills 142, 188, 190, 210, 213,
    214–218, 222, 231
phonetic error correction 60, 61, 63, 141,
    195–198, 220–222, 232
    delayed correction 196
    on-the-spot correction 196
    teacher correction 182, 197
    peer correction 182, 197
    self-correction 165, 197
phonetic 'false friends' 98–100,
    126, 229
phonetic/phonological metacompetence
    153–154, 155, 231
phonetic script *see* phonemic
    transcription
phonetic transcription *see* phonemic
    transcription
phonotactic constraints 153, 157, 232
    segmental 158–159
    sequential 160–164
pleasantness of foreign accents *see*
    acceptability
poems in pronunciation training 141,
    178–180, 170, 232
pre-fortis clipping 82, 84, 163
pronunciation and intelligibility 69,
    71–76
pronunciation and spelling 35, 37,
    60, 80, 81, 84, 91, 92, 93, 94,
    95, 100, 103, 104–110, 112, 114,
    118–119, 124–126, 138, 158,
    159, 160, 162, 167, 171–172,
    174, 175, 201, 217, 223
pronunciation games 143, 147, 167, 171,
    176, 182–187, 214–218, 232
pronunciation in language examinations
    5–6, 56, 141, 199–200, 223–224, 226
pronunciation instructors
    native 5, 12, 35–36, 37, 65, 154
    non-native 6, 12, 15–16, 27, 36,
    37, 154
pronunciation of inflectional suffixes 62,
    63, 156, 168–169

Queen's English 9

Received Pronunciation (RP) 9, 10, 24,
    30–32, 49, 50, 51, 53, 54, 55, 65, 78,
    158, 175, 228
rhotics 76, 79, 83, 84, 85, 86, 87, 90
rhythm 17, 78, 83, 88, 111, 113, 114, 115,
    138, 159, 214

Scottish English 29, 30, 31, 50, 52–53
Second Language Acquisition (SLA) 1, 33,
    38, 105
'segmentals vs suprasegmentals' debate
    110–117, 229–230
sentence stress *see* nuclear stress
songs in pronunciation training 141, 142,
    143, 178, 214–218, 232
South African English 9
spelling pronunciation 94, 125, 130, 132,
    133, 135, 136, 172
spelling and pronunciation 35, 37, 60, 68,
    80, 81, 91, 94, 95, 171, 229, 232
strong and weak forms 17, 62, 78, 83, 85,
    86, 87, 90, 112, 114, 131

tapping (flapping) of /t/ 77, 84, 85
technology in pronunciation training
    165–166, 193–194, 232
'top down' approach 110–117, 230

ultimate phonetic attainment 7, 38

visual learners 164–166, 167, 172, 193
voice quality *see* articulatory setting
vowels
    vowel contrasts 57, 63, 82, 85, 87, 88,
    89, 91, 111, 112, 116, 117, 129, 130,
    131, 132, 133, 134, 135, 136, 220,
    221, 222, 229
    vowel length (quantity) 77, 82, 85, 86,
    88, 89, 116, 117, 131, 134, 135, 136,
    210–212, 229
    vowel quality 18, 77, 82, 85, 86, 88, 89,
    116, 117, 131, 132, 134, 135
    long schwa 77, 83, 84, 85, 220, 221, 222
    schwa 17, 62, 86, 102, 131, 132,
    137, 159
    word-final vowels 159
vowel reduction 17, 85, 86, 87, 88, 89, 90,
    114, 117, 131

washback effect 5, 56, 226
weak forms *see* strong and weak forms
Welsh English 30, 50, 53
word-final obstruent devoicing 92,
     116–117, 132, 133, 135, 136, 163,
     201, 210–211

word linking 89, 112, 158, 210, 211, 212
word stress 60, 62, 77, 85, 86,
     87, 88, 89, 90, 112, 113, 114,
     116, 117, 130, 139, 154, 169,
     220, 229
words with several liquids 128–129, 139